Familiar
"Leadership"
Heresies
Uncovered

Familiar "Leadership" Heresies Uncovered

by
an inside look at the Bible

the Eden Heresies (Gen 2-3, 1 Tim 1-3)
the Headship Heresies (1 Pet 3, Eph 5-6)
the Legalist Heresies (1 Cor 11 & 14)

Bruce C. E. Fleming

Resource *Publications*
An imprint of *Wipf and Stock Publishers*
199 West 8th Avenue • Eugene OR 97401

Resource Publications
A division of Wipf and Stock Publishers
199 W 8th Ave, Suite 3
Eugene, OR 97401

Familiar "Leadership" Heresies Uncovered
By Fleming, Bruce C. E.
Copyright©2005 by Fleming, Bruce C. E.
ISBN: 1-59752-038-1
Publication date 1/4/2005

Think Again! logo by MannaStudio.com

Table of Contents

vi

Foreword

Bruce and Joy have the credentials and the worldwide experience to have researched and field-tested their work in a wide variety of cultural settings. Their slogan invites the reader in: "Think some Bible passages are impossible to understand? *Think Again!*"

Rev. Bruce C. E. Fleming holds the M.Div. (Master of Divinity) and the Th.M. (Master of Theology) from Trinity Evangelical Divinity School (Deerfield, IL), and the post-graduate D.E.A. degree from the University of Strasbourg, France. Ordained by the Evangelical Free Church of America, he has been involved in co-founding several churches, schools and parachurch organizations.

This book grew out of his work in Africa, where he served as Professor of Practical Theology and was Academic Dean of the Bangui Evangelical Graduate School of Theology (B.E.S.T) in French-speaking Africa.

A popular speaker, teacher and author, he also has published numerous professional reports on the leadership of Christian organizations and nonprofit groups. He consults on ministry leadership training in French-speaking Africa.

Dr. Joy Elasky Fleming did the groundbreaking research on the Hebrew text of Genesis 2-3. Her inside look at the passage on the Garden of Eden made possible the uncovering of "leadership" heresies throughout the Bible. Joy holds a Ph.D. in Old Testament Studies from the University of Strasbourg, France. A graduate of Wheaton College (IL), she earned her M.Div. from Trinity Evangelical Divinity School. She is completing a Psy.D. in Clinical Psychology.

Joy has been a seminary professor and guest lecturer (B.E.S.T. and Bethel Theological Seminary, St. Paul, MN), college professor (Northwestern College, St. Paul, MN), high school teacher and home-school teacher.

Dr. Fleming is the author of *Man and Woman in Biblical Unity – Theology from Genesis 2-3*. Active in prayer ministries on three continents, Joy also serves in a local church ministry to international graduate students.

Joy and Bruce have been married for more than 25 years and are the parents of Christy and Mark. They make their home in Minneapolis.

Introduction

We were sitting in goat-hide sling chairs in front of his mud-walled, thatched-roof house on a low island in the middle of hundreds of square miles of roadless swamp bordering the Congo River. He was a chief of one of the main tribes among the Water People.

"Chief, Why do your people build these low mud pyramids in front of their houses?" I asked. "Oh, those! Well, the water table is just inches below the surface of our islands," he answered. "We can't go *down* to bury our dead, so we go *up* to build a resting place for them. These before you hold my ancestors," he said with a slow wave of his arm. Pointing to a patch of bare ground he said, "Here I will be buried in a large pyramid, and beside me will go smaller pyramids of the best of my wives when they die."

"Isn't it complicated to have multiple wives?" I asked, turning the subject back to the land of the living.

"Ayee! It sure is!" he heartily replied. "That's why just last week I put away two of my wives. Now I'm down to just seventeen!"

Sound like any conversation you've ever had with a local leader? It was a first for me. But it would not be my last. As a professor, pastor and anthropologist, I would have many more.

Unknowingly, most of us are locked inside the solid walls of our home culture. We assume we "know how the world works." We assume changes that are new to us are new to the rest of the world. In cultures all over the world, and down through time, others have made the same assumptions.

We all make assumptions and global judgments when it comes to topics such as "chieftainship," "signs of honor," "traditional marriage" or even "the organization of a local congregation." In reality, however, we may be similar or quite different from other cultures.

There is great interest in knowing more about "man" and "woman." Around the world there are varying, and sometimes contradictory, roles prescribed for man and woman at home, in church and in the culture.

You will discover an inside look at the "theology of leadership" in this book. Each chapter was developed following the set of Seven *Think Again* Bible Study Steps. By following these simple Study Steps a person may discover the meaning of one passage at a time and thus allow the Bible "speak for itself."

What is a "heresy"? A heresy is *a lie* about spiritual things. It is a falsehood. In this book, this word is used to label a teaching or belief that runs contrary to Scripture.

Some heresies pervert the message of salvation and keep people from finding new life in Christ. Other heresies distort the way life is to be lived in Christ, causing great individual hurt and weakening the church.

The heresies discussed in this book fall into one or both of these categories. Those who believe otherwise are not necessarily condemned as unworthy of Christian fellowship. But they are recognized as the source of great sorrow and wrongdoing in the church and a hindrance to reaching the world around it.

The word "heresy" sounds old and out of date to some people, but it is the best word to raise the red flag of warning. It means, "This teaching, or belief, is toxic! Don't feed on it! Don't give it to others! Keep it away from children and grownups too! If you find it implanted in your doctrines or practices dig it up by the roots and replace it with proper theology."

A heresy harms all those who touch it. Those holding to a false and heretical teaching are made spiritually sick and weak. Those spreading this false doctrine – knowingly or unknowingly – are liars (!) who need to be silenced and corrected. Any heresy is a serious matter, which must be dealt with seriously.

Just like cancer, a heresy cannot be ignored or tolerated. It must be cleaned out and the truth of Scripture must go in its place.

The words of Satan recorded in the Bible are heretical. Satan, the "Father of Lies" contradicts, omits, exaggerates and in other ways twists the truth into a lie.

Those who love God's Word are called to be on guard against the wiles of Satan, who is the "author of confusion." God's children are called to rightly understand and apply God's Word.

Remember, a "heresy" may *sound* like a truth that comes from God. Those who hold to it may *think* they are following God when they put it into practice. Some may *claim* that a teaching is "biblical" – when it is not. A "heresy" twists the truth. It brings death not life.

> **… Objective revealed truth is an inherent Christian doctrine ….**
> **Heresy represents the very real error of departure from that truth.**
> *Evangelical Dictionary of Theology*, Baker, p. 556.

What can be done to correct heresy? It is said that government agents who track the printing and spread of counterfeit money are trained to recognize a fake bill by spending most of their time studying real bills. The more an agent is familiar with the real thing, the easier it is to spot a fake.

The Seven *Think Again* Bible Study Steps help a student of the Bible to see the Bible as it really is; as it presents itself to us; as God speaks through it to us. By implementing these Seven Steps in your studies of the Bible you will escape inventing heresies on your own. You will also be able to spot heresies that other people may have been missing to the detriment of their own spiritual health.

Here are the Seven *Think Again* Bible Study Steps. They are presented in detail in the last chapter of this book.

The Seven *Think Again* Bible Study Steps

Step 1. *Think Again* **about what the Bible says.**

Step 2. *Think Again* **about the context of your passage.**

Step 3. *Think Again* **about the content of your passage.**

Step 4. *Think Again* **about the key image and/or idea.**

Step 5. *Think Again* **about the target verse(s).**

Step 6. *Think Again* **about the points of application.**

Step 7. *Think Again.* **What does the Bible *not* say?**

The Annotated Steps:

Step 1. *Think Again* **about what the Bible says.** Pick a target word, verse or idea you want to study. Find a Bible passage where it is located. Read a page before and after your passage in the Bible to see if it addresses the target you want to study. If it does, proceed to the following Study Steps. If not, look elsewhere until you find a more appropriate passage.

Step 2. *Think Again* **about the context of your passage.** Find the limits of the passage – the first and last verses. The passage may be as long as several paragraphs or more. Or it may be just a verse or two long. Notice how the

Familiar "Leadership" Heresies Uncovered   by Bruce C. E. Fleming
www.ThinkAgainAboutTheBible.com

passage fits into the larger context of what comes before and after it. To allow the Bible to make its own point in a verse, or a series of verses, you must first make sure you know where the flow of ideas is going and pay attention to how your passage fits into that context.

Step 3. *Think Again* **about the content of your passage.** Determine the main points in the passage. These points should receive your major attention. Recognize sub-points for what they are, subordinate points to the main points. They will not contradict the main points of the passage – instead they strengthen and deepen them.

Step 4. *Think Again* **about the key image and/or idea.** A key image or idea has an impact on the meaning of the whole passage. Find out what it means. Don't let your imagination carry you away. First, see if the simplest meaning works. Is this a real thing? If it is, take literal language literally. If the literal sense makes no sense, then move to the simplest level of abstraction and see if it fits into the flow of meaning. If not, then and only then, look for a more abstract possible meaning.

Step 5. *Think Again* **about the target verse(s).** Now is the time to study the word, the verse, or the paragraph, that drew your attention from the very beginning. Having taken the four previous study steps, now look at word order, key verbs, and the definition of various words. Come to conclusions about the meaning of the verses that specially interest you.

Step 6. *Think Again* **about the points of application.** The Bible was not written for study as an intellectual exercise. It is God's Word to us, communicating to us things God wants us to know, understand, and do. Now that you have a fresh grasp on the passage, what are you to do? Be specific.

Step 7. *Think Again.* **What does the Bible *not* say?** This study step is not often practiced in Bible study. However, if it has not happened earlier, this is the point where any heretical ideas previously attributed to the passage are identified, labeled and rejected. Practical steps to take in order to root out these false teachings are helpful to write out at this point.

7

PART I

The "Eden" Heresies

Chapter 1

"Leadership" Heresies and the Woman in the Garden
… an inside look at Genesis 2-3 (with a focus on 3:16)

Chapter Contents:

10

Genesis 3:15-17 (showing the linchpin in the middle)

God's words to:

The serpent ¹⁵I will put enmity between your seed and her **<u>seed</u>**

The woman ¹⁶I will multiply your **sorrowful toil** and your **<u>conception</u>**

The man ¹⁷Cursed is the ground … in **sorrowful toil** you shall eat of it

Genesis 3:16 (translation from Hebrew in outline form)

God's news to the woman about two things – bad *and* <u>good</u>
Line 1
^{16a}I will surely multiply your **sorrowful toil** and your **<u>conception</u>**

God's instruction to the woman
Lines 2-4
 ^{16b}With effort you will bring forth children
 ^{16c}Your desire is to your husband
 ^{16d}But he will rule over you.

12

Verses That Touch Everyone

The familiar "leadership" heresies spring from what many mistakenly think is found in the first chapters of Genesis. These are the Bible chapters we will look at first, especially Genesis 2-3.

Later chapters in the Bible might tell of a certain king here, or a certain shipwreck there. But the first chapters in Genesis are packed full of meaning. They explain why our world is a mixture of good and evil.

How we became heresy hunters.

When we were preparing to teach in Africa, we interviewed African leaders for their advice. "Don't study something *you* think might be interesting but may turn out to be of no help to us here," they said. "First, find out what the people of Africa need to know from the Bible. Do your research on that. Then, you'll be a real help to us."

Since we would be serving as missionary professors in French-speaking Africa, we spent two years in France learning the language. Our first year, we attended language school in Albertville, in the French Alps.

Our second year, we learned French by using it. Joy studied Old Testament. I studied Practical Theology. It was the first time the University of Strasbourg School of Theology had a wife and husband duo with each studying in a doctoral program of theology at the same time.

Joy focused on Genesis 2-3, having been advised that studies on the Beginning, God, Man, Woman, Temptation, Sin, Death and Curses would be quite useful in Africa. I studied the New Testament and Contextualization of Theology in Africa.

Then we headed for Africa. Our first months there, all the library and course notes I had taken down during class lectures and from my research in the libraries in France were stolen. The thieves apparently thought my metal portable filing box was a strong box for valuables. When they saw only papers inside, they got rid of them and just kept the box!

What could I do next? I couldn't leave Africa to go back to Europe to retake my courses. There were new professors at the University. Different courses were being offered. I felt the loss deeply. All that work was lost!

For months we prayed, "God, is there any way to bring good out of this evil?" Was it somehow possible to pick up my studies and go on? Was there something else God wanted me to study? The answer came a year later when we moved deep into the rain forest to teach in a small theological institute.

Out our front door, down the hill, under the dark green shade of towering avocado trees, past the end of the grass airstrip and then the whitewashed clinic, came the end of the mile-long dirt path. From that point you could only turn right or left down the main road, which was only a one-lane rutted track, crowded on both sides by thick rain forest.

To the right, you came to the first mud-walled, thatched-roof huts in a line of villages that belonged to people from the Mono tribe. To the left, you soon found a larger village. These people were from the Ngombé tribe. Their villages lined the mud road away to the west. In this extraordinary location, in the lush hills of northwestern Congo, Joy and I took turns raising our toddler daughter and teaching courses to students who were preparing for pastoral work in village churches in the Congo.

The initial coming of Christianity to new culture groups anywhere in the world almost always results in a marked improvement in the status of women in those groups. To my surprise, I found that after 25 years of mission work and church planting, the status of women had *not* improved in the Mono and Ngombe villages that lined the Bosobolo Road. In fact, their lowly status in the two tribes remained remarkably as it had been before the arrival of Gospel in their area. Why?

As a Practical Theologian, I began digging to find what had been taught, and what had *not* been taught, by the first missionaries and African pastors. What had been done right? What had been misunderstood? What had been done wrong?

I interviewed older believers in their villages and took notes. I searched the school library, the archives, and the shelves in the various offices. My searching paid off, as I found dust-covered, yellowing booklets that had been used in Bible and Practical Christian Life training during the early years in the school.

I further discovered that "leadership" heresies were being taught in the village churches. This was hindering the growth of the Christian women and men in their faith and their ministry. It was disrupting their home life as well!

Many of these "leadership" heresies were based on misinterpretations of Genesis 2-3. Additional heresies, based on these faulty interpretations of Genesis warped the understanding of modern readers of key New Testament passages as well. I realized that here was the Biblical research and writing God had for me to do.

As Joy and I each tackled tough passages, we began to spot faulty translations into modern languages from the Hebrew Old Testament and the Greek New Testament. Working from the original languages, we began to peel away centuries of faulty interpretation and arrived at clear expressions of the passages we were studying.

Familiar "Leadership" Heresies Uncovered   by Bruce C. E. Fleming
www.ThinkAgainAboutTheBible.com

We taught what we learned to the students and believers around us. It was a privilege to see their troubled expressions turn to ones of recognition and joy as the Bible studies progressed.

What about heresies on the Fall of the man and woman?

It is hard to grasp how *far* the human race has fallen without knowing how *high* God intended us to be. In Genesis 1, we learn about the creation of everything from nothing. When all was created, God said it was "very good."

In Genesis 2-3, we learn about the Garden of Eden. Chapter 2 focuses on details about the creation of the first couple. Genesis 3 tells us about their temptation and fall into sin and death. The perfection of life in Eden in Genesis 2 stands in sharp contrast to the death and sin experienced in Genesis 3.

> **It is hard to grasp how *far* the human race has fallen without knowing how *high* God intended us to be.**

Just how far the human race would descend was not fully shown in Eden. But our race was on its way down. The Bible later records many horrible acts committed by humans. So horrible that, in Jeremiah 19:5, God says that the foul sins that were committed had never even entered into His mind!

In Genesis chapter 3, we begin to get a glimpse of the death that had come with disobedience. We see sin at work in relationships: between the humans and God, and between the humans with one another. We see the man, hostile in his dealings with both his loving Creator and his loving wife. Hideously, he sides with the enemy of them all!

When people were first warned not to shoot drugs with needles that may have been infected with AIDS, for example, they did not immediately see all the horrors that their willful actions would produce – the secondary diseases, the wasting away, the lost opportunities, the anguish; all these were not immediately evident when an infected needle full of drugs was offered to them. Similarly, the full impact of sin may not have been grasped while the couple was still in the Garden.

But *we* know. People of our modern generation can look *back* over history, and we can look *around* us in our own day, and *we can see* how hideous sin is. With this heightened sense of awareness, we are naturally drawn to the momentous events recorded in Genesis 3.

There were three participants present in that meeting at the Tree: the serpent, the woman and the man (Gen 3:6). The serpent, at odds with God, purposefully tempted the woman and the man ("you" is plural in 3:1, 4, 5) to disobey God. The woman took the fruit and gave some to the man, who was "with her" (3:6*b*).

A surprising number of errors have crept in to the interpretation of what happened when the three of them were at the Tree. These errors can be found in many places, from children's illustrated Bible storybooks to heavily footnoted theological textbooks.

In a great many cases these errors twist what happened to the woman. Many see *her* as the Temptress, totally overlooking the real Tempter!

The ancient Jewish *Babylonian Talmud* taught that in Eden there were ten curses imposed on Eve – and it listed these "curses" in great detail! Why would they ever think the woman was cursed at all? Because in her "sinfulness" and "evil intentions" she deserved it, they wrote.

What does the Bible say?

The Bible says that God imposed two curses in Eden. The Hebrew word for curse, *'arur*, is used only two times in Genesis 3. First God cursed the serpent (3:14) and God cursed the soil (3:17).

Additional "details" about Eden that are not from the Bible appear in folk tales and even in some theology. But these heretical added "details" need to be stripped away and discarded. We need to think again only about what the Bible says as it was first written in its original languages.

God's response to sin.

After the two humans are tempted by the serpent to disobey God and eat, they both eat. Immediately something happens. After sinning, they realize that they are naked. This had not bothered them before. Ever.

In a tense moment, they make clothes to cover their nakedness. These are their very first clothes. This is their very first time to be tense. Why are they acting this way? Why so many firsts? Are these the beginning signs of evil and dying?

Eventually, God comes walking in the Garden and calls out. They both come. God interviews them both. Then, God tells the serpent, and each of them in turn, what He is going to do.

Picture a classic courtroom scene. The judge looks down sternly from the bench at three offenders and begins judging the first one. The others pay close attention to what is happening, thinking, "What will the judge say to me?"

Sounding alike. God's words to the serpent – the literal Hebrew words – are organized in a very distinct pattern. Then, when God speaks to the man, His words follow the same pattern. But God's words to the woman are organized in a very different way.

Why do God's words to the serpent and to the man follow one pattern? What is it about these two that causes God to speak to them in phrases that are echoes of each other?

The serpent and the man share something in common. Each one purposefully participated in the rebellion at the Tree. God had noticed. Here are points in God's words that are common to both the serpent and the man:

- God uses the Hebrew word "**curse**" (*'arur*) in speaking with each one.

- The word "**because**" opens each speech as God explains why He is imposing a curse.

- The **object** God curses is related to each one. "Cursed are *you*," God says to the serpent. "Cursed is the *ground* …," God says to the man.

- Each curse involves **eating** and **dust**. The serpent will "eat dust." The man will eat food that will come from the cursed soil, and eventually, he will return to dust.

- Each receives a note of lasting **duration**: "… all the days of your life." These curses are unlike any other curses in the Bible. They change the way of things. Even today, the two curses of Eden are in effect.

- **Echoing Hebrew verbs** close God's words ("shoof/shoove")
  - God tells the serpent: "… bruise (*shuph*) … bruise (*shuph*)" (The serpent's head will be *bruised* by his enemy.)
  - God tells the man: "return (*shuv*) … return (*shuv*)" (The man, made out of dust, will *return* to the dust.)

A separate sound. God's words to the woman are very different from His words to the serpent and the man because her case was different. She had not purposefully participated in the rebellion at the Tree. God had noticed this too.

She had been deceived, or tricked. God's words to her reflect this. The words addressed to her are different in grammar, logic, tone and content.

The common elements that are found in God's words to the serpent and to the man are missing in God's words to the woman:

- The Hebrew word **"curse"** (*'arur*) is not used.
- The word **"because"** is not used.
- The woman is not cursed, nor is anything cursed because of her.
- God does not speak to her about **eating** or **dust**.
- The words of **duration**, "all the days of your life," are not used.
- There are **no echoing Hebrew verbs**.

Here is a literal translation of Genesis 3:16.
Genesis 3:16 begins with an introductory phrase followed by four lines of words in which God speaks to the woman. Only a total of 11 Hebrew words are used in Lines 1-4. (Note: Often, it takes several English words to translate a single Hebrew word. In the following diagram, hyphens are used to show the extent of each individual Hebrew word.)

Genesis 3:16: God said to-the-woman,

Line

	#1	#2	#3	#4
1	Multiplying	I-will-multiply	your-toil	and-your-conception.

	#5	#6	#7
2	With-effort	you-will-bring-forth	children.

	#8	#9
3	Your-desire	[is] for-your-husband

	#10	#11
4	But-he	will-rule-over-you.

This diagram saves us the trouble of learning Hebrew to understand this verse. The English words in the diagram are literal translations of the Hebrew words in the verse.

Put together they do not sound like normal English. This is because they are not English. They represent words of a different language. By carefully looking at each of these eleven Hebrew words we can come to a correct grasp their meanings.

Heresy alert! Too many people skip over the differences between God's words to the woman and God's words to the serpent and the man. God's carefully chosen words to the woman are treated instead as if they are just one more parallel speech to one more willful rebel. This is one of the sources of the Eden heresies on leadership.

Misreading what God says to the woman in Genesis 3:16 is one of the sources of the Eden heresies on leadership.

Both Good News and Bad News

[16] Line 1: Multiplying, I-will-multiply   your-toil   and-your-conception

What did you say? It's likely that very few people set out to promote heresy. Perhaps nobody does. But since Genesis 3:16 has been used as a source of heresy it is especially worth looking at to make sure none of us gets it wrong.

The way to make sure we understand this key verse is to look at it carefully, word for word. In verse 16, after the introduction – "And God said to the woman…" – there are only 11 more Hebrew words in what God says to the woman. Reading them and understanding them will not be too difficult. The difficulty will be in not getting tangled up in any of the misinterpretations that have been built up around these words over the centuries.

        #1   #2   #4
Words 1, 2 and 4: "Multiplying, I-will-multiply   and-your-conception"

Hebrew words #1 and #2. God starts His words to the woman by repeating a verb in a way that shows emphasis in Hebrew. This verb is – "to multiply."
Literally, in 3:16 God says:

Multiplying, I-will-multiply

Translations make this sound more conversational by saying:

I will *surely* multiply

This is the verb God used when He told the woman and man "to multiply":

God blessed them and said to them,
"Be fruitful and *multiply*, and fill the earth...."
(Gen 1:28)

The *protevangelium*. In Genesis 3:15, in His final words to the serpent, God prophesies that the woman's "seed" (*zera'*) will defeat the Tempter. Bad news for the Tempter, but good news for the woman and all humanity!

In theology textbooks, this prophecy is known as the *protevangelium*, or the very first mention in the Bible of the good news of salvation. God's words in 3:15 are addressed to the Tempter, but are overheard by the woman.

God then turns to the woman. He twice uses the verb – "to multiply" – in the emphatic way a promise is started. He confirms to her, with word #4, the good news of her coming offspring.

In verse 16, God uses another Hebrew word that fits better with the poetic sound and alliteration of verse 16. Instead of the word "seed" or "offspring" (*zera'*), as in verse 15, God uses the Hebrew word "conception" (*heron*).

Thus, three of God's first four words to the woman in verse 16 assure her that, though she is under the sentence of death because of her disobedience, she will indeed conceive, making possible God's fulfillment of the *protevangelium* of verse 15, the promise of the Seed who will defeat the Tempter.

What's so special about "multiplying"? Not much, when it is used in the ordinary way. But it is *very* special when the verb "to multiply" is repeated for emphasis (as an "infinitive construct"). This is done only three times in the Old Testament. All three occur in the book of Genesis: in 3:16, 16:11 and 22:17.

In Genesis 16:11 and 22:17, "multiplying, I-will-multiply" introduces the promise of having "offspring." The Hebrew word that follows is "seed" (*zera'*), which refers to those who will come after (children, grand children, great grand children, and so on), or to put it another way, those who will be one's descendance. In both Genesis 16 and 22, God says,

Multiplying, I-will-multiply your seed

God makes this promise to Hagar in Genesis 16:10. God's words to Hagar, "I-will-surely-multiply" include the word "seed" and encourage her.

Familiar "Leadership" Heresies Uncovered   by Bruce C. E. Fleming
www.ThinkAgainAboutTheBible.com

I-will-surely-multiply your *seed* (*zera'*)
so that they shall be too many to count.

After Abraham shows his faith in regards to the sacrifice of his only son Isaac, God blesses Abraham and makes this promise to him in Genesis 22:17,

Multiplying, I-will-multiply your *seed* (*zera'*) ...

In Genesis 22, the surrounding context reads as follows in 16-18:

By myself I have sworn, declares the Lord, because you have done this thing, and have not withheld your son, your only son, indeed I will greatly bless you, and *I will surely multiply your seed* as the stars of the heavens, and as the sand which is on the seashore; and your seed shall possess the gate of their enemies. And in your seed all the nations of the earth shall be blessed, because you have obeyed my voice.

God's words to Abraham: "I-will-surely-multiply ..." are in the context of a *blessing*. They initiate the promises of numerous offspring, overcoming his enemies and bringing great blessing to all the nations of the earth.

In Genesis 3:16, the promise of offspring is made to the woman in the Garden. This time, the word "conception" (*heron*) is used, which fits the alliteration of the Hebrew words in Line 1:

"I will surely multiply ... your *conception*."

The word "seed" (*zera'*), that is used in Genesis 16:10 and 22:17, is present in the context of God's words to the woman. It's counterpart is found several words earlier, in Genesis 3:15.

The announcement that the woman in Eden would surely conceive, meant that the Deliverer who would vanquish the enemy was on the way. This was wonderful news! Despite the fact that some people teach the heretical idea that bearing children is a curse the woman must suffer, the opposite is true.

Hebrew word #4 is a *singular collective noun*. This means that it is a singular noun that has packed within it the promise of many. The word "seed" in verse 15 is also a singular collective noun.

Looking back from our perspective in history, we identify the promised "seed" of verse 15 as Jesus. He was just one person. But the singular collective noun "seed" had packed into it the whole line of descendants who would be born from Eden to Mary in Bethlehem. (These descendants are listed in Luke 1.)

Hebrew word #4 in 3:16, *heron*, is also a singular collective noun. The Hebrew word means "conception" or "pregnancy." God personally assures the woman that she will have "conception." This singular collective noun of promise, in 3:16, is linked to the singular collective noun promised just before, in 3:15.

Here are the words that God spoke to the serpent and to the woman, that link the two verses:

> v. 15 ... between your seed and her *seed.*
> He shall bruise you on the head
> And you shall bruise him on the heel.
> v. 16 I-will-surely-multiply ... your-*conception*

Joy was six months pregnant when we first arrived in Africa. We noticed right away that people in Africa hold the opinion that having children is not a chore but a blessing. Everyone enthusiastically shared our anticipation and joy at the coming birth of our first child!

The words to the woman in Genesis 3:16 convey a great promise! First of all, they remind her of God's mandate to be fruitful and *multiply* (1:28). But more than that, in spite of her sin, apparently God will not annul that mandate as far as she is concerned, nor will God curse her (like the serpent in verse 15). Instead, God promises her that she will surely *conceive a child.*

Later, these first words of promise are elaborated on and expanded in God's promise to Abraham. This is all part of the history of God's promised Deliverer, the Savior of the world!

Heresy alert! Many people, however, have not noticed the good news God gives to the woman in the Garden. They assume that God's words to her are just as stern as His words to the serpent. They hold the same view as the ancient pagan religions that looked down on women like Pandora. But the first woman was no Pandora! This was not how God treated the one who received the promise of multiplied conception.

Many people even speak of "The Three Curses," as if there were a "curse" in God's words to the woman. They think God cursed (1) the serpent, (2) the woman, and (3) the man. Counting curses this way, they are wrong two out of three times! Only on the first count are they right, the curse on the serpent in verse 14.

In short order, the Hebrew word "curse" is used a second time in the Garden of Eden, in verse 17. But God only curses twice. He only curses the serpent and the soil. God curses neither the woman nor the man!

Hebrew words #3 and #4. To understand the rest of Genesis 3:16, it is best to keep in mind all four Hebrew words of Line 1 – especially the three positive ones, which are shown below in bold:

> #1 **"Multiplying,"** (positive)
> #2 **"I-will-multiply"** (positive)
> #3 "your-sorrowful-toil" (*'itsebon*)
> #4 **"and-your-conception."** (positive)

Even though God confirms the good news about conception in Line 1, there is also bad news to announce. God says the woman will surely experience "*'itsebon.*" What is *'itsebon*?

Of all the words the woman might have expected to hear, this negative word likely would not have been one of them. It describes something wholly new to her experience. In the Eden she knows, there has been no *'itsebon.* How could this happen? She will have to wait a moment for God is not going to tell her. But we can find out right now.

The word *'itsebon* is used only three times in the Bible. All three occur in the first five chapters of Genesis – in 3:16, in 3:17 and in 5:29. A careful look at the context in which this word is used helps define its precise meaning.

Defining the bad news.

(1). Genesis 5:29 gives us a clear definition of *'itsebon.* In 5:29, the parents of newborn Noah give him a name that expresses their hope that life will be better with this child around. They hope that he will provide relief from the *'itsebon,* or "**sorrowful toil,**" they are experiencing as the result of the curse on the soil:

> … called his name Noah, saying, "This one will comfort us concerning our work and the **sorrowful toil** [*'itsebon*] of our hands, because of the ground which the Lord has cursed."

This *'itsebon* is not just any generic kind of "work." The English words "work" or "toil" are not nearly as precise as the Hebrew word. *'itsebon* is a very specific kind of toil, a "sorrowful toil." It means: "the-sorrowful-toil-which-results-from-God's-curse-on-the-soil."

24

(2). Genesis 3:17 describes the historic moment when *'itsebon* comes to be. It results from the curse God imposes on the soil because of the man.

In 3:17, God curses the ground. God then tells the first man how this curse will impact him. The man will experience something new. It will be *'itsebon.*

> Cursed is the ground because of you;
> through **sorrowful toil** (*'itsebon*)
> you will eat of it all the days of your life.

The man will experience this "sorrowful toil" as a direct result of God's curse on the ground. This curse will make raising food from the soil much harder. It will raise sweat on his brow. Every time this happens, it will be a sorrowful reminder of why he is experiencing this *'itsebon.*

(3). In Genesis 3:16, the woman hears from God that she will experience *'itsebon.* For her, this announcement is a *proleptic prophecy.*

A proleptic prophecy foretells the result, but not the cause of the result. That is explained later. God tells the woman that she will experience "sorrowful toil" (*'itsebon*), but she is not told where it will come from, why it will come about, nor what it will feel like.

She learns much more when God addresses the man. She overhears that it will come about because of the curse God will impose on the soil "because of the man" (3:17). But the woman too will experience *'itsebon,* as she walks the same earth and works in **sorrowful toil** the same cursed soil as the man.

The meaning of the word *'itsebon* in verse 16 is explained in verse 17. Here is how *'itsebon* is linked in verses 16 and 17.

3:16 I will multiply your **sorrowful toil** and your conception

↓

3:17 Cursed is the ground … in **sorrowful toil** you shall eat of it …

Heresy alert! Perversely, a number of modern language versions of the Bible do not translate *'itsebon* the same way in verse 16 and verse 17. This obscures both its precise meaning and how the two verses are related. Those who unwittingly use these translations are vulnerable to being taken in by the "leadership" heresies.

This kind of "toil" has nothing to do with childbirth. Check your own Bible. Does it clearly show that God promises to multiply two things in 3:16, sorrowful toil *and* conception? This is the "bad news / good news" of Genesis 3:16. God guarantees that not only one thing ("sorrowful toil" – the bad news) will occur, but another thing ("conception" – the good news), will come to pass. The bad news is that the woman will experience "sorrowful toil" as she works the soil alongside the man outside of Eden.

This kind of "sorrowful toil" has nothing to do with childbirth.

Many translations incorrectly make it look like God promises a change in only one thing, and that thing occurs at the end of nine months of pregnancy. Many Bible translations make up a phrase that looks like God only promises *one* thing. They make it impossible to see God's announcement to the woman of impending *itsebon*. They omit, as well, the clear reference to "conception." They render the last part of Line 1 as if God promised the woman only multiplied "pain-in-childbearing"!

This mistranslation of Genesis 3:16 gives the impression of some kind of a "curse" imposed by God on the woman, when instead God treats her very carefully and very kindly. It is extraordinary to learn, that what God actually said and did in the Garden, is very different from what many have been led to *think* He did.

Here is the source of many "leadership" heresies. To think that God curses the woman in the Garden can lead through mistaken "logic" to all kinds of false beliefs and damaging practices.

**Mistranslations of 3:16 give the impression
that God imposes some kind of a "curse" on the woman,
when instead God treats her very kindly.**

This misleading of the church by faulty translation is so unnecessary! The old *King James Version* of the Bible did a much better job of translating these Hebrew words into English. New translations into modern languages around the world can still be corrected in future editions. They must be!

Where do translations go wrong?
Sometimes, when translating the Old Testament into a modern language, it is acceptable to drop the Hebrew word "and." For example, "and" can be dropped when it is found in a grammatical construction called a *hendiadys*.

When translators encounter a true hendiadys, they push the words together to indicate a single idea. Here's a helpful explanation of a hendiadys:

> A hendiadys is a way of combining two Hebrew words
> so that one of the words defines the other.

There is **no hendiadys** in Genesis 3:16. Yet, this is just how many modern translators have treated Line 1 of Genesis 3:16. They have dropped the word "and" and have attempted to make sense out of the remaining words. This is where they have ended up seriously mangling the thought of Line 1!

Older translations, some of them very old, did not make this mistake. In the first translation of the Old Testament more than 2,000 years ago, this line in Genesis 3:16 was not translated as if it had a hendiadys. This ancient translation, the *Septuagint*, clearly used the word "and" surrounded by two nouns. This way of translating "and" was done in the already mentioned *King James Version* of 1611, and in the more modern *New English Bible* of 1970.

So *why* do other translations drop the "and"? This is not a mere matter of quibbling over conjunctions.

Hunting for a hendiadys. One crisp autumn, Joy's study of this topic led us to New England. This area of the country is especially beautiful when the leaves change color. It is also the home of several renowned research schools and libraries. So she scheduled a visit with an Old Testament professor at a famous school and asked me to accompany her.

As we went down the half flight of stairs to his office entry, a few copper colored leaves swirled around our ankles in the autumn breeze. Inside, his office was crammed with books.

We found space to sit and talk about the "and" in Line 1 of Genesis 3:16. "Professor, would you look at this Hebrew 'and' and tell us what you see?"

His comments, punctuated by long pauses as he reflected deeply, ran something like this:

> Here we have an example of a hendiadys – two things joined by 'and' to mean a different thing.
> … Yes, an example of a hendiadys. … Of course, *this* one doesn't look like your ordinary hendiadys. The typical indicators are not present. …
> In fact, there is nothing in the grammar to indicate that the words in this verse should be combined as if there were a hendiadys present.

The words *could* very well be read normally as two separate things with 'and' in between joining them. … But, even though *this doesn't look anything like a hendiadys* and it could be correct to say there is no hendiadys here … we know that it is a hendiadys.

"Thank you so very much, professor," Joy said when the time came to a close. As we climbed up the stairs into the breeze and the leaves that greeted us, one thing was perfectly clear from our hour-long discussion on the word "and." There *wasn't any reason* to drop it out.

There wasn't any reason to push the words together in Line 1 even though the professor had said, "We *know* it is a hendiadys." Perhaps he was influenced by the writings of others who had passed along the incorrect assumption that this was a hendiadys. In mathematical language, they thought that Line 1 read, *a (b+c) = ad*. According to them, a new thing, *d*, was the result of God's actions.

Certainly, this had become a widely held view. But, the professor's observations, made in front of us, clearly showed that the widely held view wasn't necessarily correct.

Without squeezing the words of Line 1 into a hendiadys, the math in Genesis 3:16, Line 1, is easy to calculate: *One* thing, plus *one more* thing, joined by the word "and" adds up to *two* different things – "sorrowful-toil *and* conception." It does *not* add up to one new thing – "pain-in-childbearing"!

Do the math. To illustrate how the Hebrew grammar in Line 1 works, it may be compared to the *distributive property* in mathematics. In math language, the distributive property looks like this:

$$a\ (b+c) = ab + ac$$

The left side of the equation is equivalent to the right side of the equation. The "a" term is simply distributed to each of the other two terms, "b" and "c." The result is that both the left and right sides of the equation are equivalent.

In the case of Genesis 3:16 the left side of the equation is "God will surely multiply." The right side of the equation has two elements. The resulting meaning is that (a) God will surely multiply (b) "sorrowful-toil" and also that (a) God will surely multiply (b) the woman's "conception." As in the math equation above, God is going to multiply, not one, but two things.

Rise and Fall in Eden. What the professor's words revealed about the imaginary hendiadys, fit well with what Joy had discovered about the passage in other ways. Line 1 *had* to be the multiplication of two different things in order for the verse to fit in with the structure of the rest of the verses in the overall passage in Genesis 2-3.

The verses on the Garden of Eden are organized into seven Sections that mirror each other in a parallel way (in a *chiasm*). Usually the most important idea in this kind of parallelism is placed in the middle, which in this case is stated in Section D. The first three Sections are mirrored by the last three Sections of the passage.

Together, these Sections make up the record of all that happened in the Garden of Eden. In the first three Sections, Genesis 2:5-15, 16-17 and 18-24 (or A, B and C), *God* is at work. Everything becomes more complete, and better and better.

The fourth section, 2:25 (or D), is the height of creation. God has ended His creative work. All is very good and harmonious.

In the last three Sections, Genesis 3:1-5, 6-7 and 8-24 (or C', B' and A'), *sin* is at work. Everything goes downhill!

For Hebrew readers of Genesis 2-3, this grouping of words into seven Sections is aesthetically pleasing. In Genesis 2:5-3:24, the *form* of the Hebrew words corresponds to the *content* of the passage. The way the passage is organized is as if the first four sections are to be read with a smile, while the last three are to be read with a frown. Understanding the *form* of Genesis 2:5-3:24 is important because it corresponds to the *content* of the passage.

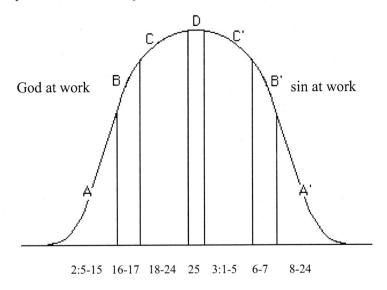

Familiar "Leadership" Heresies Uncovered   by Bruce C. E. Fleming
www.ThinkAgainAboutTheBible.com

Here is another way to diagram the same parallelism of the seven Sections:

Section A – Genesis 2:5-15

Section B – Genesis 2:16-17

Section C – Genesis 2:18-24

Section D – Genesis 2:25

Section C' – Genesis 3:1-5

Section B' – Genesis 3:6-7

Section A' – Genesis 3:8-24

Discovering parallel linchpins.
In Genesis 2:5 to 3:24, Section A is mirrored by Section A' (pronounced "A prime"). Joy knew, that the more she learned about Section A in Genesis 2, the more she might be able to understand Section A' in Genesis 3.

In her studies, she came across an article by Professor Isaac Kikawada who had discovered an "interlocking crossover point," or *linchpin*, in Genesis 11. In a footnote in his article, he mentioned that he had also found an interlocking crossover point in Genesis 2:7-9, with 2:8 at the center. His footnote didn't mention anything about Genesis 3.

According to Kikawada, in the Genesis 2 linchpin, two key words linked verse 2:8 to the verses before it and after it. One pointed back to the previous verse. One pointed forward to the following verse.

According to Kikawada (*Rhetorical Criticism*, p. 24), in verse 8, God brings together both plant life and humanity. Kikawada showed that this important "linking" takes place not only in *what* the words say but also in the *way* the words are arranged. The initial Hebrew word of verse 8 points down to the first word in verse 9. The last Hebrew word in verse 8 points back to the first word in verse 7. The interlocking crossover point, as diagramed in Hebrew by Kikawada, is shown below. (Note: Hebrew is written from right to left.)

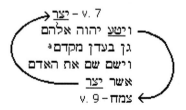

Familiar "Leadership" Heresies Uncovered by Bruce C. E. Fleming
www.ThinkAgainAboutTheBible.com

Here is how the linchpin in 2:7-9 looks in literal English:

(7)   God *__formed__* the man from the dust …

(8) God **planted**…and… *__formed__*

(9) God **made grow** trees from the ground…

Joy realized that Kikawada had made a major discovery in Section A that could help in understanding Section A'! Since Section A' mirrors Section A, was there also a linchpin in Section A'? As far as she could tell, no one had ever written about a linchpin in Genesis 3.

She checked the Hebrew of Section A' to see if it had a verse with key words that linked it to the verses around it. She found them, joined by "and" in Line 1 of verse 16. Genesis 3:16 contains the linchpin for Section A'!

As in the first linchpin, there are two distinct words, one that links to the verse before it and one that links to the verse after it. The Hebrew word, "conception," in verse 16 links to the word "seed" in the verse before it, and the Hebrew word "sorrowful-toil" (*'itsebon*) in verse 16 links to the same word, "sorrowful-toil," in the verse after it!

This precise way of arranging these words did not happen by accident. It is one of the ways Hebrew is used deliver information in a memorable way.

The use of the links in this linchpin meant that God's words to the woman in verse 16 were linked to two elements in the speeches before and after it, to the serpent and to the man. No wonder many people have "felt" like verse 16 is just another speech in a 1-2-3 progression of speeches from God to the three participants in the Great Disobedience. But linchpin links don't indicate parallelism. They communicate their own meaning. God's speech to the woman is very different from His parallel words to the serpent and the man.

Here is a diagram of the linchpin in Genesis 3:15-17,

```
(15)        I will put enmity   …   between your seed and her seed

(16) I will surely multiply your sorrowful toil and your conception

(17) Cursed is the ground … in sorrowful toil you shall eat of it
```

When modern language translations don't clearly translate the Hebrew words "sorrowful toil" and "conception," the average reader can't begin to notice the linkages between these three verses. Is it any wonder then, that incorrect assumptions, even heresies, are drawn from the words in translations that really don't come from God's words to us in the original Hebrew Old Testament documents?

> **Incorrect doctrines (heresies) are built upon these words.**
> **Our modern translations give us words that are not found in the Bible!**

Most modern translations make it look like God is multiplying just one thing, and it is one big *bad* thing! How horrible!

Here is how two modern translations present Line 1. Notice how the two parts of the linchpin are not discernable, and that it looks like God promises to do something extra, something bad, to the woman:

NIV: "I will greatly increase your pains in childbearing"
NASB: "I will greatly multiply your pain in childbirth"

Translated into English like this, the Hebrew words that link Line 1 to verses 15 and 17 cannot even be guessed at. Furthermore, where does the idea of *pains-in-childbearing* come from?

"Conception" was a good and natural event when God created woman. It remains a good and natural event. Yet these translations make it appear that God somehow "zaps" the woman and turns "childbearing" into a bad thing!

"Zapping" the woman with pains in childbearing turns conceiving children into a punishment when the babies are born. Where has this idea come from? How much damage has been caused by this idea, which is foreign to the Bible?

The mistaken idea of "the Temptress." One day, during our studies in Europe, my professor took our class on a trip to another city for a walking tour. When we visited the medieval cathedral, he showed us its sculptures standing out from their stone backgrounds.

He helped us appreciate the stories they told – "Here is a choir of angels." "Here are the disciples."

Then the professor showed us the statue I will never forget. "This is Eve," he said with his thick German/Alsatian accent. "See! She is holding out an apple and has a smile on her face. She has been standing like this for 700 years."

He motioned to us to step up close and look behind her. We were shocked to see stone snakes imbedded in her shoulders, writhing down her back! The professor commented, "This shows what the sculptor thought of her motivation. He thought *she* was *the Temptress*. In front she looks beguiling. But in back she shows signs that she is in league with the serpent!" he said.

This medieval idea is not what the Bible teaches. The Bible says the Tempter in the Garden was the *serpent*. That is why God cursed the serpent Tempter. And that is one of the reasons why, when we look for a curse on the woman in the Hebrew text, we find none.

Who is right? When all is said and done, the grammar and the context of Line 1 of Genesis 3:16 help us determine its meaning. God promises two things. Each one ties in to the immediate context through the linchpin construction.

Translations that make it look like God takes supplemental action against the woman in regards to childbearing are incorrect. Disengaged from the actual words of the passage, they promote speculation that leads to heretical teachings on the part of the woman in the Great Disobedience and on her place in the home and in the world.

Here is a translation of Line 1 that is faithful to the text and the context:

"I will surely multiply your sorrowful toil and your conception"

Teaching, Not Stuttering (Line 2)

[16]Line 2: "With-effort you-will-bring-forth children"

As we have seen, many modern translations stray from the meaning of the Hebrew words in Line 1 of verse 3:16. What is worse is that translations of Line 2 continue and even complicate further this confusion.

Here is how two modern versions present Line 2 in English:

NIV: "In pain you will bring forth children"
NASB: "In pain you shall bring forth children"

In the end, most modern translations make it sound as if God is doing little more than stuttering and repeating what was given as their translations of Line 1. Let's look at Line 2 more carefully. At this point God assumes the role of teacher. He continues to instruct the woman through the rest of verse 16, in Lines 3 and 4. In this teaching section, she learns about life on earth as a "dead person" with a mortal body, married to another person with a fallen nature.

In these lines, God becomes the "Great Instructor."
He teaches the woman details about "life after death."

In Line 2, God explains to the woman what giving birth with a mortal body will be like. This addresses the natural question that springs from the last word in Line 1, "*conception*."

Line

	#5	#6	#7
2	With-effort	you-will-bring-forth	children

Hebrew word #5. Nine months after conception (Hebrew word #4) comes childbirth. And outside of Eden (where God knows she and the man will soon find themselves), childbirth will be different for the woman. She will not give birth in the Garden of Eden, but in a hostile environment. She will give birth with a mortal body subject to difficulty and even death.

With great gentleness, God describes for her what she will experience. He uses the word "effort," or *'etsev*. When she begins to experience this *'etsev*, she must know that this will not be what it feels like to die but the beginning of the delivery of her child.

The Hebrew word "effort" is a common word, one that is not used only a few times in the Bible. It is used in various places as a general term not limited to childbearing. It means "effort," "labor," or "hard work."

Deep winter in Minnesota brings snowdrifts in one's driveway, or even across the road. It is not unusual for someone to get stuck in a snowdrift several feet high. When that happens, it is usually possible to push the car out, with help.

Those who do the pushing have to strive mightily to help the driver get enough traction and momentum to move the car out of the drift. The work is not painful, necessarily, but it takes great effort, teamwork and a lot of perspiration to push the car out.

This is what is meant by Hebrew word #5 – **"with-effort."** In this way the woman will bring children into the world.

Heresy alert! Once more, it appears that teaching that God added "pain" to the childbirth process is just not correct. It is *not* what Line 1 said. And it is *not* what Line 2 says either.

Hard as it is to believe, this false teaching, that woman was subjected by God to painful childbirth, has been used to justify the withholding of help to a mother in childbirth. It is even recorded that a woman who took an herbal pain reliever was sentenced to death for supposedly going against God's will that women suffer from pain in childbirth!

Jungle hospital. Joy gave birth to our first child in a mission hospital in the steamy rain forests of northwestern Congo, then called Zaire. As we drove to the hospital in the mission pickup truck, palm trees stood sentinel duty outside, a red-tailed African gray parrot flew overhead and, nearby, a ten-foot high termite hive was tinted pink by the setting sun.

There was no ultramodern delivery room available. The setting was more like a field hospital in time of war. The doctor, who had driven the pickup truck, excused himself to go across the road to turn on the diesel-powered generator. Then we had electric lights and Joy had a fan in that stifling room.

The medical staff was superb. The lead doctor was ably assisted by two other doctors. Both were Harvard Medical School graduates. Plus, there were several fine nurses in attendance.

A nurse and I were on either side of Joy as we timed her breathing. We had bought a book on natural childbirth while we were still in France and Joy had studied it and practiced the breathing exercises.

It was *very* hard work, thirty-six hours of hard work (most of the time was at home before coming to the hospital). She received no medication of any kind. I admired her great effort, which was followed by exhaustion and exhilaration, as Joy gave birth to our firstborn, Christy!

Seven years later, we had just returned from Africa and were in Minnesota when it came time for Mark to be born. This time Joy asked in advance if she might have an anesthetic, only if and when she needed it. The staff assured her that would be just fine.

She waited until that moment did arrive, and asked for an anesthetic. "Oh, it's too late to ask for that now," she was told. "You should have asked *earlier* in the process. Taking anything this close to the delivery is not possible now."

And so, once in a jungle hospital, and once in a western hospital, she experienced very "natural" childbirth. She gave birth through her own intense *effort* (and with God's help). When God explains this sort of childbirth to the first mother-to-be in Line 2, He describes it to her in such a way that she will understand what is happening without the benefit of having watched any other human mother give birth before.

Line 2, in Genesis 3:16, is extraordinarily sensitive, clinical and respectful. *"Effort"* – hard physical work requiring endurance – is going to be her experience in childbirth. This description of how the first woman will experience *birth* with her mortal body, contrasts with what God tells the man when He addresses him, telling him about the *death* of his mortal body. In both cases, God teaches the first couple what to expect, giving them insight into the implications of their mortality as fallen human beings.

Instructions in three lines.

God's words to the woman in verse 16, Lines 2-4 are words of description and of teaching. In them, God tells the woman what her physical experience will now be like.

God also knows that she is married to a dead man. Her husband was a willful participant in the Great Disobedience and signs are already showing that his relationships with God and his wife have been corrupted.

Very soon they will find themselves outside of Eden with the way back barred by armed angel warriors. With supreme urgency and maximum use of His every word, God instructs the woman in Lines 2, 3 and 4.

The changes. Two changes that will have a physical impact on the woman:

– There is now *death*, and she has a mortal (or death body) – the consequence of sin (foretold in Gen 2:17).

– There will be the *curse on the ground*, with its "sorrowful toil," which will be the result of a separate act of God. (Gen 3:17).

Having disobeyed God's prohibition, her body is now subject to difficulty and death. The kind of "effort" required for childbirth, spoken about in Line 2 of Genesis 3:16, comes in the context of a fallen world and a body now subject to mortality. But God does not curse her body, as He just did to the serpent. The changes she will experience come from other causes than a curse, or a "zap" from God.

Dealing with dyslexic translations. The evening after the Old Testament professor told us about the hendiadys of Line 1 (that wasn't there), I was still having a hard time sorting it all out. The meaning of Lines 1 and 2 was hard for me to see.

This, I found out, was because various mistakes in translating the Hebrew words had been piled one on top of the other. Also, the many familiar theological teachings that had been built on these mistaken foundations bothered me. Numerous phrases from sermons, articles and even hymns, that followed the faulty translations, ran through my mind.

For my first step, I decided to be content with what had become clear for me – God was multiplying not *one*, but *two* things in Line 1 of Genesis 3:16. I decided to leave it there and sleep on it.

When I discussed it with Joy the next day, things became clearer. It helped to realize that not only had people mistranslated Lines 1 and 2, but they had also *intertwined* the Lines, inserting *mistaken elements* from one Line into the other! No wonder it was hard to sort out!

Sorting this out in the following diagrams illustrates how the Hebrew words have been mistranslated and misplaced. For me, it is a sad exercise to have to untie this knot of mistranslations. They should be clearly translated and trustworthy lines and not require this effort. But, such is the case.

Here are Lines 1 and 2, translated word for word. Remember, because it sometimes takes several modern language words to translate one Hebrew word, each Hebrew word is numbered and is indicated by the equivalent English words linked by dashes:

Diagram 1. How these Lines are written in Hebrew

1	2	3	4
Multiplying	I-will-multiply	your-sorrowful-toil	and-your-conception

5	6	7
With-effort	you-will-bring-forth	children

Modern translations, however, make Line 1 (words 1-4) and Line 2 (words 5-7) look as they might appear to a dyslexic reader. They mix words and meanings, and even make some words disappear. They do this by taking words from positions #5 and #6 in Line 2, and using them in Line 1, in positions #3 and #4.

To make matters worse, the words that are moved around from one position to another are not correctly translated! First, here are the words that are commonly mistranslated (the key Hebrew words are in parentheses):

Diagram 2. Notice the words that will be mistranslated (bold)

1	2	3	4
Multiplying	I-will-multiply	your-**sorrowful-toil**	**and**-your-**conception**
		(*'itsebon*)	(*heron*)

5	6	7
With-**effort**	you-will-bring-forth	children
(*'etsev*)	(*yalad*)	

The third diagram shows the final dyslexic version that is found in most of the Bible translations we own today.

First, notice that "your-sorrowful-toil" (*'itsebon*) from Line 1, and "with-effort" (*'etsev*) from Line 2, are treated as if they both mean the same thing. Though *'itsebon* and *'etsev* sound somewhat similar, and may come from the same root, they do *not* mean the same thing! And neither one means "pain in delivery."

Secondly, notice that "conception" (*heron* from the end of Line 1), and "bring-forth" (*yalad* from Line 2) that comes nine months later, are confused with one another. In the process an incorrect thought is pasted over the end of Line 1 – "in childbearing" – even though this not the right way to translate the word *heron*.

Here is the resulting dyslexic version presented to us by modern translations, with the displaced, and the replaced, words underlined. (A sense of familiarity to these words may make them "sound" right to you, but beware – this is a flawed and misleading "translation.")

Diagram 3. The dyslexic version

1	2	5	6
Multiplying	I-will-multiply	your-**pain**-**in-childbearing**	

3	6	7
In-**painful toil**	you-will-bring-forth	children

Stuttering? With the Hebrew words mixed up and mistranslated as shown in Diagram 3, the two lines become strangely redundant. Line 1 appears to be all about painful childbirth and Line 2 looks like it is about painful childbirth as well.

In this misleading version, Line 2 sounds like little more than a repetition of Line 1. The real Hebrew word #3 ("sorrowful-toil-because-of-the-curse-on-the-soil") disappears, and it seems that God is imposing some *new* pain *just for the woman* when she brings forth children! All this, contradicts the message of the Hebrew words in Line 2 which consist of gentle instruction as God tells the woman about the physical consequences for her of mortality and death.

In the rearrangement of Lines 1 and 2 of verse 3:16, the original word meanings are changed as follows:

- It sounds as if God is multiplying not two things, one good and one bad, but just one big bad thing.

- Obscured and lost is the resemblance to Genesis 16:11 and 22:17, "I will surely multiply your seed (descendance or offspring)."

- The linchpin, and its connection of multiplied conception with the promise of a deliverer in verse 15, in the *protevangelium*, is lost.

- The linchpin, and its connection to the curse on the soil in verse 17, is lost.

- The meaning of *'itsebon* is obscured and confused. *'itsebon* is made out to mean "pain" or "*painful* toil" instead of the uniquely God-caused "sorrowful-toil-because-of-the-curse-on-the-soil."

- *'etsev* is made out to mean "*pain*" and not "effort" or "work."

- From Line 2, the verb "you-will-bring-forth" (children), is borrowed and reshaped into a noun and placed in Line 1. In so doing, 'itsebon is misapplied to childbirth, instead of to the soil.

- A preposition is invented to smooth over the changes to the text, making it seem more sensible. It replaces a pronoun. Thus, "*your*-conception" becomes "*in*-childbearing" or "*in*-childbirth."

This deceiving mix-up is eerily reminiscent of Genesis 3:1-5 where the serpent craftily rearranged the word order of God's command of 2:16-17 and turned the meaning of God's words completely upside down.

Tracking responsibility. In Line 1, God carefully tells the woman He will take action and cause two things to come about. In Lines 2-4, God takes no further action. He explains to the woman what will come about now that she has a mortal body and a sinful husband.

In Line 1, God is the agent who acts ("*I* will ...."). In Lines 2-4, God simply teaches the woman what she will experience because of the results of her sin.

In Genesis 3:16

God is responsible
for the changes announced in Line 1.

Sin and death are responsible
for the changes God explains in Lines 2-4.

Hebrew words #6 and #7. In the second part of Line 2, God uses the Hebrew verb *yalad* (word #6) to describe "bearing children." It means the woman will "bring forth," "bear," "beget." This same word *yalad* is used extensively in the genealogical lists (it is translated by the quaint sounding word "begat" in the King James Version).

The woman already knows from God's words to the serpent in 3:15, and His words to her in Line 1 of 3:16, that she will become a mother. But the last word in Line 2 adds a very exciting detail!

Up to this point, each time God referred to her offspring, He used words that could have stood either for one, or for many. These *collective singular nouns* were: "seed" (verse 15) and "conception" (verse 16). But at the end of Line 2, God uses the *plural* Hebrew word "children," clearly indicating that whoever is her first child will not be her last!

Familiar "Leadership" Heresies Uncovered   by Bruce C. E. Fleming
www.ThinkAgainAboutTheBible.com

She will have a multiple number of *children* (word #7). After she gives birth to her firstborn, another is sure to come.

Heresy alert! If God *had* found it right and proper to curse the woman, changing her body in some distorted way, *then* one could assume that she must have been a terrible sinner to merit such treatment. The common, and incorrect, way to translate Lines 1 and 2 makes it look like this is what happened.

It is not hard to see how some might build on this idea of "woman – the terrible sinner." But this turns the truth upside down. It twists the meaning of the words of the Bible.

A Desirable Desire (Line 3)

[16]Line 3: "Your-desire [is] to-your-husband"

At this critical moment in her personal history, as the woman is face to face with God, she waits to hear if He has more details to reveal. God does not disappoint her.

When the woman and the man were beginning their life together, God had judged all of creation to be "very good" (Genesis 1:31). In Line 3, as He continues to teach her, God takes care to reinforce what is *still* good.

The *Evangelical Dictionary of Theology* says that the man and the woman "accuse each other" before God. That may be how the story is often told, but it is *not* what Genesis tells us. This is an example of a contradiction of what the Bible really says.

Attitude check. When God interviewed the woman in Genesis 3:13, He asked her,

"What have you done?"

She replied clearly and simply,

"The serpent deceived me, and I ate."

In God's Garden courtroom she told the truth, the whole truth and nothing but the truth. The truth of her words was immediately confirmed in verse 14. God said to the serpent, "Because [not "if"] you have done this...."

The truth of the woman's reply is confirmed further in the New Testament:
- In 2 Corinthians 11:3, Paul speaks to all Christians as he refers to Genesis 3, "the serpent *deceived* Eve by his craftiness."

- In 1 Timothy, Paul compares himself (1:13) with others who had gone astray (2:8-12) when he writes in 2:14, "the woman *being deceived* fell into transgression." Having *first* been deceived, the woman *then* sinned.

When Joy was studying the fables that have been encrusted onto Genesis 3:16, she found that many people, both ancient and modern, claim that the woman sinned on purpose. Not only were they in wrong on this point, she also found many claiming that she sinned more than one time, in *additional* ways. This is *not* what the Bible says, and the extra sins they incorrectly fault her for need not be repeated here (some of them are quite foul). What the woman *did* do in the Garden was to participate in the Great Disobedience – in a state of deception.

In His justice, God takes into account the state of a sinner's heart. Those who sin without realizing what they are doing are treated differently from those who deliberately sin. For example, in the Old Testament the sacrifices required from someone who sinned in ignorance were fewer in number than those required for someone who had sinned on purpose (Numbers 15:22-31).

God judges a wrongdoer based on the attitude of the heart,
based on whether a sin is committed
purposefully or ***unintentionally***.

In her disobedience, the woman had been deceived into eating. She did not eat in open rebellion against God. In her heart, she sinned "without malice aforethought."

Hebrew words #8 and #9. In Line 3, God helps the woman do a reality check on her heart. God confirms to her the "desire" she has for her husband. In relation to him, her desire is also "without malice."

Before and after. When God made the woman, the man was clearly thrilled. He burst into poetry (2:24). Together, the couple was not ashamed (2:25).

Then, the serpent came along. He deceived the woman into eating and this is what she admitted (3:13). When she shared the forbidden fruit with the man, it was in a deceived state – not as Satan's assistant.

When God speaks to her in Line 3, her "desire" is still for her husband and God says so. Line 3 says this without using a verb. Translators appropriately supply the verb "is" to indicate her state of being. Her desire for her husband is still her state of being.

The Hebrew word used to describe her heart is *teshuqah*, or "desire." In 3:16, God checks the woman's heart and, yes, she still *desires* her husband. The word "love" has not been used in the Bible anywhere thus far, but it fits here.

However, the word "desire" is not used to describe the man. God will comment on his attitude in Line 4. God's evaluation of the woman's heart in Line 3 will serve as a measuring point when the state of his heart is compared to the loving desire of his wife.

Her "desire" for her husband is her state of being.

Heresy alert! One respected twentieth century commentator got Line 3 very wrong. He said that the woman's desire in Genesis 3:16 was the outgrowth of her earlier desire to lead her husband into temptation. As a result, he continued, she had developed a crazed and sinful desire, "bordering on nymphomania."

Is this what the Bible says? No! But when this idea has been included in commentaries, or sermons, or other places, it has provided the foundation for heretical teaching on the imagined "meanness" and "evil intent" of woman. This idea must be uncovered, labeled as incorrect, removed from our understanding of the woman's "desire" and be replaced by the correct meaning.

Others have attempted to compare her "desire" to the desire depicted in the word picture in Genesis 4:7. This verse is outside of the chiasm of which 3:16 is a part, the passage of 2:4-3:24.

The "desire" mentioned in Genesis 4 is part of the next passage. What we learn from that occurrence is that "desire" (*teshuqah*) is not necessarily a sexual term because it is used in a non-sexual way in the account of Cain and Abel.

The word *teshuqah* is used only one other time in the Old Testament. In Song of Solomon 7:10, *teshuqah* describes Solomon. His lover refers to his "desire" in these words – "I am my beloved's and his *desire* is toward me."

The word "desire" is not used when God describes the man in Line 4. But God's evaluation of the woman's heart will serve as a measuring point when the state of the man's heart is compared to the loving *desire* of his wife.

Familiar "Leadership" Heresies Uncovered   by Bruce C. E. Fleming
www.ThinkAgainAboutTheBible.com

Time to review. Here is a summary of what has happened up to this point in God's words to the woman in Genesis 3:16:

- The serpent and the man each knowingly defy God. God's words to them follow a common pattern.

- The woman sins after being deceived by the Tempter, whom Christ later calls the "Father of Lies." God does not speak to her as to the other two.

- God does not say to the woman, "Because you..." as He does to the others.

- God does not utter any "curse" (*'arur* in Hebrew), as He does for the other two. God does not curse her *body*, as He did the body of the serpent. He does not curse any *thing* because of her, as He will because of the man.

- God tells the woman about the "sorrowful toil" she will experience, as will the man, when they work the cursed soil.

- As for God's creation mandate to be fruitful and multiply (Genesis 1:28), God commits Himself to ensuring that she will conceive and that she will bear more than one child.

- The woman's seed, or offspring, will include a coming Deliverer who will crush the woman's enemy.

- God tells her how she, as a mortal mother, will now experience "effort" in her experience of childbirth.

- God observes that the woman still "desires" her husband.

The Fallen Guy (Line 4)

[16]Line 4: "But-he will-rule-over-you"

Have you ever noticed, that when you go somewhere for the first time and then return, that the return trip seems shorter? On the way out, every detail is new to you. The trip seems endless. And in one sense it is, because you have never come to the *end* of this trip before.

But on the way back, the trip seems shorter. You know both ends to the trip. The details are no longer unfamiliar to you. You are more relaxed and confident. The woman in the Garden of Eden was on a trip she had never taken before. Each step was new. She had just learned important things about herself from God. Now, she needed to know one thing more – what about the man? Indeed, God did know more about him than she had noticed.

- God knew that the man had purposefully rebelled and sinned.

- God also knew that the man was in a continuing state of rebellion.

- When the man spoke up first and defended himself alone in 3:12, God took note that the man did not mention the serpent and that he defiantly accused both the woman and God of being the sources of his difficulty:
    > The woman whom *You* gave to be with me,
    > *she* gave me
    > and I ate.

Hebrew words #10 and #11. Aware of all this, God tells the woman about the state of the defiant man's heart. God warns her of troubled waters ahead: "he will rule over you."

A ruler "out of line." It is hard to exaggerate how strange these last words must have sounded to the woman! This new thought was difficult to grasp.

- Up to this point, only *God ruled over* the humans.

- The *humans* were *co-rulers over* the rest of God's created world.

As God ruled over them, the humans ruled over the fish, over the birds and over the animals (1:28). But the idea of *one* human ruling over *the other* was totally out of place.

If this were true, then who was ruling over the other human?

- God had not told either one to rule over the other.

- The one who did this would be disobeying, breaking God's order.

- One human would have chosen self rule and rejected God's.

- The one ruled by the other human would be faced with a terrible reality: "We each owe obedience to God, so how do I deal with this one who is trying to rule me instead?"

Familiar "Leadership" Heresies Uncovered   by Bruce C. E. Fleming
www.ThinkAgainAboutTheBible.com

In God's words to her in Line 4, the warning of man's rule is described, but not endorsed. It is identified by God but not instituted by Him. **Heresy alert!** This ruling of one over the other is the act of a sinner. It is not something God imposes. To believe so is the root of another "leadership" heresy in Eden.

This ruling of one over the over is the act of a sinner. It is described, but not endorsed. It is not something God imposes. Claiming this is *God's* will is another "leadership" heresy.

Speaking for himself. When God interviewed them after the Disobedience, the man spoke up first. He spoke for himself only. They had both eaten. They had both felt ashamed. They both tried to hide themselves from God. But the man separated himself from the woman. He spoke as if he were once again the only human on earth and separated himself from the woman. When the man spoke he also separated himself from God. Instead of confessing his sin, the man was defiant. He first accused the woman, and then God (3:12)!

Back to God's blueprint. When He walked the earth, Jesus Christ, the woman's promised Seed, preached the *opposite* of *ruling over one another*. He said, "If anyone wants to be first, that one must be the very last, and the servant of all" (Mk 9:35).

The Apostle Paul taught Christians that a sign of being filled with the Spirit was to *not* rule over one another. Instead, he called for all those who were filled with the Spirit to practice a reciprocal and mutual self-submission:

"Be submitting yourselves to one another ..." (Eph 5:21)

Created to be allies. In Genesis 2, when God created the woman, He described her in relation to the man. In two meaningful Hebrew words, *'ezer kenegdo*, God described how the two were designed to go together. They were made for each other! Once together, they were to be a resourceful and satisfied pair, at home together in Eden.

Modern language versions of the Bible translate these two Hebrew words in confusing and contradictory ways. But there really is no cause for confusion. The two words in Genesis 2:18 are not that hard to translate.

Familiar "Leadership" Heresies Uncovered by Bruce C. E. Fleming
www.ThinkAgainAboutTheBible.com

46

An *'ezer kenegdo* is someone who works together with another, as they help each other through sharing their strengths.

As for the word *'ezer*:

- The majority of times it is used in the Bible, it is used to describe *God*. In Deuteronomy 33:7, God is the *'ezer* of Judah. The NIV translates this as: "Oh, be his *help* against his foes." He is the *'ezer* who *helps* with His superior strength.
- The Bible also uses *'ezer* to describe one king who *helps* another as allies in battle. The word *'ezer* refers to someone who helps by sharing his strength with another (as Pharaoh in Isaiah 30:1-5).

As for the word *kenegdo*:

- This word creates a picture of two people facing each other.

- It can be translated as "vis-à-vis," "conspicuously facing," and "corresponding to."

The woman is *'ezer kenegdo* to the man. Thus, she is "a corresponding ally" or "corresponding partner" to the man.

From the moment of her creation, this is who the first woman is. This is who she and her husband together are made to be.

In their discussions with God, no doubt the woman learned how God had described her, even before her creation. She understood that God had intended to create them both, and how He had created them. Her understanding was correct and needed no modification. They were created to be partners and allies.

Medieval heresies! While Joy and I were studying in Strasbourg, France, I had the opportunity to gain access to a centuries-old copy of Calvin's translation of the Bible into French.

It was very different from modern Bibles in the way it was laid out on the page. There were no verse numbers. Instead, in the left and right side margins there were the letters A, B, C and D to set off each quarter of the page!

There, and in a copy of Calvin's *Commentaries*, I saw that Calvin had misinterpreted the word "ally," or "help," (*'ezer*) in Genesis 2:18.

How could he have done that? Calvin was a first generation Reformer of the false doctrines and practices that had grown up over the centuries within the late medieval Church. He managed to address, and set right, many things. But not everything.

The Roman Catholic theologians of his day operated within a hierarchical church. Like these theologians, John Calvin held to the idea that woman had been created to be subservient to man; she had been created to be the man's *junior* partner. I was surprised to read Calvin's comment on 2:18. He described the woman as being "like a cook's helper."

Calvin's incorrect understanding of the meaning of the Hebrew word *'ezer* was passed on to his followers. The results of this fundamental mistake gave a false tilt to much of the rest of the theology he wrote. This incorrect theology persists among his adherents to this day and is another root of "leadership" heresies!

According to Genesis 2:18 rightly understood, the woman was not the man's junior partner, or assistant. She was made to be the man's ally; one who corresponded to him.

> ²:¹⁸And the Lord God said, "It is not good for the man to be alone; I will make an ally [*'ezer*, or "help"], corresponding to him [*kenegdo*, or vis-à-vis]."

Word #10. In Genesis 3:15, God described, and put His stamp of approval on, the woman's conflict against the serpent. This was part of God's good plan. It would culminate in the defeat of the Tempter, the serpent. As to her loving relationship with the man, God makes no change, and endorses no new arrangement between the two. *But*, He warns her, "but he" has changed.

God makes no change, and endorses no new arrangement between the two.

A wise person once remarked that, throughout the ages, God's strength, purity, love and justice has been forgotten. Apart from the true God, humans create gods and spirits that are corrupt. They are pictured as having all the flaws that sinful humans see in themselves, because fallen humans cannot imagine anything higher than themselves.

In much the same way, people who look back in time from outside of Eden, have difficulty imagining a truly good picture of sinless spouses interrelating with each other.

Those who look back to Eden, have difficulty imagining sinless spouses relating to each other.

This is one reason the first chapters of Genesis are so important. They go beyond our fallen imaginations and introduce us to how it was, and what God designed us to be! It tells us how we were meant to be, as individuals in our relationship with God, and as an individual with our spouse.

Familiar "Leadership" Heresies Uncovered   by Bruce C. E. Fleming
www.ThinkAgainAboutTheBible.com

Word #11. In Line 4 of Genesis 3:16, when God began to speak about her husband, He used the Hebrew word "but-he...." Hebrew word #11, "but-he-will-rule-over-you," describes the man dealing with the woman very differently from how God had created them to interact!

According to Genesis 1-2, the two humans were the perfect couple, "made for each other." God, the original and supreme authority, had delegated authority to them both as co-rulers over the animals and the environment.

In 1:26, referring to *both* the man and the woman, God had said,

> Let us make humanity in our image, according to our likeness;
> *let them rule over* (*radah*, in Hebrew) the fish of the sea,
> over the birds of the air, and over the cattle, over all the earth and
> over every creeping thing that creeps on the earth.

The Hebrew verb for "rule" (*radah*) in Genesis 1:26 and again in 1:28, is assigned to the man and woman as their appropriate task. Together they are to "rule over" the rest of God's created realm. God has to use a different Hebrew word in Genesis 3:16 (*mashal*) to describe the man who takes things into his own hands.

In Lines 3 and 4 of Genesis 3:16, God paints a striking contrast between the woman and the man:

- She has experienced their Edenic relationship, described in 2:25, and her desire is still for him.

- The man, on the other hand, has already accused God and the woman (3:12), and he will presumptively rule over her apart from God.

God doesn't want her to be surprised by this drastic change. She will be living in a fallen world with this aggressor. God's last words to her alert the woman to the man's adversarial stance.

In Genesis 3:16, God does not tell the man to rule over the woman. God is not even speaking to the man in this verse.

God does not tell the man to rule over the woman.
God is not even speaking to the man in this verse.

When God says – "he will rule" – that is not news, as both she and he "ruled" over creation. But what comes next must have been shocking to the woman, "… over *you*."

This is similar to learning that her partner is a walking dead man. God warns her that she is the bride of this dead man who plans to rule over her. Not a pretty picture!

Comforting Words to the Woman

We have witnessed God's solemn but gentle words to the woman in Genesis 3:16. In the eleven Hebrew words of Lines 1-4, God explained the consequences of her sin and her mortality in a matter-of-fact way, while also giving her good news – and reinforcing it.

God spoke with her face to face. He did not demote her from subduing the earth nor from ruling over the animal realm.

He confirmed to her the good news of a coming Seed who would vanquish her enemy, the Tempter. She learned that family life would continue and that she would have children. But she also learned that she would be dwelling with a presumptuous and adversarial spouse.

From our position in history, we know that their first child's name was Cain. Alas, he was not the promised One. He did not go after the serpent and crush him. Instead, he took after his father. And Cain himself became a monstrous sinner.

Children of Eve? We can choose to be children of the defiant Adam. Or, we can choose to take after Eve.

During the Exodus, God symbolically combined events from the Garden, and the coming death of Christ on the cross, into an object lesson of saving faith (Numbers 21:4-9). To teach the Israelites to stop sinning and to look to Him in faith, God sent poisonous serpents among the rebellious people. He then had Moses attach a bronze serpent to a pole and lift it up.

Anyone who obeyed God and gazed on that serpent was saved by faith from death by snakebite. Jesus later explained that the snake on the pole was symbolic of his death on the cross for our sins.

Anyone in our generation who by faith looks to Jesus to be saved from death will be saved as well. On the cross, Jesus gained victory over that serpent who precipitated the rebellion and death of all humanity.

Just as Moses lifted up the snake in the desert, so the Son of Man must be lifted up, that everyone who believes may have eternal life in him. For God so loved the world that he gave his one and only Son, that whoever believes in him shall not perish but have eternal life. (John 3:14-16, TNIV)

The Bible brings us the good news that the woman's promised Seed has been born. Her Offspring, Jesus, came and was wounded by the serpent. But on the cross He triumphed over the Tempter, over sin and death.

We may grow wise by observing around us the deadly consequences of the Great Disobedience. We can choose, like the woman, to learn from the God who promises redemption and we can place our faith in the Promised One, Jesus Christ. By the transforming power of Jesus, we can choose to live a life of redeemed relationships, unlike those tainted by the Fall.

Think Again! Consider the following answers. Do you agree?

1. Who did God install as leaders over the earth? (Genesis 1:28?)
The man and the woman were co-rulers over the earth and all its creatures

2. Was one created to be leader over the other? (Genesis 2:20)
No. They were a matching pair of humans (suitable partners)

3. How did the real leader, God, respond to the disobedience against Him?

- The serpent who rebelled on purpose was cursed.

- The man who sinned on purpose (a 1st degree sinner) saw the soil cursed because of him.

- The woman who sinned only after she was deceived (a 2nd degree sinner) received no curse and received the promise of the Savior.

Chapter 2

"Leadership" Heresies and the Man in the Garden
... an inside look at Genesis 2-3 (with a focus on 3:17-19)

Chapter Contents:

- **A Fresh Translation of Genesis 3:17-20**
- **Creation Basics: Man, Woman, Marriage**
- **God's Judgment of the Man (3:17a-b)**
- **God Instructs the Man (3:17c-19)**
- **What About the Tempter?**
- **What's Ahead for the Man and the Tempter?**

Here is a **fresh translation** of God's words to the man in Genesis 3:17-19, and the man's actions afterwards, recorded in verse 20.

[17a]To the man He said, "Because you listened to the voice of your wife and ate from the tree about which I commanded you saying, 'You must not eat from it,'

> [17b]Cursed is the ground because of you
>> [17c]In sorrowful toil (*'itsebon*) you will eat of it
>> all the days of your life.
> [18]Thorns and thistles it will produce for you
> and you will eat plants of the field.
> [19]By the sweat of your face you will eat bread
> until you return to the ground
> since from it you were taken –
> for dust you are and to dust you will return.

[20]And the man called the name of his wife Eve, for she would be mother of all living.

Creation Basics: Man, Woman, Marriage

Joy was three years old when her family moved across town to a house in south Minneapolis. It was winter in Minnesota.

By the time outdoor play weather warmed the air she was four. Joy went out and came across a neighbor girl playing outside. Her name was Nancy and she was just about Joy's age.

Joy was shy. She firmly planted her feet and clasped her hands behind her back, self-consciously swiveling her upper body to the right and then to the left.

"I like your cowboy hat," Nancy said, trying to make four-year old friendly conversation.

"How did *you* know I had a cowboy hat?" Joy asked, surprised that this new friend already knew about her favorite hat!

Then she noticed the hat string hanging around her own neck and became aware of the weight of her hat on her back. She had been wearing it all the time! Nancy had noticed. It wasn't hard to see. It was red!

Sometimes others can see something about us better than we can see ourselves. This was certainly true of the man in the Garden and his Creator. The man had rebelled and disobeyed God. Right away he and the woman had sensed the change and made something to cover themselves. But God could clearly see his sinful state. He saw the man was in the grasp of rebellion and had the weight of sin on his back.

Just as Nancy's words caused Joy to realize she was wearing her cowboy hat, and that this was clear to all, so God's words to the man in Genesis 3:17-19 revealed to him his fallen and rebellious state. A fresh look at these verses uncovers some surprises!

Just the facts please. There are so many misconceptions about the man in the Garden of Eden it is necessary to think again about what Scripture really says in Genesis 2-3.

These verses show us what happened in the beginning. They also impact our understanding of the New Testament, because various New Testament passages refer to what happened in the Garden of Eden.

Unlike the woman in the Garden, the man and the serpent acted deliberately in the Great Disobedience. In the previous chapter the focus was on the part of the woman. In this chapter, special attention is paid to God's words to the man in Genesis 3:17-19.

Everything in the first three chapters of the Bible is full of meaning. In Genesis 1, we learn sweeping information about the creation of everything from nothing. When all is created it is "very good." Next, Genesis 2 gives details about the creation and the beginnings of marriage. In Genesis 3, the temptation and Fall of the man and of the woman is recounted.

In Genesis 1-3, God uses the Hebrew word " 'adam", or "Adam," to refer both to the man *and* the woman. In Genesis 1:26-27 God says,

> [26]Let us make (hu)man (*'adam*) in Our image....
> [27]male (*zakar*) and female (*neqebah*) He created them.

What happened "in the beginning" has often been recounted with much imaginative embroidering. The actual text of the Bible is spare in its details, and the whole period of life in the Garden is told so quickly, that many people have yielded to the temptation to add details that aren't in the Bible.

The "details" they add are inevitably influenced by the biases and limited knowledge of their own time and place. These additions more often have hurt than helped our understanding of what happened in the beginning. Some have lead to heretical claims and false doctrines.

A silly scene. One Christmas season our family was invited to take a guided tour of a museum's presentation of Christmas items from around the world. One of the displays that caught our attention was an old Nativity Scene.

The detailed wooden pieces had been carved and painted in seventeenth century Belgium. Amusingly, the little town of Bethlehem looked more like seventeenth-century Brussels. The skyline was typically Belgian, complete with stairstep rooflines and cable hooks high in the front of each building to be used to winch heavy furniture up to the windows of the narrow upper floors!

Of course, the artist who made this Nativity Scene did not know that it looked ludicrous – and even silly. Nor did the people of that time and culture laugh at the display's anachronistic errors. They likely thought the work was quite good. Some probably even copied it when they made Nativity Scenes of their own.

You get the picture. For thousands of years, people have invented anachronistic scenes of the Garden of Eden for themselves and for others. But, most of their depictions have been riddled with errors.

Common errors people have made in their imaginings about the first man in the Garden will be uncovered along the way in the coming pages. But the main focus will be to grasp what *is* said in the Bible, especially about the basic topics covered in the pages on Eden.

Who is "man"? There was no form to fill out, no birth certificate to be signed, when the first human was "born." Therefore the Bible refers to him simply by pronouns such as, "he," "him" and "his." When he shares a pronoun with the woman, as in Genesis 1:28, the pronoun "them" is used.

Not only do verses 1:26-27 refer to them both as "Adam," Genesis 5:2 reports that, at creation, God "... called *their* name Adam." This would be the equivalent in modern days of simply calling them "Mr. and Mrs. Adam."

["Adam" became the name of the man alone only when he took it for himself after the Fall (3:20). Therefore, in these chapters, the first man is not referred to by the name "Adam" for any events prior to Genesis 3:20. Instead, the terms "the man," "the woman" and "the human beings" are used.]

The name "Adam" is actually a play on the Hebrew word "ground" or "earth." *'Adam* (human) is made (2:7) from *'adamah* (ground). In English, one might say, "Earthling" is made from "the Earth."

God creates the man before the Garden of Eden is planted (2:8). God plants the Garden and then places him in it to cultivate and keep it (2:9-15).

God's first recorded words to the man (16-17) are a command,

> From any tree of the garden you many eat freely; but from the tree of the knowledge of good and evil you shall not eat, for in the day that you eat from it you shall surely die. (NASB)

Who is woman? In Genesis 2:22, while the man is unconscious, God takes a part of the man's side and creates the woman. When he wakes, in 2:23, the man declares that this new person God has made is not a simple clone of himself. They each are separate, unique adult human beings.

He recognizes her as a *female* human being and himself as a *male* human being when he speaks:

> She shall be called *woman* for she was taken out of *man*.

In the next verse, 2:24, the writer of Genesis uses these same two words to give details about marriage:

> For this reason a *man* (groom)
> will leave his father and his mother,
> and give his loyalty to his *woman* (bride)
> and they will be one flesh.

According to Genesis 2:23-25, Mr. and Mrs. Adam were adult human beings, of different genders, who were married to one another. Even after God created the man, for a while, creation was "not good." This was because there was just *one* human and he was *alone* (2:18). The man learned that no other creature on earth was an appropriate companion to him. He was the sole human (19-21).

In dramatic fashion God announced in verse 18 that He would make yet another human being, but He delayed doing so in verse 19, and longer still in verse 20, building the suspense.

Finally, God created the woman in verses 21-22. But He put the man to sleep while He did so. Not until the moment described in verse 23 were the two humans introduced to each other by God.

A playful paraphrase. Here is a paraphrase that reflects the drama that builds in Hebrew fashion in this report of the creation of the other human:

[18]"**My creating is not yet done,** young man, but I'm going to finish!
[19]"**I've done a lot,** and this menagerie of animals is great. They are even made a lot like you – from the earth. Now, to take stock of how far I've come in the creation process, note what is here so far. Name all you see."
[20]"**Are you ready? I'm really going to do it.** Think of what has been done so far and what this means." [Technically, this is called "suspension of the resolution." The man names each animal but finds no partner corresponding to him.]
[21-22]"**I'm doing it now. But you can't look!**" God creates the woman, and the woman meets her Creator.
[23-24]"**OK. All is finished. Now look!**" God brings the woman face to face with the man. The man responds, "Wow! You sure did it!"

As discussed previously, God used two Hebrew words to describe the new human being He was about to create. These words may be translated into English as "ally" (or "help") and "corresponding-to." Together, they mean "corresponding partner." In verse 18, God observed that without this person, without this corresponding partner, creation was "not good."

When the woman was created, the situation changed from "not good" to "very good." The man joyfully recognized that she was his counterpart. God's work reached completion with her creation. Their marriage was a joyful fulfillment of God's creation.

What about naming? Before the woman was created, God told the lone man to name the animals. When he did, the man used what can be called a "naming formula." This formula was made up of two parts, the verb "to call" (*qarah*) and the noun "name" (*shem*).

The Hebrew text says the man *called* their *names* when he gave each animal the name of his choice. Something like this Hebrew "naming formula" is used in old English whenever a king or queen names someone saying, "I now *dub* you with this *name* ..." Some have suggested that having the privilege of naming the animals is an example of ruling over the animals.

When God creates the woman, God does not instruct the man to name her. When the man meets the woman for the first time, he does not use the naming formula on her; in fact, he does not name her in any way. According to Genesis 2:23, when the man meets the woman, he responds with a joyful and poetic outburst recognizing that she alone, at last, is the female-human who is his counterpart in all of creation.

Knowing God. When the man was made, for a time he and God were alone in the world (2:7). When the woman was made, the man was sound asleep. Practically speaking, the woman and God were alone in the Garden until God introduced the woman to her husband-to-be (2:21-22).

Each one had been handmade by God. Each was brand new. Each one had spent time with the Creator before meeting their spouse-to-be.

Each one spent time with the Creator before meeting their spouse-to-be.

God gave these first two humans the gift of spending life together as partners in marriage. In fact, God was the first matchmaker.

The three steps in marrying.

Marriage is something God designed for man and woman to share. The first marriage was God's will. This couple was designed as male and female to know one another, to share life together, to raise a family and rule over the earth.

Sounds like a beautiful life in the Garden of Eden, doesn't it? That is what God designed for them, and for all their children – including us! How do we know this relationship was intended by God to be lived out by all their children, including us? It says so in the next verse in Genesis, in 2:24.

Verse 24 does not describe something that went on in the Garden. It is a word of commentary added from the later perspective of when Genesis was written down. [Moses had years of conversation with God during Israel's wandering in the desert. One of the eyewitnesses of the Garden of Eden, its designer, God Himself likely provided these details to Moses.] For example, verse 24 refers to the man leaving his father and mother. The first man had no physical "father and mother" to leave. But this principle would be true for all future men.

This first couple did not have a human mother or father attending their wedding. Instead, their Creator "parent" was present.

Here is what is involved for all other humans who marry – three basic steps. These steps are described by three verbs: 1) "to leave" (*'azav*), 2) "to cleave" or "to be united" (*davaq*), and 3) "to be" (*hayah*).

Taking these three steps together transforms a single man and a single woman into a married couple.

> 2:24For this reason, a man will **leave** his father and mother
> and **be united** to his wife
> and they **will become** one flesh.

Jesus confirmed this pattern when some Pharisees tried to trap Him in a question about divorce (Matt 19:3), "Is it lawful for a man to divorce his wife for any and every reason?" Jesus used the occasion, recorded in verses 4-6, to state that our very maleness and femaleness is at the base of marriage (see Gen 1:26-27), and it is meant to last for a lifetime.

> "Haven't you read," he replied, "that at the beginning the Creator 'made them male and female,' and said, 'For this reason a man will leave his father and his mother and be united to his wife, and the two will become one flesh'? So they are no longer two, but one. Therefore what God has joined together, let man not separate." (NIV)

The word in Genesis 2:24 that introduces the three steps in getting married is "for" or "therefore." A basic rule in Bible interpretation is always to find out what a "therefore" is *there for*.

Looking back from verse 24 the "therefore" refers to the fact that they were humans of different genders. The man (a male human) and the woman (a female human) were designed for marriage. In His answer to the Pharisees, Jesus states that marriage is designed to last a lifetime.

Of course there are exceptions that fall into the category of celibacy. Jesus never married. Neither did the Apostle Paul.

Verb #1 – "To leave." Marriage is designed to be a one-time, public event. It involves a man "leaving" his parents, the ones from whom he came. His parents and others in society all know that this man is leaving his father and

59

mother to marry his wife. There is no sneaking away. No hiding the fact. In this very intimate union of two people, society is involved.

Interestingly, Genesis 2 pictures the *man* as the one who leaves his family of origin, unlike wedding ceremonies in many cultures in which the woman does the leaving.

Verb #2 – "To be united." This second Hebrew verb is a rare one. To find out what it means, it is helpful to observe how the word is used in another Bible passage where the meaning is clear. It is clear in Ruth 1:14, because its meaning is illustrated both in Ruth's words and deeds.

After Ruth's husband dies, her righteous Jewish mother-in-law Naomi decides to return to Israel. Ruth, a Moabite woman who came from a pagan culture, chooses to be united to Naomi. Some translations translate this verb as "to cleave," "to cling to" or "to join her life" to Naomi. From Ruth's life, we see clearly that verb #2 involves deep commitment.

The depth of this union is made clear in Ruth's declaration to Naomi:

> 16-17Where you go I will go, and where you stay I will stay. Your people will be my people, and your God, my God. … May the Lord deal with me … if anything but death separates you and me.

Ruth's union with Naomi is a deep personal commitment on more than one level. Not only does she pledge Naomi her loyalty to stay with her, but they share a spiritual unity as well – they trust in the same God.

Verb #1 involved the man the action – "to leave." *He* leaves *his* parents. Verb #2 involves "the transferring of one's loyalty." Who does this? According to Genesis 2:23, again it is the *man* who transfers his loyalty to his wife as *he* gives his heart to her.

> … a *man* will leave his father and mother
> and *be united* to his wife …

The uniting of a husband to his wife was designed by God to be a close-knit union of worshipping individuals, united in heart and mind.

Verb #3 – "To be." This third verb involved in marrying, is completed by the Hebrew words, "as-flesh" and "one." These words indicate two levels of union they are to share as a couple. They are to be united physically and emotionally. Emotional oneness is part of their physical union.

[This is one reason why sexual intercourse with anyone other than one's spouse is forbidden in the Bible. Physical union with anyone else shreds the emotional oneness of their marriage.]

What about kids? Some people think that having children is "what marriage is all about." Children are to be expected, as indicated by the Creation Mandate recorded in Genesis 1:28. But children are not mentioned in this passage on marriage in Genesis 2. And the verb for sexual union is only one of three that describes marrying.

After the man publicly "leaves" his parents, and after he transfers his loyalty to his bride, then the two become one. Whether they have children or not, they are married and united for life because they have taken the three steps of marriage.

Heresy alert! Here is where several marriage heresies have inserted themselves. For example, in some places in the world, a marriage is not considered complete until a child is born. If, after some time, the couple remains childless, the marriage is considered null and void!

I personally have spoken to church congregations in Africa on this subject. Several times I have read the marriage steps in Genesis 2:24 as if *four* steps, not just three, were involved in marrying.

Out loud, I would read one step at a time. After reading each step I would ask rhetorically, "Isn't that so? "Mmmmm!" they would reply in the typical hum meaning agreement.

Deliberately, I laid before them the following steps and got their response.

"Step #1. Leave?" I proposed. "Mmmmm (yes)" was their reply.
"Step #2. Be united?" I suggested. "Mmmmm" they hummed.
"Step #3. Become one? I wondered. "Mmmmm!" they agreed
"Step #4." (I added) "If they have many children? "Mmmmm!"

Usually, not everyone in such a congregation would have their own Bible, but I knew that some would be following along. After proposing Step #4, I would pause – as long as it took. Finally, someone would speak up and make a tentative correction, "It doesn't say anything about children, I think."

Of course it doesn't. But their shared cultural beliefs were so strong that they reflexively agreed that "having many children was a requirement" for a successful marriage! They had changed the biblical definition for marriage.

This is sad news in cultures where medical help is lacking and many men and women are infertile. What a terrible heresy to spread in the church, because it condemns a woman who has no child, to an eventual abandonment by her husband, an abandonment that will be looked on with approval by the community! "Maybe his next marriage will be a *real* one."

False! Heretical! Get rid of this horrible judgmental attitude toward the childless wife! Repent!

Familiar "Leadership" Heresies Uncovered   by Bruce C. E. Fleming
www.ThinkAgainAboutTheBible.com

Teach that children are among the many blessings God may give us, but don't even imply that God designed more than just these *three* steps to getting married. Keep clear in the minds of all, that God designed marriage between a man and a woman, and that His three steps are sufficient to launch a happy lifelong marriage.

'Leadership' heresies. The German theologian, Peter Beyerhaus, once stated, "It is just as important to say what we *don't* believe as it is to say what we *do* believe." Following his advice, the next paragraphs indicate *correct*, and *incorrect*, theological statements on leadership.

For example, in Genesis 3:12 when the man describes his marriage partner and their marriage relationship, he does *not* say, "the woman you gave *to* me; the woman you made for me to lead." He says to God, "the woman you placed here *with* me."

There is a "here-with-ness," and a "side-by-side-ness," to the marriage relationship. Two adults turn toward each other and unite in the sight of their families, society and God.

Here are several other commonly held "leadership" heresies. They are contrasted with correct statements based on Genesis 1-2.

1. **Incorrect**: "Man, more than woman, was created to rule the earth."
   Correct: God gave dominion to them both as co-regents (1:28-30).

2. **Incorrect**: "Woman was created to be man's subordinate."
   Correct: When the man was alone his situation was "not good." God created a female adult human being, and then there were two. Neither was alone. They were allies; corresponding partners (2:18).

3. **Incorrect**: "The man was created first in chronological order and is therefore "first," or greater, in importance or power."
   Correct: God did His creation work in ascending order of importance: from inanimate to living plants, to animals, and finally to humans. God could have made the two humans simultaneously. But making the woman from the man's side underlines their common essence in humanity. Marriage underscores this again. God took one and made two. In marriage, two join to become one. Neither is greater.

4. **Incorrect**: "The man had a part in making the woman and therefore exercises control over her."
   Correct: A "part" of the man served as material for making the woman (like "dust" served as raw material for making the man). But the work of creation was all God's own. In fact, the man was asleep when God

did His work. The man was not a participant, consultant, or even spectator in the work of woman's creation.

5. **Incorrect**: "In a Christian marriage, the husband is the leading figure."
    Correct: Two adults join together. The man leaves his parents and transfers his loyalty to his wife. Then they can join in sexual union and there is the possibility of having children. Each knows God and serves God before they meet and marry. During marriage each continues to follow God, while they also serve God together in their joint responsibilities. In heaven there is no marriage (Matt 22:30). Each one's primary loyalty to God will continue.

6. **Incorrect**: "The purpose of marriage is to have children."
    Correct: It is possible to have an excellent marriage without children (as many childless couples have learned).

God's Judgment of the Man – 3:17a-b

The reason
[17a]To the man He said,
"Because you listened to the voice of your wife and ate from the tree about which I commanded you saying, 'You must not eat from it,'
God's action
[17b]Cursed is the ground because of you,
[17c]In sorrowful toil you will eat of it all the days of your life.
[18]Thorns and thistles it will produce for you and you will eat plants of the field.
[19]By the sweat of your face you will eat bread until you return to the ground since from it you were taken – for dust you are and to dust you will return."
Historical account
[20]And the man called the name of his wife Eve, for she would be mother of all living.

When we were growing up, my little sister Debby had a way of making me look like the guilty one whenever something went wrong. To my great frustration, my Dad always believed her and I got in trouble!

My Mom knew better. She would get to the truth of the matter before any punishment was handed out. She also took into account whether an accident had taken place or whether a bad attitude was behind the matter.

Getting to the truth. This is how God operated after the man and the woman ate from the tree. God came and interviewed them both to see what they would say.

When the serpent came as Tempter (Gen 3:1), he deceived the woman into eating (3:6*a*, 13). The man, who was with her, was not deceived. He chose to disobey (3:6*b*, 17).

The punishment for their sin was death. Death, as their punishment, is not specifically mentioned in Genesis 3. It isn't necessary to do so. It had been foretold. It is an unseen fact behind all that is said and done in verses 14-19.

As God passes judgment on the three participants in the Great Disobedience, God curses the serpent and foretells his doom. Then, in verse 16, God takes time to explain to the woman important details about her new mortality. He also warns her about changes for the worse that were already present in the man.

God's words to the man.

Verse 17 starts with the introductory phrase, "And God said to the man." Had the man assumed that God had forgotten him? He had not. In verse 17, God turns to the man wearing the fig leaves and addresses him personally.

Raise your hands! Often, we have asked large groups, small groups, and even individuals to tell us how many times they think God made a curse in the Garden of Eden.

Once? Sometimes a person picks this answer. Twice? Perhaps a few choose this one. Three times? More choose this one. Four times? Most opt for this one. Some even opt for more than four curses! Why is this so?

It is helpful to think in terms of the three Latin legal categories: (1) *de jure* – according to *law*, (2) *de facto* – according to *fact*, and (3) *de senso* – according to *perception.*

In Genesis 3, many people have the "impression," *de senso*, that God deals with the serpent, and the woman, and the man in parallel ways. What applies to one member of this trio, they *assume* applies to the other two.

In fact, however, God's words to only two of them are similar – the serpent and the man. To assume otherwise has lead to heresy. As was pointed out earlier, there are a number of distinct common points in God's words of judgment to the serpent and to the man (in the Hebrew text): with each of them God uses the word *curse*; he begins his words to each of them with "*because*" – and so forth.

Why the fig leaves? Genesis 3:10 reports that the man told God he hid himself because he was afraid and was naked. Whose fault was that?

Was the man implying that God stopped short when He created the world and everything in it? Should God have gone on to create clothes? Was it God's fault that the man felt naked? What about the man's fear? The man was experiencing symptoms that stemmed from a deep-rooted problem. Not focusing on these symptoms or their cause was an exercise in denial.

God asked the man, in verse 11, "Who told you that you were naked? Have you eaten from the tree of which I commanded you not to eat?"

God had spoken to him earlier about this tree. In fact, God had given him a command not to eat from this one tree. Disobeying God was his sin.

Denial and deflection. At this point, surprisingly, the man resorts to denial and engages in some deflective finger-pointing. Of the four personalities in the Garden of Eden, the man could point to *himself* – he had made his own wayward choice. Or he certainly could point to the *serpent*, attributing to him, his responsibility in being his Tempter and thus his enemy.

Instead, the man mentions neither of these. Rather, he tries to implicate the other two personalities in the Garden!

It is true that the woman had given him the fruit, but not maliciously, not with the intent of the Tempter. Nevertheless, he pointed a finger at her! In verse 12, he began his defense with, "the *woman* ...." Then, after pointing to the woman, the man blamed *God* for his action!

The *woman* whom *You* gave to be with me,
she gave me from the tree and I ate.

Such an audacious retort to God's questions came from a person who had hardened his heart by sinning deliberately. In this way, his sin was different from that of the woman. The New Testament confirms that he was not deceived (1 Tim 2:14). He ate the fruit with his "eyes open," that is, with full and conscious awareness of what he was doing.

When God turned to question the woman in verse 13, she replied in three (Hebrew) words: "The-serpent deceived-me and-I-ate." She pointed correctly to her deceiver, described accurately what the serpent did, and acknowledged what she had done wrong.

Heresy alert! The woman and the man each ate of the fruit. Both were guilty of doing what God had told them not to do. Yet there was a difference in their understanding, and thus a distinguishable difference in the guilt of each.

The man – not deceived by the serpent – sinned nevertheless. He deliberately dethroned God from His proper and rightful place as Sovereign of his life and decided to rule over himself in God's place.

The man adopted the "leadership" heresy which was behind the words of the Tempter:

"God is not in charge of you. *You* be in charge of your own self."

Heresy alert! When the woman ate the fruit, she had not decided to take charge of her own life in place of God. Her act did not involve conscious rebellion. She was deceived into thinking the fruit was good, and so she ate some of it. To make more of her sin than the Bible does is to open a multitude of ways by which to depart from the path of revealed truth and venture onto heretical grounds.

Here is a summary of the differences in the heart of each human sinner:

- The *man* pointed this way and that, away from his own sin. When he pointed toward the woman and God, the man acted in his own "wisdom."

- The *woman*, on the other hand, answered God's question directly and pointed to her deceiver – the serpent. She had disobeyed, but she had not willfully rebelled, and she did not do so now.

When God then turned to the serpent and next to the woman (3:14-15 and 16), the man may have thought, "Aha! The others are in trouble, while I, in my new wisdom, am fooling God!" Perhaps, the man's denial and deflection were working. Perhaps, the new "wisdom" the serpent promised him was making the difference. Maybe he really could engage God in a verbal duel and win!

In verse 17, however, God turned to the man.

Your turn! After describing the man unfavorably in His warning to the woman in verse 16, Line 4, God turns to the man with words of judgment that brush aside the his attempt at diversionary tactics.

God gives the man no room for escape as He describes exactly what took place when the man disobeyed and ate. Pointedly, God refers to each detail of the man's words in his attempted deflection.

Had the man pointed to the woman? Then God would start there. In verse 17, God refers to the man's own words and then states his real sin (note the words placed in bold for emphasis), that of disobeying God's prohibition:

Because you listened to the voice of your wife and **ate** from the tree about which **I commanded** you saying, '**You must not eat** from it' …

Heresy alert! God mentioned to the man details about the woman because the man had mentioned her when he tried to deflect God's judgment. God adds a surprising detail that the man hadn't mentioned. How did God know she had said something? God had seen and heard all that had happened. Hiding from God had been a futile and ridiculous effort.

Some people suggest that the man's sin was to listen to his wife. That would make her his Temptress. No! No! No! That is not what bothered God the Judge. The Bible does not teach that, "a wife is *not* to be listened to." In fact at a key point in history (Gen 21:12), God explicitly directed Abraham, to "listen to" his wife at a point where he was inclined to disregard her. In the Garden, the man sinned not because he listened to his wife but because he disobeyed God.

What were you thinking? God judges the intents and motives of the heart. Deliberate rebellion merits a corresponding response. This is the heart of all justice. How did this apply in Eden?

God imposed two curses in Eden in response to deliberate evildoing. In so doing, God dealt justly with the participants in the Great Disobedience in Eden.

God judges the intents and motives of the heart.
Deliberate rebellion merits a corresponding response.
This is the heart of all justice.

Elsewhere in the Bible, God takes into account both the sinful act and the state of the heart of the sinner. Here is an example (Ex 21:12-14, italics added):

> Anyone who strikes a man and kills him shall surely be put to death. However, if he does *not do it intentionally*, but God lets it happen, he is to flee to a place [God] will designate. But if a man schemes and kills another man *deliberately*, take him away from my altar and put him to death.

In the New Testament, when Saul (later Paul) sins, God judges him based on the state of his heart. As a result, he is judged much differently for *his* blasphemy, because he sinned "in ignorance and unbelief" than the two blasphemers who rejected their good consciences and sinned in deliberate rebellion against God (1 Tim 1:12-13, 19-20).

"Cursed is the ground because of you." When God addressed the man (verses 17-19), His first act of business was to identify the man's sin and the state of the man's heart when he sinned. The sentence of death for sin had already been announced. It was non-negotiable. Spiritual death had already occurred. Physical mortality was already at work.

1st or 2nd degree? Because the man purposely sinned, in addition to the penalty of death, God also imposed a curse. In modern courts of law, a distinction is made between premeditated, or deliberate, 1st-degree murder, and unpremeditated murder, or 2nd-degree manslaughter. Looked at in this way, the fallen man is guilty of "disobedience in the 1st degree."

The crafty serpent received a curse because of its intentional rebellion against God. For the man, as well, additional punishment is merited: "Cursed is the ground because of you...."

Heresy alert! At this point in Genesis a detour question is sometimes asked, "If the man *wasn't* deceived, *who failed* to deceive him?" An incorrect answer deflects us from correct theology into all kinds of heretical speculation.

Many blame the woman! The Son of Sirach said, "From the woman was the beginning of sin" (*Ecclus.* 25.24). Augustine called the woman "the Tempter's accomplice" (*City of God XIV*)!

Others claim that since the woman in the Garden was deceived, somehow this shows that all women are more easily deceived than men. But, Genesis does not teach this! Neither does the New Testament.

Brauch, in *Hard Sayings of Paul* (p. 263) points out,

> [Paul did not share] with his rabbinic tradition the view that women were *inherently* more deceivable. This is confirmed by the fact that Paul uses Eve's deception in 2 Corinthians 11:3-4 as an *illustration* of the possibility that *all* believers in Corinth, both men and women, may be deceived and led away from faith in Christ.

Who or what is cursed? The man heard God address the serpent. He heard God say to the serpent, "Because *you* have done this, cursed are *you*...." When God began speaking to the man, he may have anticipated receiving a similar punishment, "Because *you* have done this, cursed are *you*...."

But, God does not curse the man. Instead, God deflects the curse. It hits the ground ('*adamah*, in Hebrew) from which the man ('*adam*) was made, "Cursed is the *ground* because of you...." Whew! That was close.

The grace of God is a marvel! Neither human is cursed – neither the woman who sinned after being deceived – nor the man who sinned in the first degree.

The loving Creator treats them justly but graciously. They both die, but neither one is cursed.

God Instructs the Man – 3:17c -19

After the curse on the soil is imposed because of the man, God, as his divine teacher, explains to the man how death and the curse will affect him.

The man learns (1) that he will experience a new "sorrowful toil" because of the curse on the soil. He also learns (2) that indeed his days are numbered. He will die and return to the dust.

Lesson One: "Sorrowful Toil"

Had the man desired to be like God? God teaches the man that as a result of the curse on the ground he will experience something new but completely undesirable: "in 'sorrowful toil' you will eat of it all the days of your life…."

The Hebrew word for "sorrowful toil" is 'itsebon. The curse on the ground will make raising food much harder. The man will have to toil over it. This toil will raise sweat on his brow, and every time this happens, in sorrow he will remember why the ground has been cursed.

The woman has already heard from God, in verse 16, that she will experience this same "sorrowful toil." For her, the announcement was a proleptic prophecy. The result was foretold but the cause for the result was not immediately given.

Now the woman overhears where this "sorrowful toil" will come from, and why it will come about. It comes about through God's curse on the soil because of the sin of the man. She will experience this sorrowful toil as she walks the same earth and works the same cursed soil as the man.

Rare news. The Hebrew word for "sorrowful toil" is a rare word. It is used only three times in the Bible: Genesis 3:16, 17 and 5:29. The meaning is precise.

The meaning of 'itsebon is explained clearly in Genesis 5:29. This 'itsebon is the "sorrowful toil" that resulted from the curse God placed on the ground. The parents of Noah were weary of this 'itsebon and looking for relief from it:

This "sorrowful toil" is caused by God's curse on the soil.
It comes from working the ground the Lord cursed because of the man.

In Genesis 3:17, God pronounces the curse on the soil. He then explains the *'itsebon*, or "sorrowful toil," that will directly result from it.

Cursed is the ground for your sake;
In sorrowful toil (*'itsebon*) you will eat of it all the days of your life.

Heresy alert! Many English translations make it appear that when God told the woman about impending the "sorrowful toil" (*'itsebon)* in Genesis 3:16, He told her about something unique to her. They make it look like something is imposed on the woman because of what she did. However, *'itsebon* in verse 16 is the same "sorrowful toil" spoken of in verse 17 that is the result of the curse God places on the ground.

The "sorrowful toil" has nothing to do with her being a woman, or with her bearing children. It has everything to do with working the cursed soil, which she and the man begin to do as soon as they are outside the Garden.

The man and the woman had been undisputed rulers over all the animals and plants. Now, the cursed soil will produce unwanted thorns and thistles (verse 18). The man will experience difficulty and diminished returns as he works the smitten ground. As one of the fallen rulers over the soil, he will have a recalcitrant and rebellious subject.

By the sweat of your nose. I have vivid memories of the first time I worked in a farm field. I had volunteered to help my elderly uncles who were pulling thistles out from among the plants they wanted to grow.

The thistles had hairlike thorns that left little stinging welts on my fingers. As I bent over my work, my hands were covered with dirt. I wanted to wipe my brow, but in doing so I only smeared dirt on my face and gained no relief.

As the sweat ran down my face unchecked, some ran down my glasses tracing little rivers on the lenses and making it difficult to see. I took them off and tucked them away. Without my glasses to divert the drops of sweat, I soon learned that they ran to the tip of my nose, gathered in size and weight and then plunged in a series of bulging drops to the dust below.

The precise Hebrew words in Genesis 3:19 are not "by the sweat of your brow" but, "by the sweat of your nose...." Of course it is! Irritating it is too!

In verse 19 God says to the man:

By the sweat of your nose you will eat bread
until you *return* to the ground
since from it you were taken –
for dust you are and to dust you will *return*.

Lesson Two: Dying

God explains the man will live on ... for a while. It will be some time until the physical process of death in his mortal body is complete.

Death arrived in judgment when he disobeyed and ate the forbidden fruit. He had overheard that the woman would live on a while longer too. She would live to see the birth of multiple children. Now the man learns that though he will live on for a while, he is on Death Row.

God solemnly teaches the man that his body will turn back into the dust from which he had been made. God could have added plenty of graphic details on the horrors of physical decomposition. Instead, God explains simply that the man's mortal body will cease to live and will return to the dust.

God moves the subject from sweat dropping into the dust, to dust swallowing up the man's remains! It is all very clear.

Of course, *we* believe in death. It is indisputable to those of us who read these words from the perspective of a world filled with thousands of years' worth of graves. We know that no newborn child will live forever.

The first man knew too well that death was not built into his being. It was not part of the world God had created that was "very good." Death was a foreign element that invaded human life only upon the commission of sin.

Even today, the sensitive human spirit cries out against the "unnaturalness" of death. We were not made to die. Death was not in our original blueprint. *We* can sense it and we hate it!

A sentence in a few sentences. God's words in the Garden are packed with meaning but are few in number. It is sufficient that God's words are spoken in "open court."

- The man overheard God speak to the serpent about the coming Victor who would crush his head.

- He overheard God's words of concern to the woman, alerting her that the man's heart was no longer full of a loving desire for her.

- God knew that the man intended to rule *over her* – even though God had not given him dominion to do so.

- The man also hears that the soil will be cursed because of *him*! He learns of the "sorrowful toil" that will result.

And then, God's words of judgment and description come to an end.

Rebel with a curse. There is a pause in Genesis 3. It comes between God's words to the three participants in the Great Disobedience (14-19) and His further actions that end with banishment from the Garden (21-24). God let stand the sentence of death and, because of the man, God also placed a curse on the soil.

Then, the fallen man seizes the initiative! Verse 20 records:

And the man called the name of his wife Eve,
for she would be the mother of all living.

At first glance this verse seems simple enough. But the preceding context shows us otherwise. His action follows hard on God's words of judgment of him as the rebellious sinner. Will the man demonstrate remorse or repentance? No. The rebellion continues. In verse 20, the man engages in another rebellious act.

Name calling. When the woman was created, the man was sound asleep. When the man woke up, he acknowledged God's creative work but he didn't name the new human (2:23).

The man's exuberant response expressed his wonder that this person, – "corresponding to himself" – was now present through God's creative work. He recognized that she was the female-human (*'ishshah*), who corresponded to the male-human (*'ish*).

Neither *'ishshah* nor *'ish* was a name. These words denoted the gender of a human being: "woman" and "man."

It was a different matter when the "naming" of the animals took place. A distinctive "naming formula" was used as described in Genesis 2:19-20. (This formula appears in Gen 4:17, 25, 26; 5:3, 29; 11:9; and elsewhere.)

But after the Fall, the man presumes to name the woman even though God had not told him to do so. Shockingly, he uses the naming formula and gives her a name in the way he gave a name to the animals.

In this way, the man presumes to "rule over" her. The man gives her a name that is different from the one God had already given her (Gen 5:2). Giving the woman a separate name creates distance in their marriage, not unity. The man is not willing to share with her the same name.

He takes the name "Adam" for himself and chooses to give her another one. He discards the name God has given her, and calls her name "Eve." It is the first time they don't wear the same names. It is another sign of sin's deadly fruit.

Here is a translation (with words italicized for emphasis) of (Gen 3:17-20):

[17a]To the man He said,

> "Because you listened to the voice of your wife
> and ate from the tree about which *I* commanded
> you saying, 'You must not eat from it,'

[17b]"*Cursed* is the ground *because of you,*
[17c]In *sorrowful toil* you will eat of it
all of the days of your life.
[18]Thorns and thistles it will produce for you
and you will eat plants of the field.
[19]By the sweat of your face you will eat bread
until you return to the ground
since from it you were taken –
for dust you are and *to dust you will return.*"

[20]And the man *called the name* of his wife Eve, for she would be
the mother of all living.

In the beginning (Genesis 1-2), God created both the man and the woman. They each knew God their Creator. They knew one another. They were allies, corresponding to one another. They were a couple, able to have children and raise a family that would fill the earth. They had work to do. Their Creator delegated to them the task of ruling over the world he had created.

Together with God

ruling over creation
before the Fall

Familiar "Leadership" Heresies Uncovered   by Bruce C. E. Fleming
www.ThinkAgainAboutTheBible.com

After the Fall, the man further disrupts what God began. He seizes power for himself and rules over the woman, placing her into *his* kingdom. This kingdom has radically different authority structures. A barrier of sin comes between the humans and their rightful Lord. God's sovereignty over them, and all relationships descend into dysfunction.

Rebel ruler ruling the other ruler   *Both separated from God*

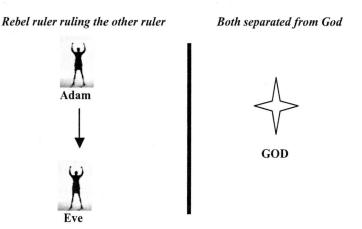

Misrule and separation after the Fall

Trible (*Rhetoric*, p. 128) describes the changes that took place:

> ... distinctions within one flesh became oppositions. ... Division followed, yielding 'opposite sexes.' ... the man [*ha-'adam*] turned against the woman and betrayed her to God (3:12). Yet, according to God, she still yearns for the original unity of male and female: 'for your man [*'ish*] is your desire [*teshuqa*].' Alas, however, ... the man will not reciprocate the woman's desire; instead he will rule over her. Thus she lives in unresolved tension. Where once there was mutuality, now there is a hierarchy of division. ... His supremacy is neither a divine right nor a male prerogative. Her subordination is neither a divine decree nor the female destiny. ... God describes this consequence but does not prescribe it as punishment.

Out of Eden. In Genesis 3:21, God clothes the man and the woman with garments of animal skins. In the remaining verses in Genesis 3, they are banished from the Garden. Here at the end of this long passage (2:4-3:24), as in the opening verses in Genesis 2, there will be no one in Eden. In 3:24, the guardian of 2:15 is banished from the Garden and angelic guardians are assigned to guard it against him! In Genesis 2, everything about creation became better and more complete until all was created and the first family was living in the Garden. Then, in chapter 3 everything took a downward plunge.

Genesis 2-3 is written as a unit, with the facts tightly interwoven into their literary structure. What happened on the way up in chapter 2 is mirrored in the parallel section in chapter 3 on what happened on the way down. The following diagram shows this.

The mirrored sections of Genesis 2:5-3:24

A 2:5-15 God creates the man and places him *in Eden*
   B 2:16-17 God's *command to obey*
      C *2:18-24 God works to* complete *humanity*
         D 2:25 In relationship with each other and with God
      C' *3:1-5 The deceiver works to* destroy *humanity*
   B' 3:6-7 God's *command disobeyed*
A' 3:8-24 Results of disobedience and expulsion *from Eden*
   Part I   8-13   Interrogation
   Part II 14-19   God as Judge and Teacher
   Part III 20-24   Aftermath and expulsion from Eden

What About the Tempter?

The strange voice in Eden. There are many stories about the serpent in the garden. They add all kinds of details that are not found in the record in the Bible.

As stories, they may or may not be interesting. But as for truthfulness, they must be discounted. What the Bible says is sufficient for us to understand the intent and character of the Tempter.

God created the man and the woman and brought them together (Gen 2:18-25). A serpent would have been seen and named by the man in Genesis 2:20.

But this particular serpent was different. It spoke and had a will. And its will was against God. In Genesis 3:1-5, the serpent had much to say, but it fell silent as God spoke to it in verses 14-15.

The temptation. Verses 1-5 record that the serpent purposefully tempted the woman and the man. It used a plural "you" (as in "you two" or "y'all") each time it spoke, in Genesis 3:1, 4, 5. Its counsel was aimed at them both.

The Tempter was wily. After it initiated the conversation, it cast doubt on the loving and benevolent character of God. It twisted the truth, encouraging reflection in such a way as to challenge God's authority: "To think that God has said 'You shall not eat from *any* tree…'!"

If *this* had been what God had said, God's prohibition would have been exceedingly difficult to obey. All trees would have been off limits.

But God had not said that. He had said that the couple could eat from any and every tree of the Garden except for one. That one tree was clearly identified. The consequence of eating only from it was death.

The Tempter misquoted God's words of Genesis 2:16-17. Slyly, it slid the negation ("not") from one part of God's words to another. The result stood God's prohibition on its head! This rearrangement of God's words carried a whole different meaning. It changed the words of the prohibition into words that seemed a refutation of God's actual words.

The woman came to the defense of God and His word. Her words demonstrated an attitude of faithfulness and obedience to God. But the Tempter pressed its attack with incredible boldness. It flatly contradicted both the woman and the truth of God's words – "You shall not surely die!"

Continuing its frontal attack, it imputed evil motives to God, claimed to know what God knew, and implied that God was holding out on them:

> For God knows that in the day you eat from it, your eyes will be opened, and you will be like God, knowing good and evil.

Making claims that swung from one extreme to the other, the Tempter insinuated that *God* had said the fruit of *any* tree would be bad to eat. Then, the Tempter focused on just the one tree, claiming that eating from *that tree* would be good. It claimed they would attain great knowledge and become like God. The Tempter was acting as if it knew as much, and even more than God. Jesus later would call the Tempter "the father of lies" (Jn 8:44). A formidable foe!

The tree did seem to correspond to what he deceptively said. It *was* attractive and appealing as food. It *was* aesthetically pleasing, and it *seemed* to offer the potential of giving success, cleverness and insight.

A condemnation and a prophecy. God cursed the serpent forever more to "eat dust." Ironically, *eating* was how the humans disobeyed. Had the serpent tempted them both to *eat*? Now the serpent would eat the stuff from which the man had been made!

The Hebrew verb "to bruise" is used twice at the end of God's words to the serpent (3:15). God uses the verb *shuph*, to "bruise" or "crush," to tell the serpent that it faces ultimate defeat.

As for the descendance or seed of the woman, God says, "He will bruise you on the head and you shall bruise him on the heel." Had the Tempter shown itself to be God's enemy? God would defeat it and bruise its head through the seed of the woman!

The promise. Isaiah foresaw the bruising of the promised Seed, "He was wounded for our transgressions, bruised for our iniquities...." (Isa 53:5). But this "bruising" did not mean ultimate defeat.

God's words in Genesis 3 revealed that the woman's offspring would be the ultimate Victor. God would incorporate the serpent's strike at the Deliverer into His plan of salvation for humanity.

What's ahead for Adam and the Tempter?

Childlike simplicity is often the straightest path to truth. The end of the serpent-Tempter will be certain destruction. The prophetic words in Genesis 3:15 foretell that the Deliverer will "crush his head."

Jesus' closest disciple, the Apostle John, received further details about the serpent, which he wrote down in the last book of the New Testament, the Revelation of John.

The words of Revelation are filled with references to the events that occurred in the Garden. Note the sobering parallels (in bold type) in these verses from the end of the Book of Revelation:

> [20:1] And I saw an angel coming down from heaven, having the key of the abyss and a great chain in his hand. [2] And he laid hold of the dragon, **the serpent of old**, who is the devil and Satan, and bound him for a thousand years, [3] and threw him into the abyss, and shut it and sealed it over him, so that he should not **deceive** the nations any longer....

> [10] And **the devil**...was thrown into the lake of fire and brimstone (where the beast and the false prophet are also) and they will be **tormented** day and night **forever**. ...

[15]And if anyone's name was not found written in the book of life, he was thrown into the lake of fire. …

In his final chapter, John quotes the words of Jesus and comments on them:

[22:13]"I am the Alpha and the Omega, the first and the last, **the beginning** and **the end**." [14]Blessed are those who wash their robes [in the sacrificial blood of the Lamb, Jesus], that they may have the right to **the tree of life** … (NASB)

So all is not lost! Even though the Garden of Eden, which contained the tree of life, was sealed off after the Great Disobedience, it will be available to all who have placed their faith in the victorious Offspring of the woman.

It is not clear whether the first man placed his faith in the promised Child and had his name written in the book of life.

Here's what we do know:

- Genesis 3:20. We see him continuing his willful sinning as he usurps God's authority and rules over the woman, the other co-ruler of creation.

- Genesis 3:22. We see him driven from the Garden lest he put forth his hand and eat from the tree of life.

- Genesis 3:24. We see that supernatural beings are set as a guard against his return to the tree of life!

- Genesis 4. We note that he fathered a number of children, including Cain and Abel, and Seth.

- Genesis 4:5. We learn that he lived a total of nine hundred and thirty years, and then he died.

- Job 31:33. We note that he is referred to by Job, but not on account of his faith. In fact, the contrary is the case: "If I covered my transgressions like Adam by hiding iniquity in my bosom."

A day is coming when people will be thrown into the lake of fire. Will Adam be among them? The Bible doesn't deny it, nor does it expressly state it. It does not tell us.

The more relevant question applies to the people of our generation. Are our names written in the Book of Life? Is yours?

The Apostle Paul soberly took into account the life of the first Adam. But Paul's focus was on the Messiah, Jesus Christ, whom he called the second Adam in 1 Corinthians 15. In this passage it is certain that he had the events in the Garden of Eden in mind. Because of Christ, he saw victory over Satan available to all who believe.

[45]…"The first human, Adam, became a living soul"; the last Adam a life-giving spirit.

[47]The first man was from the earth, earthy [made of dust]; the second … is from heaven. [48]As is the earthy, so also are the earthy; and as is the heavenly, so also are those who are heavenly.

[50]I declare to you, brothers and sisters, that flesh and blood cannot inherit the kingdom of God; nor does the perishable inherit the imperishable.

[53]For this perishable must put on the imperishable, and this mortal must put on immortality.

[54]… then the saying that is written will come true: "Death is swallowed up in victory."

> [55]"O death, where is your victory?
> O death, where is your sting?"

[56]The sting of death is sin, and the power of sin is the law [57]but thanks be to God, who gives us the victory through our Lord Jesus Christ.

[58]Therefore, my dear brothers and sisters, stand firm. Let nothing move you. Always give yourselves fully to the work of the Lord, knowing that your labor in the Lord is not in vain.

Think Again!

1. What was the first Leadership Heresy in Eden?
Answer: *God is not my leader.* This was at bottom the serpent's lie.

2. What was the second Leadership Heresy in Eden?
Answer: *Someone else can be leader.* This began an infernal competition.

3. If God is not over all, which "god" might be over the others?
Answer: (1) The Serpent and (2) the man decided to compete against God.

4. What was the third Leadership Heresy in Eden?
Answer: *Someone other than God can be leader over another human.*

God gave the man and the woman the command to *rule over* the earth and all that was in it. Both were under God's own rule. But the man stepped between God and the woman to try to usurp God's rule.

Chapter 3

"Leadership" Heresies and Church Leaders
... an inside look at 1 Timothy 1-3 (with a focus on 2:8-3:15)

Chapter Contents:

Paraphrase of 1 Tim. 2:8-3:7*

Correcting wayward overseers in Ephesus
[8]Timothy, I want the injurious men among the overseers to pray and prophesy in church lifting up holy hands without anger and disputing. [9]Likewise, I want the injurious women among the overseers to adorn themselves with modest apparel that promotes self control – not with improper hair plaiting, along with its gold and pearls, and costly clothing – [10]Women overseers preaching godliness are adorned by good work. [11]Let the wayward women overseers learn in quietness and with all studiousness (in subjection to teacher and studies). [12]I am not permitting them to teach men in an incorrect way, but to quietly learn. (Why do I recommend gentle treatment?) [13]Well, God formed the two in the Garden, Adam and then Eve [14]and Adam was not deceived, but Eve was deceived (as I had been) and to that degree became a transgressor. [15a]Eve placed her faith in the birth of the Child and so will be saved,
[15b]as will these women if they persevere in faith, love, sanctification and self-control.
[3:1]**"Faithful is the Word" (Jesus the *Logos*)!** so if any of these (in 2:8-15) aspires to return to oversight, that one desires a good work. [2]Here's a list of important practices and traits this man or woman must display:
An overseer must be without reproach –
a faithful spouse, temperate, serious, modest, hospitable, a good teacher, [3]not an excessive drinker or pugnacious, but patient, not contentious, and not avaricious, [4]ruling his or her own household well, having one's children in subjection, [5](for if someone doesn't know how to manage his or her own household, how can that one take care of the church of God?), [6]not a recent convert, so as to avoid the danger of being puffed up with pride, and falling into the same condemnation as the devil received. [7]Also, it is important to have a good testimony from outsiders, so as not to fall into disgrace and the devil's snare.

*Insights: Study verses 11-12 in their context, which starts in verse 8 and likewise in 9. Verses 11-12 form one unit of thought in Greek. The main point of the passage is in the main verb of 11, "Let learn!" In verses 13-15a Paul explains why he recommends gentle correction for these wayward overseers.

Chapter Introduction

The new snowfall was a foot deep one morning! It was beautiful. My son and I hopped into the car and drove over to my mother-in-law's house. We pulled into the left side of the driveway in front of her two-car garage. Soon a jet of white flakes was shooting into the air. I handed the roaring machine to Mark, who was 13 at the time, to finish clearing the right half of the driveway and headed in to talk to his Grandmother.

At the door to her house, I tossed the car keys to Mark and shouted, "When you finish snowblowing that side of the drive, move our car over into the spot you've just cleared. Then you can clear the rest of the drive." I thought my directions were simple enough. I pictured him backing the car straight out and driving it back in on the right side of the driveway.

What I didn't know was that for some time Mark's Grandmother had given him permission to do some complex maneuvers with her car. He would back it out of the driveway and into the street. Then he would drive down the street to the end of her lot, turn the car around, drive back and pull into her driveway.

This day, the street was already deep with fallen snow, plus a thick drift had been piled up by a passing city snowplow! When Mark got into the car he backed it into the street and decided to park in front of the house. Halfway into the drift he got stuck!

The driver of a passing delivery truck saw his predicament, stopped and pushed him out. Then, Mark pulled the car into the cleared side of the driveway.

Happy ending? Not completely. He hadn't followed directions and had gone astray. I told him that he wouldn't be permitted behind the wheel any more *until* he was taught, and until he learned well, to drive in wintry conditions!

When Paul wrote 1 Timothy, Timothy was working in "wintry" conditions. Paul had left Timothy behind to correct certain members of the church at Ephesus who were into deep drifts of error. Paul wrote with a full heart, advising his younger colleague how to deal with each one who needed correction and discipline.

Paul's letter is a surprisingly hopeful one. From his own experience of receiving God's correction, he instructed Timothy to graciously restore to ministry those who had wandered astray. He encouraged Timothy himself, that he might remain faithful.

Much as I restricted our son from driving *until* he was corrected, Timothy had to stop those at Ephesus who were acting in error. They, in turn, were to accept his discipline. *After screening*, those who proved themselves faithful could be put back into service.

Familiar "Leadership" Heresies Uncovered   by Bruce C. E. Fleming
www.ThinkAgainAboutTheBible.com

Wise Advice to Timothy

Paul recruited young Timothy to join his missionary team early in his second missionary journey (Acts 16:4). Timothy was already well instructed in the things of God by his mother and grandmother, Lois and Eunice (2 Tim 1:5). At first, Timothy worked at Paul's side. Later on he was left behind, or was sent ahead, to churches that needed attention while Paul was busy elsewhere. One day Paul left Timothy in Ephesus, the great city of Asia Minor where the church had been planted for some time. A number of Christian workers had labored in Ephesus. Paul himself had spent much time there. His co-workers, Priscilla and Acquila, had built up the church even more. It was here that Paul left Timothy to correct certain persons who had gone astray and caused trouble through their false teaching and bad behavior.

Appropriate corrections. There are many different ways to correct a wayward person. Some people who mistakenly go astray simply need a word of correction. Others deliberately reject the truth and grow malicious in their attitude. These people need to be dealt with firmly. Paul left Timothy to deal appropriately with each one in the church at Ephesus.

In his letter, strikingly, Paul uses himself as a prime example of someone who needed correcting. He calls himself the "chief of sinners" and then lists three specific sins of which he had been guilty.

In the first half of the letter, Paul focuses on himself and on the overseers who had gone astray at Ephesus. As he refers to his own sins, one by one, Paul instructs Timothy how to deal with similar offenders. He devotes the second half of his letter to Timothy, and ends with the exhortation, "O Timothy, guard what has been entrusted to you …" (6:20).

According to The Book of Revelation, Paul and Timothy were successful in correcting the false teachers and in teaching the rest of the Ephesians not to be led astray by any more false teachers! The Ephesians received this praise:

> I know your deeds, your labor and your perseverance, and that you cannot bear those who are evil. And you have tested those who say they are apostles and are not, and have found them to be liars …. (Rev 2:2)

Paul's background. In his early years, when Paul was a disciple of the respected teacher, Rabbi Gamaliel, Paul followed the strictest practices of Judaism as a Pharisee. But this did not make him loving and righteous. Instead, he became vicious.

86

Paul was present at the execution of Stephen, the first Christian martyr (Acts 8:1). He, then, became an instigator of more persecution against the church. He "made havoc of the church, entering every house, and dragging off men and women, committing them to prison" (Acts 8:3, NKJV, *cf.* 1 Cor 15:9).

"Breathing threats and murder against the disciples," he asked for official support from the High Priest to go outside of Israel, to enter the synagogues in Damascus, to arrest any who claimed to follow this Way of Jesus and to bring them as prisoners to Jerusalem.

Striding with a heart full of fury, he was brought up short on the road to Damascus by the resurrected Jesus who spoke to him (Acts 9:3-20)! Jesus told Paul that he was a persecutor of the Messiah. Paul never intended to do that. He had set out from Jerusalem intending to "sanitize" the synagogues by getting rid of the followers of Jesus. Having met Jesus himself, he arrived in Damascus physically blind, and convinced that *he* had been spiritually blind.

Had Paul wanted to work outside of Israel in the distant synagogues? Jesus would assign this territory to him. But Jesus changed his mission. Instead of persecuting the followers of Jesus, he would bear the name of Jesus wherever he went. To the amazement of all, "Paul the persecutor" became "Paul the preacher." In synagogue after synagogue he affirmed that Jesus was the Messiah, the Son of God!

By the time he writes to Timothy, Paul is a veteran who knows from experience that the word of the gospel is trustworthy, and that Jesus, the Word of God, is always faithful. Paul develops this theme in 1 Timothy, his letter about disciplining wayward overseers.

1 Timothy is written in three distinct sections:

- the **first** section concerns **Paul** himself (1:1-17)

- the **second** concerns wayward **overseers** (1:18-3:16)

- the **third** section concerns **Timothy** (4:1-6:12).

Three Keys that Unlock 1ˢᵗ Timothy

When I was a boy, I discovered that a word looks backward when viewed in a mirror. My Dad playfully explained that I could "fix" that problem by looking in a second mirror. That way I could make the letters come out looking normal. After a while, I grew tired of all that and got rid of the mirrors altogether.

Many years later, I took a course on 1 Timothy from the British Bible scholar, John R.W. Stott. I had just begun seminary. Stott's love for the Bible and his lessons were wonderful! But I was troubled when he explained that there were a number of "points of dispute" among scholars on the meaning of 1 Timothy.

Usually, he told us how he thought a point of dispute might be cleared up. Carefully, he would show us how a mistake in interpretation, or in logic, led some to draw the wrong conclusions. I wondered if these people weren't reading 1 Timothy with a mirror. I thought of the saying,

> A Biblical text taken out of context can be used as a pretext for teaching practically anything!

But, sometimes Stott presented two different points of view and stated that, as far as he could tell, either view might be correct.

In the great number of commentaries that have been written about 1 Timothy are found very different interpretations of its passages. They even disagree on ways that 1 Timothy should be put into practice in daily life. Much of this confusion is due to the fact that the structure of 1 Timothy, and the purpose of its sections, have been misunderstood.

To understand 1 Timothy, one must first determine its overall structure. Then each passage, each verse and word, can be placed in its proper context.

There are three "keys" that unlock the book's structure and the meaning of its contents, including the so-called "difficult" passages of 1 Timothy. While many people have noted the first key, few or none have made use of keys number two and number three to unlock the meaning of 1 Timothy.

Here are the three keys:

- The **Mission** – reason for the letter

- The **Logos** – central place of Christ

- The **Outline** – Paul's three sins

This can be restated as (1) the *people* (to whom the letter is written), (2) the *pun* on *logos* (on the life-changing power of Christ), and (3) the *points* (the three parts in the first chapters of 1 Timothy).

Key #1: The Mission – Correct false teachers at Ephesus.

This letter reminds Timothy of his mission and gives him written directions for fulfilling it. His is to correct wayward overseers at Ephesus. Verse after verse has to do with overseers.

Timothy's mission is to correct overseers who have gone astray.

Timothy is tasked to give these wayward overseers two instructions, what *not* to do and what *to* do:

– They *must not* teach false doctrine (1:3, overseers were teachers 3:2)
– They *must* practice love, maintain a pure heart, a good conscience, and a faith without hypocrisy (1:5, 19).

Key #2: The *Logos* – Central pun on the power of Jesus, the Word.

In 1 Timothy Paul makes reference to Jesus using a phrase that holds a potential pun in Greek. He uses this important phrase at three strategic places in his letter. The phrase has no verb, but "is" may be inserted and used as the verb. Here are the three words of this important phrase:

	1	2	3
Greek	*pistos*	*ho*	*logos*
English	faithful [*is*]	the	word

The challenge of dealing with any phrase with a double meaning is: (1) to notice that more than one meaning is *possible*, (2) to accept that multiple meanings *may be intended* and (3) to determine each time *which meaning* (or meanings) is being used.

The last word in the phrase is – *ho logos*. It has two possible meanings:

- "the Word," as in Jesus Himself who is *the* Logos
- "the saying," as in a slogan or a well-known truth.

The first Greek word – *pistos* – can mean either "faithful" or "trustworthy." Its meaning depends on which meaning of *logos* is intended. Either one, or both, of these meanings in Greek may be intended:

Meaning #1		**Meaning #2**	
pistos	*ho logos*	*pistos*	*ho logos*
faithful [is]	the Word (Jesus)	trustworthy	[is] the saying

Meaning #1 stands alone as a complete thought: "Faithful is Jesus, the Word." Meaning #2 does not stand alone. A saying must accompany it: "Trustworthy is the saying...."

Since Paul is using this potentially "punny" phrase in his own letter, he may, of course, use the phrase *pistos ho logos* however he wishes. It is very likely that he and Timothy had made puns on the words in this phrase many times as they worked together, walked the long roads together, and listened to each other's sermons.

I love to pun! Those who know me well have heard my puns many times before. After they have heard my puns, the fun for me is to keep them guessing as to *which meaning* of a possibly punny word I am going to use!

**To understand a "punny" phrase
one must choose the intended meaning.
Pick the wrong meaning and it turns to nonsense.**

The first time Paul uses this potentially "punny" phrase (1:15), he keeps Timothy guessing.

1. Paul's primary meaning is that the Word Jesus, the Logos, has been faithful to him and that Jesus made Paul into a faithful servant!

2. Paul adds a second meaning too, by attaching a specific saying to it. Both options of the pun focus on the central place of Christ.

The second and third times Paul uses this phrase (1 Tim 3:1 and 4:9), it is easy for Timothy to spot Paul's meaning. Paul simply uses the primary meaning of the phrase – "Faithful is the Logos, the Word Jesus." Elsewhere, Paul used "faithful" in the same way (1 Cor 10:13) – *pistos ho theos* or "faithful is God."

Just as the Word Jesus made Paul fit for service, He could make the wayward overseers fit for service (3:1). The Word Jesus also could keep Timothy faithful (4:9-10) in his own difficult ministry.

Here is an overview of how the phrase is used these three times. It will become clear that this phrase points to the three sections of 1 Timothy.

Section 1: Paul and "the faithful *logos*"(1:15). Paul reports in 1 Timothy 1:13 that he had been a wayward sinner. In verse 15 he calls himself the worst of sinners! When he encountered "the faithful Word," Jesus Christ, Paul was turned in the right direction, and for the rest of his life he brought word of the Word Jesus as the Apostle of Jesus to the Gentiles.

Paul and the early Christians were familiar with using the Greek word "*logos*" to stand for "Jesus." For example, the Apostle John used *logos* for Jesus as he opened his Gospel in John 1:1,

> In the beginning was the *logos* (Jesus),
> and the *logos* (Jesus) was with God,
> and the *logos* (Jesus) was God.

The Greeks were fascinated with ideas of the mind and with sayings full of meaning. They had high respect for the word. In the context of 1 Timothy, Paul used the word *logos* to refer to Jesus. Jesus was the "word" of truth. In fact, Jesus was *the* "Word."

In 1 Timothy 1:15, after beginning the verse with *pistos ho logos* (faithful is the Word) referring to Jesus, he turns to a second possible meaning of the word *logos* and spells out a trustworthy "saying," namely, "… that Christ Jesus came into the world to save sinners…." What a great pun!

According to the first and primary meaning of the pun, the *Word* Jesus turned Paul around and saved him.

According to the second meaning of the pun, the "*saying*" came true in Paul's life, "… that Christ Jesus came into the world to save sinners…."

Section 2: Overseers and "the faithful *logos*"(3:1a). Paul uses his key phrase a second time in 3:1a. Before he uses it, in 2:8-15 Paul prescribes discipline for the wayward men and women overseers of the church. Then, Paul points to Jesus who faithfully restored him. Jesus – the faithful Word – could make them faithful again for service (3:1b-16)!

**Paul focuses on the wayward men and women overseers of the church.
The faithful *logos* could make them fit for service again.**

Section 3: Timothy and "the faithful *logos*"(4:9). The third time Paul uses his key phrase, he reminds Timothy of the foundation of his own ministry. Timothy was well-trained by his godly grandmother Lois and his godly mother Eunice (2 Tim 1:5). He was young when he joined Paul's ministry team (Acts 16:1-3). Timothy was still relatively young when Paul wrote 1 Timothy (4:12). For Timothy, "the faithful Word" (4:9) made him fit for ministry too. Paul refers to the faithful Logos almost at the beginning of the Section which focuses on Timothy. Paul makes clear that he has the faithful Savior in mind when he continues,

> [10]... because we have put our hope in the living God, who is the Savior of all people, and especially of those who believe.

I once heard an evangelist tell of being hosted in a home where the little child in the family had memorized most of the songs the adults sang in church. Frequently, this little one would sing these songs while playing. One day the speaker was amused to hear the little one singing these words: "Years I spent in vanity and pride, caring not my Lord was crucified...!"
Neither this little one, nor Timothy had spent years in sin and degradation. All the better! Jesus the "Word" had been faithful early in Timothy's life and ministry, and would keep him faithful to the end.
Heresy alert! Many have missed the primary sense of the Greek phrase in 1:15, that Jesus is the Word. They only catch the sense of "a faithful saying." This becomes a problem when people look only for a "saying" in 3:1. Here, Paul uses only the primary sense of the phrase. If someone really wanted to find an applicable "trustworthy saying" in 3:1 (or in 4:9), they could think back to the one Paul cited in 1:15. But for those who insisted on finding a phrase of some kind, they must make up a phrase of some kind, and then give it a meaning of their own devising. When they do, they can miss the meaning of the passage.

Key #3: The Outline – The three parts to 1 Timothy 1:18-3:15.

In his letters, Paul often gives an outline as a preview of the main points he is going to cover. In this way he helps his readers anticipate and retain his thoughts.
Most early Christians were illiterate. Even those who could read, usually did not have their own copy of Paul's letters. Usually, someone would read his letter out loud to a group of listeners. By hearing the outline of Paul's thoughts to come, they could more easily remember his teachings.

As soon as I learned of this, I checked to see if Paul had used a preview outline in 1 Timothy. I found it in 1 Timothy 1:13! It does not cover the entire letter, but it does provide a three-part outline for the Section that deals with correcting the wayward overseers at Ephesus.

In chapter 1, prior to verse 13, Paul listed many different kinds of sin. In verse 15, he refers to himself as the "worst" (NIV) or "chief" (KJV) of all sinners. But he lists *only three sins* that actually applied to him.

He spells out these sins in verse 13. As a sinner, he had been:

- "a blasphemer" (of the name of Christ)
- "a persecutor" (officially commissioned to do so)
- "injurious" (disruptive to the life of the church).

After listing these sins, Paul takes each sin in order, and discusses it in his Section 2.

These sinners corresponded to Paul's three sins:

- blasphemers (1:18-20, Hymenaus and Alexander)
- persecutors (2:1-7, who had power to persecute)
- injurious ones (2:8-15, sowing discord in church).

I grew excited as I observed that Keys #1, #2 and #3 all come together in this Section of 1 Timothy!

Paul refers to those who:

- need correction because they are guilty of
- his own three sins,
- and *pistos ho logos* serves as the turning point in 3:1a.

Paul had set out to be righteous but had become a *blasphemer*. He thought he was doing good as a *persecutor*, officially sanctioned by the High Priest, but in doing so he had persecuted the Messiah (Acts 9:5). He had attempted to be zealous for the law of God, but instead he had disrupted the people of God by his *injurious* behavior. The faithful *logos* (1:15) had set Paul right and this same faithful *logos* (3:1) could do the same for the false teachers in Ephesus!

Don't let English get in the way. Many people have found it difficult to understand some of the old words and phrases used in the *King James Version* (KJV) of 1611. Just like the old English used by Shakespeare, many words are difficult for modern readers to understand. Many of the KJV's English terms don't mean now what they used to mean. Some of the old words aren't used at all and are incomprehensible to modern readers.

Here, for example, is how the KJV translates 2 Timothy 2:5, in a way that is difficult for modern readers to grasp:

> [5]And if a man also strive for masteries, *yet* he is not crowned, except he strive lawfully.

This is one reason why new translations are produced. They update the Bible using a more modern vocabulary. The *New International Version* (NIV) of 1973 translated this verse in a way more comprehensible to modern readers:

> [5]Similarly, if anyone competes as an athlete, he does not receive the victor's crown unless he competes according to the rules.

However, the English language has changed since 1973, especially in the precision by which one refers to men and women. Before 1950, grown men were often referred to as "boys" and adult women were often referred to as "girls." That has all changed.

When I was young, I remember thinking it strange when older relatives called the two bachelor uncles who still ran our ancestors' family farm, "the Boys." They were well into their 70s!

Before 1950 the word "men" also could be used to refer to both men *and* women. But this has changed too. Common English usage in the 21st century does not use the word "men" inclusively, but spells out "men and women" when both genders are meant. When the word "men" is used, modern English speakers assume it refers to males only.

I doubt that my grandmother was bothered whenever a preacher referred to our mixed congregation of men and women as "men." But recently, a well-respected leader, who is a woman, confided to me that she was made to feel "very uncomfortable" when a speaker repeatedly addressed the dozen or so people in the room as "men." Did he mean to exclude her?

In 2 Timothy 2:5, the KJV used the word "man" to translate the Greek pronoun *tis*, which is gender neutral and doesn't designate whether the person is male or female. In 1973, the NIV clarified this use of *tis* by using the pronoun "anyone." But the NIV also used the masculine pronoun "he."

The 21st century English usage of *tis* in 2:5 is found in *Today's New International Version* (TNIV), of 2001:

> [5]Similarly, *anyone* who competes as an athlete does not receive the victor's crown except by competing according to the rules.

It is very important for modern language translations to be as clear and precise as possible. Then, readers can learn God's word in their own language, and with confidence they can put into practice what they learn.

In 1 Timothy 1:3, Paul used the Greek pronoun *tisin*, meaning "certain persons," to indicate that Timothy was to correct *any and all* overseers at Ephesus who were wrongdoers, male *or* female. The KJV translated this clearly:

> [3]As I besought thee to abide still at Ephesus, when I went into Macedonia, that thou mightest charge *some* that *they* teach no other doctrine.

The NIV introduced a degree of confusion, however, when it translated *tisin* with the English word "men." The TNIV has corrected this with a clear English translation for *tisin*:

> [3]As I urged you ... command *certain persons* not to teach false doctrines any longer....

According to 1 Timothy, *both* men *and* women were guilty of false teaching, and *all* were being corrected by Timothy.

Paul's Three Sins

Sin #1. Blasphemy (1:13; 18-20).

Beginning with His meeting with Paul on the road to Damascus, and in the days that followed (Acts 9:3-19), the risen Christ took extraordinary action to turn Paul around. Before his conversion, Saul (his former name), the Jewish Pharisee, persecuted Christians with all his might, following his sense of Jewish righteousness.

Then, Jesus revealed Himself to him as the true Messiah, long-promised by God. Paul was confounded. Instead of rightly defending orthodoxy, he had been sinning against God's Holy One. Nevertheless, his actions issued from honest intention and God took that into account.

The case of some of the false teachers at Ephesus was very different. In the first chapter of 1 Timothy in verses 3-11, Paul lists their detestable sins and contrasts them with descriptions of true love.

After listing his own sins and reflecting on his own encounter with Jesus, the faithful Word (1 Timothy 1:12-17), he then describes the situation of those who sinned in the ways he had sinned.

Paul names two sinners who were guilty of his first sin of "blasphemy." In 1 Timothy 1:19-20, Paul observes that Hymenæus and Alexander had rejected their good consciences. They had sinned deliberately. For this, Paul gave them over to Satan for "education through punishment." They were to be taught in a way appropriate to their willful disobedience – Satan would teach them! The verb Paul uses in 1 Timothy 1:20, "to be taught," is quite different from the verb he uses later in 2:11, "to learn." These different verbs correspond to the situation of the ones who needed educating. The hearts of those in 2:11 were different from the two blasphemers of 1:19-20.

Two levels of sin. When Paul said he was the worst sinner (1:15), he didn't mean he was "just like" all sinners in every way. Nor did he mean that he had committed "every sin" there was.

Even as the worst of sinners, Paul had not been an intentional sinner, like the sin of a killer guilty of premeditated murder. In 1 Timothy 1:13, Paul specified that he had sinned "in ignorance and unbelief."

This is an important distinction that should not be overlooked. The Old Testament drew a distinction between *defiant* sinning and *unintentional* sinning, or, as it might be called today, "first degree" and "second degree" sinning. Numbers 15:22-31 developed this subject at length and strongly condemned blasphemy when it was purposeful, or in the "first degree." But Paul blasphemed "in ignorance." He had blasphemed in the "second degree."

Philo of Alexander drew this distinction in *The Sacrifices* (11, 48). He taught sin could come from "sinful wickedness" or from "untutored ignorance." He wrote,

> Ignorance is an involuntary state, a light matter, and its treatment through teaching is not hopeless. But wickedness is a willful malady of the soul, and its action is such that to remove it is hard, if indeed it is not hopeless.

God knew the state of Paul's heart. He called Paul to ministry because his heart was "in the right place." Paul, the "worst of sinners" found grace and forgiveness in Jesus. Astoundingly, this sinner was appointed to be Jesus' Apostle to the Gentiles! Through this experience in his own life Paul learned to discipline with mercy as well as with firmness.

When Timothy read the early lines of his letter from Paul, his "charge" to correct false teachers loomed large. No doubt he was encouraged as he read

Paul's own testimony that Jesus, the faithful *logos*, mercifully had turned him around, made him fit, and placed him into service. But, from Paul's treatment of the two willful blasphemers, he learned that sharp discipline must be applied to those in the church who willfully insist on sinning.

Sin #2: Persecution (1:13; 2:1-7).
Many commentators and theologians can't understand how the first seven verses in 1 Timothy 2 fit into the structure of Paul's letter. They have missed the continuing development of his thought through each of his three sins.

Some have suggested that Paul "strung his ideas together in 1 Timothy in a rather haphazard manner." Some have suggested that the first seven (or eight, or nine) verses of the chapter form a unit that stands alone from the context around it. Not surprisingly, these interpreters have found the main idea of these verses hard to identify and the theories they have proposed to defend their interpretations are contradictory!

The meaning of these verses should be no great mystery. The first seven verses in 1 Timothy 2 are Paul's discussion of his second sin, that of being "an official who persecuted" the church. Paul knew all about officials who could wreak havoc on the church. 1 Timothy 2:1-7 references Paul's own past:

- when he persecuted the church
- when he was converted
- when he ceased persecuting the church.

In his request that "prayer be made for all" (2:1), and especially those in positions of power (2:2), his focus is twofold. First, Paul expresses his concern that the church might progress in peace (2:1-3). On this count, Paul had personal experience. He had been an official persecutor of the church before his conversion and then, after his conversion, he had experienced the other side of persecution (*cf.* Acts 19:23-41).

In Ephesus, where Timothy was, there had been a riot that almost turned into a bloody persecution of the Christians (Acts 19:23-41). Knowing the damage that persecution could cause, Paul wanted Christians to be spared from it as much as possible. Thus, he commanded that prayer be made to that end.

Second, Paul wants to see the persecutors come to know Christ, just as he himself had come to know Christ as a persecutor (1 Timothy 2:4-7). He was still grateful that he had been saved. No wonder he instructs that prayer be made for the salvation of others who were just like he had been. He knew that if *he* could be saved, no other persecutor was beyond hope (1:16)!

The Book of Acts reports what happened when Paul stopped his persecutions; the church experienced a period of peace (Acts 9:31):

[31]Then the church throughout Judea, Galilee and Samaria enjoyed a time of peace. It was strengthened; and encouraged by the Holy Spirit, it grew in numbers, living in the fear of the Lord. (NIV)

Paul wanted all those who had the power to persecute the church to let the church grow in peace. In addition, he hoped they would themselves come to a saving knowledge of Christ (2:4)! Some in Caesar's own household apparently were believers. Rulers of synagogues and other leaders had come to Jesus. He called for prayer that more would come to Jesus.

Paul wanted all those who had the power to persecute the church to let the church grow in peace.

If anyone hesitated to accept Paul's optimistic advice about persecutors, he had news for them. In verses 5-7, he energetically repeats the gospel and points to himself as an example of the saving power of God for all people.

As for how to deal with those who were capable (or guilty) of persecution of believers, Paul recommends that serious, and detailed, prayer be made – petitions, prayers, intercessions, and thanksgivings (*cf.* Ephesians 6:18).

Sin #3: Injuriousness (1:13; 2:8-15).

After finishing the discussion of his second sin, Paul turns to the sin that Timothy was charged to correct in Ephesus. It corresponded to Paul's third sin – the sin of *injuriously* disrupting the church. Versions of the Bible translate the Greek word for Paul's third sin, named in 1:13, with different words, such as "injurious" and "insolent."

There is no single English word that corresponds exactly to this Greek word. "Injurious," properly understood, is perhaps the best choice. It indicates someone whose actions are inappropriate and do harm.

The actual Greek term used in 1:13 is too harsh to be used to describe Christians, no matter how inappropriate their behavior might be. The only other place it occurs in the New Testament is in Romans 1:30 as part of the list of the deeds of depraved sinners. It comes in between "God-haters," and "arrogant and boastful...." So, instead of using that word in 2:8-15, Paul simply describes the acts of those who are disrupting the church at Ephesus without labeling them. He instructs Timothy to correct people such as these among the overseers in the church.

Dare to discipline. During our first years of marriage, while Joy finished her degree in seminary, I worked at starting a new church in a working-class, river town in Illinois. I got a job as a school bus driver to earn some income and to get to know the area.

I thought I would get to know the families of the children on my routes and our congregation would grow from them. But it didn't work out that way.

School bus drivers spend much of their time parked outside school buildings waiting for the students to come out. Since I had three afternoon routes, I found myself waiting with my bus in a line with other buses in school parking lots three times a day, five days a week. Often, a bus driver would park and climb into another bus to chat and pass the time. Frequently, the subject turned to complaints about everyday problems.

By the grapevine, everybody knew I was "the preacher" and they often unburdened themselves to me. I would listen and pray for them right there in the bus. Several of them gave their hearts to Christ! That was the first step in addressing their problems.

Before I knew it, we had a new and growing church made up of converted school bus drivers! These people had lived hard lives and many still were living in difficult situations. Christian growth for them was often a case of "two steps forward and one step back," or worse.

To help these new believers grow, a ministry team was assembled, consisting of Joy and myself and several mature believers, one each from three sister churches in the area.

One of the most active of the new Christian bus drivers had been a hard drinker. She had a very loud voice and had been known in town for having the foulest vocabulary around. Her conversion to Christ was glorious! The difference in her life was evident to all. She began to treat her colleagues with respect. She lavished care on her previously neglected family. As she became involved in the ministry team of the new church, she did all she could to help it grow. And grow it did!

Just before our first Easter service she organized a children's choir. She taught the children songs and bought bolts of beautiful cloth that she made into lovely robes for each child. Then, she took a big step back. The night before Easter, she called our house. She was drunk and depressed. She was angry, loud, and out of control. Worst of all, she had just gone out into her back yard and had made a bonfire out of all the children's lovely new choir robes!

Easter Sunday morning she had a terrible hangover. The children were devastated not to have the robes they had hoped to wear. They could hardly sing. More difficulties occurred in the months that followed. Time and time again, she would fall. Each time we prayed with her and helped her get back on the right track, she made progress and ministered to others in her vast circle of friends. But then, in one way or another, she would disrupt the church mightily. A mature Christian from a sister church advised us to restructure our ministry team and assign her to a quiet period of probationary discipline. It was hard to do, because most of our new contacts still came through her.

Late one afternoon after our school bus routes were over, our ministry team huddled in a quiet corner of a local restaurant and explained to her that we wanted her to spend a quiet period of time on the sidelines receiving further training, while others carried on the ministry. Our hope was that, eventually, she could minister again.

This discipline was in the spirit of Paul's assignment to Timothy. Rather than advancing God's work (1:4), some of the key people in the church had gone astray.

Paul described the big picture as follows (1:3-7, TNIV):

> [3]As I urged you when I went into Macedonia, stay there in Ephesus so that you may command certain persons not to teach false doctrines any longer [4]or to devote themselves to myths and endless genealogies. Such things promote controversial speculations rather than advancing God's work – which is by faith. [5]The goal of this command is love, which comes from a pure heart and a good conscience and a sincere faith. [6]Some have departed from these and turned to meaningless talk. [7]They want to be teachers of the law, but they do not know what they are talking about or what they so confidently affirm.

Starting with 2:8, Paul spells out how Timothy is to deal with injurious members of the leadership team.

Correcting Injurious Overseers

Paraphrase

> [2:8]Timothy, I wish for the men who pray and prophesy during worship to do so correctly lifting up holy hands without causing anger and disputing.
> [9]Likewise, I wish the women who pray and prophesy during worship to adorn themselves with modest apparel that promotes self-control – not with improper hair plaiting, along with its gold and pearls, and costly clothing – [10]Women preaching godliness are adorned by their good works.
> [11]Let those women overseers who were wayward learn in quietness and with all studiousness. [12]I am not permitting them to teach men in an incorrect way, but to learn in quietness.
> [13]Why? For, God formed the two in the Garden, Adam and then Eve [14]and Adam was not deceived, but Eve was deceived and to that degree became a transgressor. [15]But she would be saved through the Child who was to come, as will these women if they persevere in faith, love, sanctification and self-control.
> [3:1]"Faithful is the Logos," so if any one of those you are correcting aspires to oversight, that one desires a good work!

After dealing with blasphemy and persecution of the church, his first two sins, Paul moves on in 2:8 and following to deal with those who are guilty of his third sin, injuriousness.

This advice is not addressed only to Timothy. It is also Paul's advice to the entire church at Ephesus. Even though when he began the letter it was addressed to Timothy alone (1:2), Paul ends his letter with the closing phrase, "Grace be with you," and the "you" was *plural* in Greek (6:21). Thus, in verses 2:8 and following, Paul spells out serious advice, which he expects Timothy and the others at Ephesus to carry out.

Reading ahead. Sometimes reading ahead spoils the drama in a book. In this case, however, reading the most important part of the passage helps the reader keep in mind what the passage is saying.

When Paul was changed by the faithful *Logos* (1:12-17), he ceased to be the sinful envoy of the rulers in Jerusalem. He became Christ's envoy to the non-Jewish world. Everything that Paul recommends in 1 Timothy 2:8-15 leads up to the high point of 3:1. The wayward overseers that Timothy corrects can be made faithful, and fit for service, by the faithful *Logos*. The service in which they were once engaged – oversight – they will be encouraged to consider once again (3:1*b*).

> **The sinning overseers being disciplined by Timothy can be made fit again by the faithful *Logos* (3:1); they can aspire to serve the church once more.**

It is important to keep in mind that "chapter" and "verse" numbers were added many centuries after Paul wrote. For whatever reason, a chapter break was placed between 2:15 and 3:1, just before Paul's second use of the key phrase "faithful is the Logos." Readers today come upon this chapter break and assume there is a break in Paul's flow of thought between chapter 2 and chapter 3, but such is not the case.

Tendencies toward clericalism. In many churches, throughout the centuries and down to the present day, people have felt it necessary to reserve a *special chair* in the meeting room for the overseers. They refer to overseers with a *special title*, such as "the Reverend," "Bishop" or even "*Senior* Pastor." And most overseers have accepted the special chairs and titles offered them!

Following this mindset, a person might logically expect the discussion on correcting the wayward overseers in Ephesus in 2:8-15 to stand out more clearly than it does. It has been wrongly assumed that these verses can't really be a discussion about male and female overseers in the church, but somehow are about *all* men and *all* women.

However, in 3:1, Paul uses the generic Greek pronoun "anyone" (*tis*) to stand for *those who aspire to oversight*. Those referred to by this pronoun are the *women* of 2:9-15 and the *men* of 2:8.

So why doesn't Paul refer to the men and the women of 1 Timothy 2 as "overseers"? He does. Paul says it in a perfectly acceptable way. Using a typically Jewish way of storytelling, he does not refer to all the elements under consideration until he gets to the heart of his argument.

In the Old Testament each and every detail in a story or a lesson is not given at the first mention of a subject. Various elements are introduced along the way until all are mentioned in the grand summation.

Paul's identification of the injurious ones Timothy is correcting and his word of encouragement for those who successfully pass their discipline is saved until 3:1. Then Paul says that "*anyone (tis)* who aspires to *oversight* desires a good work."

As he describes them in 1 Timothy 3:2-7, those who oversee the church must be above reproach and must be able to teach, among other things. From this group of overseers came the *false* teachers whom Timothy was to correct.

Two injurious groups. Paul wants Timothy to correct two groups of injurious overseers in Ephesus:

1. *certain men*, described and corrected in verse 8

2. *certain women*, described and corrected in verses 9-15.

Paul begins verse 9 with the Greek word – "Likewise." This links verse 9 with verse 8. It is a first indication that what Paul wants done in verse 8, he wants done "likewise" in verse 9.

A second indication that Paul has two similar groups in mind is the shared verb of verse 8. Verse 9 has no verb. According to Greek grammar, when a verb is omitted the reader is supposed to reach up to the previous sentence and bring down its verb to use. The shared verb for both of these verses, "I wish," refers to Paul's desire that his recommendations be taken seriously.

By yoking both verses together with the shared verb, and by starting verse 9 with "likewise," Paul indicates that the men referred to in verse 8, *and* the women of verses 9 and following, are to be treated in a like manner – all are to be corrected – by Timothy.

---

²:⁸Timothy, *I wish*, therefore, the men ...

⁹*Likewise, [I wish]* the women ...

Target group (verse 8): *Some* **errant men.**

> 2:8Timothy, I wish, therefore, the men …

Verse 8 is not addressed to every Christian man in the world. Nor is it addressed to every Christian man at Ephesus. It is not reasonable to assume that *every* man at Ephesus had behaved in an injurious manner. But *some false teachers* had behaved improperly and *those men* were the target of Paul's concern.

Heresy alert! In 1 Timothy 2:8 and following, Paul describes misbehavior taking place *in church* while the congregation was gathered together for instruction and worship. Most modern English translations do not make this clear. For example, notice the word "everywhere" in the following NIV translation of the first part of verse 8:

> … I want the men *everywhere* to pray….

This translation makes it seem as if Paul is giving general instructions for *all* men, *wherever* they might happen to be, to go ahead and pray. Using the word everywhere makes it difficult for the reader to picture "who" Paul is correcting and "why" they are causing such a disruption.

The word "everywhere" is a misleading translation. The Greek text of this part of verse 8 contains not one, but three separate words: "in every place." This three-word Greek phrase did not refer to men "all over the world," or to "all men, everywhere."

To the Jews in Paul's day, the Holy "place" was the Temple in Jerusalem. Each local synagogue was the "place" where Jews gathered to worship and to learn. To the Christian Jews and to all believers in the early church, "the place" meant "the place where the church worships." "In every *place*" meant "every *place* a local church worships."

C. K. Barrett explains this in his commentary (Oxford, p. 54),

> … in Jewish usage 'place' meant 'meeting-place', 'place of prayer', and there is evidence (especially 1 Cor. 1:2; 1 Thess. 1:8) that it became Christian usage too. The author means 'in every Christian meeting-place'.

Preaching and praying. Just as the words "in every place" have a special meaning in verse 8, so too does Paul's use of the single verb "to pray." "To pray" is a condensed way to describe the activity of an overseer during worship. Grammarians call this type of shorthand notation *synecdoche*. It is a way of using one word to stand for several words. The more complete phrase would have been: "praying *and* prophesying." An example of the complete phrase is found in 1 Corinthians 11:4-5.

When the church was gathered for worship, "praying" went hand in glove with "prophesying." The word "prophesying" indicated *forth-telling* more than the *foretelling* that is usually associated with this word in English.

This "praying and prophesying" included prayer in the congregation and the "forth-telling" of the Word of God. Modern Christians recognize this as the "preaching and teaching" of the Word of God.

**Preaching and teaching the Word of God
was part of the activity of an overseer.**

When I was in seminary, I learned that a sermon was only worthy of its name if, when I was in the pulpit, I prophesied and *spoke forth* the words of God as they were found in the Bible. Any stringing together of mere human opinions and anecdotes counted for nothing more than an "after-dinner speech"!

When the church in Ephesus gathered together, the believers worshipped, prayed and preached the Word of God. This "praying" "in every place" in verse 8 could be paraphrased as follows:

"When you are worshipping-and-teaching in church..."

Certain men among the overseers had been incorrectly worshipping and had been teaching false doctrines. They needed to change their behavior and eliminate the harmful results of their actions.

Correcting such false teachers fell directly within the scope of Timothy's charge: to correct wayward individuals whose teaching promoted controversies (1:4). The preaching and praying of some of them was injurious to the church. Their false teaching was provoking angry disputes. Paul wants this to stop!

Paul adds, in 2:8, that these men were supposed to have "holy hands." Is this because they were morally impure, and had *un*holy, or *un*wholesome, hands? If this was the case, there was to be no more preaching and teaching of contentious doctrines by disreputable men in open worship.

Target group (verses 9-15): *Some* errant women.
As *some* of the overseers described in verse 8 were injurious, *some* of the women praying and prophesying "likewise" were injurious. Not *every* woman overseer was committing Paul's third sin. It is not reasonable to assume that every woman at Ephesus behaved in an injurious manner. But at least *some* had behaved improperly and they were the target of Paul's concern.

The Greek pronoun of 1 Timothy 3:1 ("anyone") anticipated the restoration that Jesus, the faithful Word, could provide for *these* wayward women just as was true for the wayward men. They could be corrected and restored:

^{3:1b}If *anyone* aspires to oversight, that one desires a good work.

Acceptable vs. unacceptable. As part of his advice, Paul contrasts "proper" with "improper" worshiping and teaching. He begins with proper comportment (in 9*a*). Then, he briefly describes improper behavior that needs correction (9*b*). He resumes his description of proper ministry activity (10), and, after giving some direct advice (11), he adds more details to his description of improper activity (12*a*). This can be diagrammed as follows:

(9*a*) acceptable adornment
(9*b*) *unacceptable* adornment
(10) acceptable professing

(11*a*) direct advice: let them learn

(11*b*-12) *unacceptable* professing

Direct advice. In the gap between verse 10 and verse 12, Paul uses an imperative verb at the start of verse 11. It is the only one in the passage: "Let learn!" With this verb, Paul puts an exclamation point on how he wants Timothy to correct the false teachers among the women overseers.

The presence of the imperative verb tells the reader that verse 11 is the most important sentence in 1 Timothy 2:8-15. It is a command to put into action! Do most readers who use English translations realize the important place of verse 11? Probably not.

The following outline reviews what has been discussed thus far and anticipates what will be discussed next. It also displays the key role of verse 11:

(8) **I (Paul) wish for wayward men overseers:**
to preach and pray in public worship
- with holy hands (not tainted by sin)
- with sound doctrine (not source of anger and disputing)

(9) **Likewise (I, Paul, wish for) wayward women overseers:**
(9a, 10) **a** - to dress and profess for godliness
(9b)   **b** - not behaving improperly (outward dress)
(11a)   **c - Let them learn!**
(11b-12) **b'**- improper behavior further described
(13-15a) (digression) - why such gentle correction
(15b)   **a'**- overseers (they) should behave properly

Exemplary behavior – verses 9a and 10.
Paul began by describing the characteristics of faithful women overseers. Priscilla, a first generation teacher of the church at Ephesus, would have been one of these women (Acts 18:18-19, 24-26).

Here is the list of positive characteristics:

- Orderly clothing (9a)
- Modesty (9a)
- Seriousness (9a)
- Professing godliness (10)
- Good works (10)

In France, a college "professor" is said "to profess" the lesson. The Greek verb in 1 Timothy 2:10, "professing," is used in a similar way. Godly women overseers *profess* godliness as they teach and preach, pray and prophesy.

As Godly women overseers teach and preach, they *profess* godliness.

Most English versions find other words for the verb "to profess." Some even seem to place in doubt the good motives of these women by translating the verb "to profess" in an "iffy" way. These phrases obscure the fact that these women "profess" as part of their ministry as overseers of the church. Here are two examples:

NASB. "women *making a claim to* godliness...."

NIV.   "women *who profess to* worship God...."

Familiar "Leadership" Heresies Uncovered   by Bruce C. E. Fleming
www.ThinkAgainAboutTheBible.com

In verse 10, Paul describes this ministry as "good work." In 3:1, Paul uses these same Greek words – oversight is a "good work."

Injurious behavior – verses 9b and 11b-12. Some of the women overseers had gone astray. In between verses 9a and 10, Paul begins to describe the injurious behavior of *these* women overseers (9b). In verses 11b-12, Paul gives additional details about them.

According to verse 9b, some had made inappropriate use of their hair, of gold, pearls, and costly clothing. (Some scholars note that pagan women, who served in the temples and mixed their teaching with ritual prostitution, dressed in this way. There were many such women serving in the temple at Ephesus. The Temple of Artemis was one of the Seven Wonders of the Ancient World!) Most women in Ephesus, however, could not afford such apparel. The expense was prohibitive. A pearl was valued at three times the price of gold! A costly dress ran many times the typical wage. Very few of the women could have afforded to dress in this extravagant way, for a large proportion were servants and slaves.

Here is a paraphrase of 1 Timothy 2:8-10:

> [2:8]Timothy, I wish for the men to pray and prophesy correctly during worship lifting up holy hands without causing anger and disputing. [9]Likewise, I wish the women who pray and prophesy during worship to adorn themselves with modest apparel that promotes self-control – not with improper hair plaiting, along with its gold and pearls, and costly clothing – [10]Women preaching godliness are adorned by their good works.

As an experienced partner in ministry with Paul, Timothy understood. He knew angry disputes over false doctrines did not belong in church (1:4; 2:8; 6:3-5). He recognized inappropriate dress (verse 9b).

Still, Timothy faced the question of what to do about the injurious behavior. Two very different ways of discipline were open to him. He had to take appropriate action. He could be *gentle* in the way God had disciplined Paul – who had acted ignorantly. Or he could be *firm* in the way Paul had disciplined Hymenæus and Alexander – who had thrust away their good consciences.

Timothy's Gentle Discipline (2:11-12)

Paraphrase

[11]Let those women overseers who were wayward learn in quietness and with all studiousness. [12]I am not permitting them to teach men in an incorrect way, but to learn in quietness.
[13]Why? For, God formed the two in the Garden, Adam and then Eve [14]and Adam was not deceived, but Eve was deceived and to that degree became a transgressor. [15]But she would be saved through the Child who was to come, as will these women if they persevere in faith, love, sanctification and self-control.
[3:1]"Faithful is the Logos," so if any one of those you are correcting aspires to oversight, that one desires a good work!

1 Timothy 2:11-12 forms one unit of thought in Greek. These two verses are Timothy's "orders from headquarters." Paul's instructions are emphatic, delivered with the punch of an imperative verb – **"Let learn!"**

This is the only imperative verb used in the whole passage. It is intended to reinforce what Timothy is already doing and to move Timothy to further action.

It is found within one Greek sentence that begins and ends with the prepositional phrase – "in silence" or "in quietness." This is an example of *inclusio*, a grammatical way of indicating that the words in between the repeated phrase form one unit. In this case, the repeated prepositional phrase "in quietness" indicates that verses 11 and 12 are one idea, subordinate to the command: "Let learn!"

[11]"*… in quietness* **let learn!** …[12] *… in quietness*"

If this action – "let learn!" – is the *what* of the passage, verses 13-15 present the *why* of the passage. Then, 1 Timothy 3 explains *what else* these learners are to do after they are corrected.

The main idea in verse 11 is the main idea. "Let learn!" prescribes the most important action Timothy needs to take to correct the false teachers among the women overseers. The rest of the words in verses 11-12 are subordinate to it and are of secondary importance.

Picture a pilot in an emergency situation. Frantically, he tries to get his bearings as he flies without instruments high over a cloud-covered mountain range. Anxiously he scans the horizon for some clue to indicate his location. In the distance he spots a mountaintop peeking through the clouds. By its shape he instantly knows where he is! The clouds below him cease to draw his attention. He focuses on the familiar landmark and orients his actions according to it. First things first!

In 1 Timothy 2:11, the following applies:

Rule of interpretation: "Imperative verbs receive primary attention."

The mountain peak demanding attention in 1 Timothy 2:11 is the imperative verb "Let learn!" The command is addressed to Timothy: "[You] let learn!"

This kind of learning is not the harsh "education through punishment" that was handed out to the blasphemers Hymenæus and Alexander (1:20). This is a different Greek verb – "let learn." It was a familiar verb, often used to describe rabbis at their lessons as they learned (*cf.* John 7:15).

My dog Shorty and I took a walk around the block every day after I returned from third grade class. One day, I passed by a man and a boy playing catch in their front yard. After passing them by I heard the man yell, "Billy, don't run into the street!" Without having to turn around, I knew what had happened. Billy had started to dart into the street. It was common sense. Otherwise, why would the man have shouted what he did?

When Paul tells Timothy to "Let learn!" the simple logic I used when I heard the man behind me call out to his son indicates that *someone* was *wanting to learn*. It was Timothy's job to facilitate that learning.

Timothy's work among these false teachers had borne fruit. They had ceased their sinning and were wanting to learn how to serve Christ properly.

At this point, Paul could have skipped to the content he saved until 3:1 and pointed immediately to "the faithful *logos*" who could restore false teachers. But instead, he adds more details about their injurious behavior.

Who is "woman?" In verse 11, Paul uses the Greek word "woman." This word is singular and does not have an article in front of it. It is simply "woman" – not "*a* woman," not "*the* woman," nor "the *women*." This has confused some people and has led to different views on just "who" is referred to in these verses.

Scholars who teach Greek grammar explain that an anarthrous (missing an article) noun used like this can refer to "*a certain group* of people." Since Paul used this word in the middle of describing the injurious women teachers at Ephesus, the meaning "a certain group of women" fits well with the text.

The anarthrous word "woman" refers to the *group* who behaved in the ways described in verses 9*b* and 11*b*-12. They were the ones who dressed like the pagan temple teachers. These were the ones that Timothy was to "Let learn!"

The anarthrous word "woman" refers to a *group* of women.
They had behaved in the ways described in verses 9*b* and 11*b*-12.
These were the ones that Timothy was to "Let learn!"

How **should they learn?** Learning was done among adults in Paul's day in a strictly prescribed manner. In verses 11-12, Paul says their learning should be done "in quietness" and "in all submission." Paul himself had learned this way. According to the Kroegers (p. 69):

> ... the rabbinic scholar ... was required to learn in silence. This was how one gained a knowledge of God. ... The phrase *silence and submission* is a Near Eastern formula implying willingness to heed and obey instruction ....

Heresy alert! Some commentators and preachers claim that the single prepositional phrase that comes at the end of verse 11, "in all submission," is "the key idea" to the whole passage! They even specify that this phrase has to do with "submission by wives *to husbands*." But, "in all submission" does not apply to husbands at all. "In all submission" describes a learner's proper attitude, along with "quietness."

It is helpful at this point to see an overview of these two verses in outline form, word for word as in the original Greek. (The underlined compound verb in verse 12 will be explained in the pages that follow.)

11   "**woman**" (subject: a certain group of women)

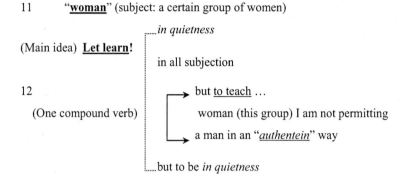

.......in quietness

(Main idea) **Let learn!**

    in all subjection

12

(One compound verb)

but <u>to teach</u> ...

woman (this group) I am not permitting

a man in an "*authentein*" way

.......but to be in quietness

The rest of the story. In verse 12, Paul builds on his instruction to Timothy in verse 11 by explaining how *he* is treating similar cases. His comments also give further indication as to the kind of false teaching in which these wayward women overseers were involved:

> [12]I am not permitting them to teach men in an (*authentein*) incorrect way, but to learn in quietness.

Verse 12 contains no command, no imperative verb. Verse 12 is an example, not a prohibition. It is a simple statement of what Paul is doing. It means: "as for me, I am not permitting...."

What Paul was doing applied to Timothy's situation. It also applies today. Wherever there are injurious teachers in the church, they must be corrected and, if possible, retrained.

At the end of verse 12, Paul closes his comment with an *inclusio* by repeating the words "in quietness."

Greeks could tie a group of words into one unit by using *inclusio*. Paul did this with verses 11-12, by using "in silence" two times, at the beginning and at the end.

Heresy alert! Some writers have claimed that, by itself, verse 12 contains *the main idea* in this part of 1 Timothy. But focusing on verse 12, takes it out of its subordinate position to the imperative verb in verse 11. Emphasizing verse 12 ignores its grammatical tie to verse 11! When verse 12 *alone* is treated as the main idea of the passage, it leads to a cascading series of errors. If verse 12 "leads the parade," verses 13 and 14 appear to be subordinate to verse 12. Instead, however, all the verses around verse 11 are subordinate to its command: "Let learn!" The imperative verb is the key idea in verses 9-15.

Some who claim that verse 12 is *the key verse* in this passage, try to buttress their argument by heaping up a pile of "apparent" cross-references from other verses that "supposedly" support their view. This is a dangerous and flawed practice, especially when these other verses are taken out of context and used incorrectly. Piling many weak arguments on top of one another does not result in one big strong argument. Instead, a big pile of weak arguments results in one big *weak* argument!

Verse 12 must be understood in its context before it is compared with verses outside of 1 Timothy.

Two verbs working together. In verse 12, Paul combines two verbs, one common and one rare, to describe the improper behavior he is not permitting. These Greek verbs are *didasko* and *authentein*. Taken together they mean, "to teach in an improper way." Teaching by women overseers was not forbidden. *Improper* teaching is forbidden, and always should be.

> **Teaching by women overseers was not forbidden.**
> ***Improper* teaching was forbidden.**

The second verb that Paul joins to the first one is an extremely rare Greek word. It is used only in this one place in the entire Bible. As such, it cannot be defined by comparing how it is used in other Bible passages.

To make its translation even more difficult, *authentein* is extremely rare in literature outside the Bible. There are *no* known instances of its use at the time of Paul, nor even within several hundred years before or after the time of Paul!

The Kroegers noted (pp. 79-80), that in the fifth century B.C., the verb *authentein* was used in association with a murderer, his kin, or even his sexual partner. Centuries *after* Paul, the verb *authentein* was associated with sinful sexual pagan doctrines and practices.

Paul was a native of Asia Minor where pagan practices abounded. At least some of the educated women converts at Ephesus could have been wealthy enough to afford the excessively expensive accessories described in verse 9*b*. Perhaps some of these women taught in an *authentein*-type way. They may have been influenced by the way teaching was practiced in the temple courts. What could Paul mean when he used the verb *authentein*? We do not know. We only know it was not the right way to teach.

One action, not two. Some translations make it look as if Paul is forbidding two separate activities – as if women are not to teach *and* they are not to *authentein* a man. However, as New Testament scholar Dr. Philip Payne explains, these two verbs are linked together by Greek conjunctions indicating that Paul has only *one* activity in mind. He is prohibiting any "*authentein*-type of teaching."

Dr. Philip Payne has shown that these two verbs, "to teach" and "*authentein*," are linked together by two Greek conjunctions.

This indicates that Paul has only *one* type of activity in mind. He prohibits any "*authentein*-type of teaching."

Wrong question – wrong answer. Many interpreters ask this passage to tell them about husbands and wives, even though it says nothing about husbands and wives. It is about teaching teachers to teach correctly.

Among those who have gone to great interpretive lengths to import the idea of husbands and wives into these verses is Martin Luther. In a lecture given on February 11, 1528, he taught that the word "man" in verse 12 should be translated, "husband." He then "reasoned backward," as he himself described it, that the word "woman" in verse 11 meant "wife."

Following in Luther's steps, many have taught, erroneously, that verse 12 is about wives and husbands. Thus, they claim that in verse 12 Paul is forbidding "wives" to teach their "husbands."

**This passage says nothing about husbands and wives.
It is about teaching teachers to teach correctly.**

Because the modern family unit has been weakened by sins of all kinds, what the Bible has to say about wives and husbands is important to discuss. There is much in the Bible that speaks to the practical issues of marriage. It is important to refer to the verses that speak about marriage. But verse 12 is not one of them!

Heresy alert! In order to discuss husbands and wives in the context of verse 12 a person has to impose made up, non-inspired ideas on the text. These ideas cover over what the inspired verse is really saying and are launching points for heretical theories of all kinds.

A typical errant claim is that verse 12 somehow presents "the biblical principle of submission." But verse 12 does not present any so-called "biblical principle of submission." Verse 12 refers to the issue of how to discipline false teachers in the church.

There is no so-called "biblical principle of submission" taught in this passage. [This raises the question if such a thing is taught elsewhere. In the passages studied in this book, none have been found.]

Clear advice. The meaning of this verse would have been clear to its earliest readers because the teaching of the rabbis was well known, that a prospective teacher was someone who "learns in order to teach and that learns in order to practice" (m. 'Abot 6:6). Paul's clear encouragement to Timothy is to "let these women learn!" He is to make sure they are retrained, as they wish, so that they might once more to be active overseers and teachers of the Word.

In case anyone questions his advice to Timothy, in the very next verses Paul adds the example of Eve. Her situation was remarkably similar to Paul's and to that of these wayward Ephesian overseers.

Like Paul, like Eve (1 Timothy 2:13-15)

Why? When a child is little, he or she begins to ask "Why?" about everything. The first "Why?" will receive a serious answer. The second "Why?" usually receives a calm response. By the third "Why?" a parent begins to wonder if it isn't about time to stop asking "Why?" Inevitably, when the child asks "Why?" again, the patient parent will explain again, and again, until what is obvious to the teacher becomes obvious to the learner.

The Gospel of Mark recounts how Jesus' disciples were slow to learn the lesson of the multiplied loaves. First, Jesus fed the 5,000 from a few loaves and fish (Mark 6:35-44). A second time, Jesus multiplied a handful of food into enough for four thousand people (Mark 8:1-9). A little while later, Jesus and his disciples found themselves in a boat with just one loaf of bread. The disciples were hungry and began to worry. Oh, what could they do in these dire straits? Carefully, Jesus talked to them about their cares and about their blindness to His power to provide for them again and again. He reminded them of all that had happened. Yet they still didn't understand (Mark 8:14-21). They needed to be told again.

In similar fashion, just in case his message has not been fully understood, Paul adds several more verses in 1 Timothy 2 to make sure his instructions about the correction of the errant women teachers are clear.

Why does he recommend retraining for these women? In verses 13-15*a*, Paul calls attention to relevant details from the Garden of Eden.

Because "intent" counts. Paul starts verse 13 with the conjunction "for" in Greek. He gives a reason "for" what he has just recommended. Then, he refers to Genesis 3. In the Garden of Eden there were two kinds of sinners. And in Ephesus, where Timothy was, there were two kinds of sinners:

1. sinners who were deceived and sinned, and

2. sinners who knowingly and defiantly sinned.

In verse 13, Paul draws a clear distinction between the first man and the first woman. By referring to their two distinct creations, he focuses attention on them as two distinct individuals.

[13]For *Adam* first was formed, then *Eve*.

The lesson of verse 13 isn't *who* was first, but that *there were two* individuals created in the beginning – first one, *then* the other. Paul further distinguishes between these two by using the names, "Adam" and "Eve."

The use of these names in their historical setting is strikingly anachronistic. The woman was not called by the name "Eve" until Genesis 3:20. Yet, Paul uses that name referring to moments in history (Gen 2) that occurred *before* she was known as Eve.

Similarly, the name "Adam" did not refer only to the man at the point in time referred to by Paul in 1 Timothy 2:13. That name could refer to them both (Genesis 5:2 – "He called their name Adam"). The man took the name "Adam" for himself, only after God judged them both.

In 1 Timothy 2:14, after having distinguished clearly between the first two individuals at Creation, Paul focuses on *how* and *why* each individual sinned.

While it is clear that each one in the Garden is disobedient to God's command, the following differences exist between them at the Fall:

1. The man is not deceived. He sins deliberately and knowingly (Gen 3:12).

2. The woman is deceived and then sins (Gen 3:13).

In the Garden, God takes these differences into account when He responds. God imposes "a curse" on the soil "because of" the man (Genesis 3:17). No "curse" is imposed because of the woman. In Genesis 3, the Hebrew word "curse" only occurs in reference to the man (and the serpent).

How does Paul know the woman is deceived? In Genesis 3:13, the woman says so, in an accurate admission to God of her wrongdoing. In 1 Timothy 2:14, Paul notes that the man is a different kind of sinner. He "wasn't deceived." This distinction, drawn between the first two sinners, is an example for Timothy.

In 1 Timothy 1, Paul referred to how God had judged him. Discerning Paul's intent, God dealt gently with him, and even put him into ministry (1:12).

In modern-day courts, even murderers are judged differently, according to their intent. There is "murder in the first degree" for those who kill on purpose, or "with malice aforethought." And there is "murder in the second degree," or "manslaughter," for those who kill but not with malicious advance planning.

In modern-day courts, murderers are judged according to their intent.

"Murder one" receives the harshest punishment. Manslaughter merits a lighter sentence.

Paul had been a second-degree sinner. How God dealt with him is the example he wants Timothy to follow in dealing with those at Ephesus who also sinned in the second degree. The women described in 1 Timothy 2:9b and 12 are to be treated (2:11) like Eve, and like Paul, who had not sinned on purpose.

To underline this, in verses 13 and 14, Paul refers to the two sinners in the Garden in a different order from when each one sinned. If Paul had been preoccupied only with details of timing in Eden, he would have referred *first* to the woman and *then* to the man. Instead, he twice refers first to Adam, who sinned on purpose.

Here is a paraphrase of verses 13-14 (italics added):

> [13]For, God formed the two in the Garden, Adam and then Eve
> [14]and Adam was not deceived, but Eve was deceived,
>   *and to that degree* became a transgressor.

Familiar "Leadership" Heresies Uncovered   by Bruce C. E. Fleming
www.ThinkAgainAboutTheBible.com

Heresy alert! Some people charge that since the first woman was deceived in the Garden, *all* women are more easily deceived than all men! But Genesis does not teach this. Neither does Paul.

Even though the man and the woman were co-regents over the earth by the Creator's decree (Genesis 1:27-30), some people claim that *the timing* in the creations of the man and the woman makes the man superior to the woman in some way.

Indeed, this was another position held by rabbis at the time of Paul. They thought that a theological consequence could be discerned behind the sequence of events in the Garden. C. K. Barrett (*Pastoral Epistles*, p. 56) quotes their midrash: "Adam was first in creation, Eve in sin."

Surprisingly, John Calvin held to this position. Even so, he found himself compelled to argue against it, admitting (*Commentaries*, 21) that any theological conclusions based on the "order of creation, appears not to be a very strong argument in favor of her subjection; for John the Baptist was before Christ in the order of time, and yet was greatly inferior in rank."

Verse 15a – Closing thoughts on Eden.

It may seem tiresome to work our way over one interpretive "bump" after another. But as every good road builder knows, it is important to keep leveling a roadbed until it becomes flat and serviceable for all those who follow.

In verse 15a, there is one more noticeable bump that needs to be smoothed out before the entire passage in 1 Timothy 2 can be clearly understood. It has to do with Paul's reference in Greek to "the Childbearing." According to the Greek in the first part of verse 15, Paul writes:

[15a]"But she will be saved through the Childbearing…

The singular pronoun – "she" – of verse 15a refers to the woman who is discussed in verses 13-14. "She" is Eve!

"The Childbearing" of Eve refers to the future birth, for Eve, of the promised Child. Mary was the physical mother of Jesus, but Eve was his ancestor. Eve's "childbearing" resulted in the eventual "childbearing" of Jesus.

The word "childbearing" is *a collective singular noun*, a single word packed with the promise of many. This way of speaking may seem awkward to the modern reader. But it is used twice in Genesis 3 when God first gives the promise of a Savior.

In Genesis 3:15, God gives the menacing promise to the serpent that the "seed" of the woman will crush his head. The word "seed" is a collective singular noun.

In the Hebrew wording of Genesis 3:16a, God promises the woman that she will have multiplied "conception." The word "conception" is also a collective singular noun.

The word "seed" (v. 15) is a *collective singular noun*. So is "conception" (v. 16).

Looking back at the Garden of Eden from the perspective of history, one can identify the promised "seed" of verse 15, and the "conception" of verse 16, as Jesus. Paul's use of the collective singular noun – "the Childbearing" – in the context of a discussion on the Garden of Eden brings to mind Eve's promised offspring. This would have been recognized immediately by Timothy and the Jewish Christians at Ephesus, as a reference to the Messiah.

Eve would be eternally saved through her forward-looking faith in the coming birth of the Child. The women in Ephesus are saved through their faith in this same Child as well.

This complete summary of Eve's situation – as a deceived sinner in the 2nd degree, who is going to be saved because she placed her faith in the coming Child – allows Paul to move on to a summation of his instructions to Timothy. He does this in the second half of verse 15 (15b).

In verse 15b, Paul changes to a plural subject, "they." Paul encourages the women who are learning, per his command in verse 11, to follow the wholesome pattern of those who have been right-living overseers all along, as he has described them in verses 9a, and 10.

He names four aspects that must be evident in their reformed lives:

[15b]if they remain in **faith**, and **love**, and **sanctification** with all **seriousness**.

More heretical detours! The first time I remember studying this verse in 1 Timothy 2 was in my seminary class with Dr. Stott. When he came to verse 15, he gave his opinion that the Greek words in the first half of the verse could be read in one of two ways.

The first way was to understand "the Childbearing," or "the birth of the Child," as referring to the birth of the Messiah. He showed how this interpretation was reinforced by the fact that the Greek word "the" is placed in front of "childbearing." This was a special childbearing, *the* Childbearing.

The other option was to take the word "childbearing" as a reference to the birth of any child. That would place the focus of verse 15 on any and all women who give birth to children.

As already discussed, the first interpretation is preferable because the collective singular word "childbearing" parallels the collective singular words used in Genesis 3. Verse 15*a* is an obvious continuation of Paul's comments on the Garden of Eden in verses 13-14. The second interpretation only raises more problems than it solves. Nevertheless, a survey of various translations shows that the majority opts for the *second* way of interpreting this verse!

To make the second option sound reasonable the translations usually change one of the pronouns in verse 15 to make everything more "harmonious." In Greek, the first half of the verse uses a singular pronoun, "*she*." The second half of the verse refers in Greek to "*they*." So these translations change a pronoun in verse 15 and make it say "she-she" or "they-they."

Here is a transliteration of the five Greek words in verse 15*a*. Note that the singular pronoun is "she," and that "childbearing" is preceded by "the."

Greek word order: she-will-be-saved   and   through   the   Childbearing

Contrast this with these samples from various English translations. *None* of them follow the first option presented by Stott – "the Childbearing." Note how the translations struggle to make sense of the verse. Some properly keep the first pronoun singular, while others make it plural. Some substitute "woman" for the Greek pronoun "she" while others insert "women"!

KJV. "Notwithstanding *she* shall be saved in childbearing"

TNIV. "But *women* will be saved through childbearing –"

RSV. "Yet *woman* will be saved through bearing children"

NIV. But *women* will be kept safe through childbirth"

Phillips. "Nevertheless I believe that *women* will come safely through child-birth if …"

LB. "So God sent pain and suffering to *women* when their children are born, but he will save their souls if …"

TEV. But a *woman* will be saved through having children"

JB. "Nevertheless, *she* will be saved by childbearing"

NEB. "Yet *she* will be saved through motherhood –"

Practically speaking, by choosing to use what Stott called "the second possible interpretation," these translations place women in an unreasonably difficult position.

In Africa, I encountered women who were *very* troubled by these translations:

- Some, because they were childless
- Others, because they experienced difficulty in childbirth
- Still others, because some of their children had not been faithful to Christ when they grew up.

Because their pastors taught (as had the missionaries who first taught them) the second option for 1 Timothy 2:15*a*, these women had been led to believe they were somehow guilty of not properly trusting in God and this had had an impact on their "childbearing." How sad!

Various African churches I encountered built their own interpretations on these translations. All ended up wrongly placing a *special onus on women* because of their supposed theological relation to "childbearing." For these women, the wrong interpretation of verse 15*a* caused them much unnecessary heartache.

The first translation option – "the Childbearing" – is obviously the better translation because it alone accords with the context of the passage. It clearly is a continuation of Eve's example from verse 13 through 14 and into 15*a*.

It does not call into question a woman's experience in childbirth. It has nothing to do with her salvation, nor does it throw in doubt the validity of her salvation.

Summary: Key elements of verses 13-15*a*.

Verse 13. Preposition "for" connects these verses to 11-12. Begins the answer to, "Why treat these false teachers so gently?" The first individuals were created by separate acts, "Adam was first formed, then Eve."

Verse 14. Adam sinned knowingly – a 1st degree sinner.
Eve was deceived, then sinned – a 2nd degree sinner.

Verse 15*a*. Singular pronoun, "*she* will be saved."
Collective singular noun "*the* Childbearing."

From Eden to Ephesus, 15*b*.

After completing his illustration from the situation of Eve, Paul moved from the woman of Eden directly to the women at Ephesus. The subject of his sentence was no longer singular – "she" – referring to Eve. He made it plural, "*they* continue."

Paul could not be certain that *every* woman in the "graduating class" who was learning in Ephesus would remain faithful, so in verse 15*b*, he used the conditional phrase, "… *if* they continue." This attitude of hopeful contingency continued in his comments in chapter 3.

In 1 Timothy 3, Paul would not say, "Each and every one of you *will certainly* minister again." Instead, he carefully lists various qualifications, and potential disqualifiers. Those who qualified would indeed be able to serve again.

Just as Eve placed her faith in the promised One, and just as Paul placed his faith in the promised One, even so the women of Ephesus could safely place their faith in the promised One, the faithful Word. They could then practice the qualities of a good overseer (2:9*a*, 10).

Here is a paraphrase of 1 Timothy 2:13-15 with the two parts of verse 15 clearly marked:

> [13]Why? For, God formed the two in the Garden, Adam and then Eve [14]and Adam was not deceived, but Eve was deceived, and to that degree became a transgressor. [15*a*]But she will be saved eternally through the Childbearing,
> [15*b*]as will these women if they persevere in faith, love, sanctification and self-control.

Made Faithful to Serve (3:1-16)

Fallen servants. When I was growing up in church, occasionally I heard of pastors who "fell into sin and left the ministry." I didn't hear any indication that these individuals were ever expected to minister again.

When I began work as a seminary professor in Africa, I met a well-known local pastor who had been removed from his duties because of a serious sin he had committed. I was startled to learn that at the end of a two-year probation period he was likely to resume active ministry. First, he would have a desk job at the district office, and eventually, he was likely to resume his work as pastor.

I had never come across a similar discipline process in the United States. My feelings were mixed. It seemed appropriately bold to have faith that God could rehabilitate this formerly fruitful servant of God, but in the back of my mind I wondered if he would ever be worthy of trust. In the church where I grew up, he wouldn't have gotten a second chance. The African church, however, was prepared to watch and see.

A little while later, it happened that he and I were each chosen to be delegates to a conference half way across Africa. On the trip, we had several occasions to talk at length and I learned why he had been removed from active ministry. His sin had been grave, but it had been precipitated by ignorance. He was sincerely repentant and had since become much better informed in the area of his sin.

Could he be rehabilitated and placed back into ministry? He could, according to the culmination of Paul's logic from chapter 2:

> [3:1]"Faithful is the *Logos*," so if anyone aspires to oversight,
> that person desires a good work!

Knowledge of the faithfulness of the Word, Jesus Christ, is Paul's basis for encouraging the overseers who were being disciplined to aspire to oversight once more. Those being corrected by Timothy, could be made faithful. After all, Paul had been made faithful!

The male and female overseers who had acted injuriously (2:8, 9b, 12a), all were included in the "anyone" of 3:1. Those of them who had repented could aspire once more to minister. This was the hope of my new African friend.

"Faithful is the *Logos*" – 1 Timothy 3a.

This is the key phrase that is the turning point for the overseers disciplined by Timothy. Any misunderstanding of these pivotal first words in 1 Timothy 3 may lead to serious misinterpretations of chapters 2-3.

How can someone misunderstand these words? It all depends on discerning how Paul uses the word "*Logos*."

The possible double meaning of the phrase, *pistos ho logos*, has already been explained. In 1 Timothy 1:15, Paul made a pun on the meaning of these Greek words: "faithful" could also mean "trustworthy," and "Word" could also mean "saying."

> Primary meaning: Faithful is the "Word"
> (Jesus)

> Secondary meaning: Trustworthy is the "saying"
> "… that Christ Jesus came into the world to save sinners."

In 1 Timothy 3:1*a*, Paul uses only the primary meaning of his potentially "punny" phrase, namely, "Faithful is the Word." The second potential meaning of this key phrase is less relevant (in 1 Tim 3:1) because these people didn't need salvation. They were already believers. What they needed was to be made "faithful" in order to be rehabilitated and once more have a fruitful ministry.

"Meaningful" puns. Some people don't see the humor in puns. The aptitude of making puns, and discerning puns, varies from culture to culture. People quickly catch on to puns in France where they are frequently used. People are less quick to catch on to puns in America where they are used less frequently.

Paul's key phrase in 1 Timothy 3:1*a* was meant to be clear and was not meant to be obscure. But over the years, many have missed its meaning.

Those who miss the primary sense of his phrase the first time around (Jesus is the faithful Word) tend to look only for an identifiable "saying" when they encounter the phrase again in 3:1. However, Paul doesn't spell out a saying the second time. He focuses on how the Word Jesus will change lives for the better.

Many scholars have gone to great lengths to come up with a saying for 3:1. A widely used edition of the Greek text used a page layout that made it look as if there was a saying in the second half of 2:15. In its next edition, however, the page layout was changed to make it look as if a saying was found in 3:1*b*. But *neither* 2:15*b*, *nor* 3:1*b*, contains a new and distinct "saying." They missed the primary meaning of the phrase!

Nevertheless, recent English translations have opted to make it look as if a saying is located in the second half of verse 1. As a result, in those translations the primary meaning of the phrase – that "Jesus the Word is faithful" – is papered over!

Here are the three Greek words of the phrase, plus the rest of the Greek words in 3:1*a*. Compare how they have been translated in these English Bibles.

Greek. *Pistos   ho logos ei   tis   episkopes orgetai*
English. Faithful [is] the Word. If anyone oversight aspires to

KJV. This is a true saying, If a man desire the office of a bishop

RSV. The saying is sure: If any one aspires to the office of bishop

NIV. Here is a trustworthy saying: If anyone sets his heart on being an overseer

NEB. There is a popular saying: "To aspire to leadership...."

124

The solution to the translation puzzle is to recognize that the primary sense of the phrase – "Faithful [is] the Word" – is the main idea in 3:1.

There are additional problems with how the rest of verse 3:1 has been translated. Some of this is related to the search for a new "saying." But much of the confusion can be attributed to a *mis*translation that occurred hundreds of years ago.

The "politically correct" *mis*translation of 3:1*b*. Not long after King James began to rule in England, he was asked by certain Puritan clergy to order that a new English translation be made of the Bible. The King authorized the work of translation. It was completed in 1611 and has become generally known as the *King James Version* (KJV).

It was a good translation for its time, prepared by fifty four of the best biblical scholars in Great Britain. But it was also a translation to be used officially by the state Church of England.

Like the Roman Catholic Church, the Church of England had a strict hierarchical structure of governance. It had a supreme earthly authority, the king. It also had archbishops, bishops, and so on.

When it came to translating 1 Timothy 3:1 for this hierarchical church, the translators worded it in a way that was "politically correct" for its time, in that it advocated a hierarchy that mirrored the structures of the Church of England.

But the translation was at variance with the Greek text. In the end, because of its flaws, the Puritans who had asked for the new translation did not accept it.

In 3:1, the KJV changed the Greek word "oversight" (*episkopes*) into the official sounding phrase – "the office of a bishop." This fit the Church of England's structure of ruling bishops who were in a (supposed) line of authority that ran from the apostles of Jesus, to the King of England, and down to them.

The translation gave the impression to its readers that there was *an office*, or appointed level of service called "bishop," and that a distinguishable group of bishops existed during Paul's time. But the words "*the office of a*" were added by the translators. No "office" is referred to in the Greek text.

In 1 Timothy 3:1*b*, when Paul used the Greek word *episkopes* it meant "oversight" as in, "if anyone aspires to *oversight*." Earle comments on the meaning of this word ("1, 2 Timothy," pp. 363-364) as follows:

> It comes from *episcopeo*, which literally means "look upon," and so "oversee, care for." ... Titus 1:6, 7 seems to suggest that "elder" (*presbyteros*) and "bishop" (*episcopos*) were the same person. An even more definite proof of this is found in Acts 20. In v. 17 we read that Paul sent for the "elders" (*presbyterous*) of the church at Ephesus. But in v. 28 he calls them "overseers" (*episcopous*).

Familiar "Leadership" Heresies Uncovered   by Bruce C. E. Fleming
www.ThinkAgainAboutTheBible.com

A "man" is not always "a male." In 17th century English usage, the masculine gender stood for both genders. As language became more gender specific in the late 20th century, it became important to translate more precisely the Greek pronoun *tis* ("a person") to reflect the fact that the Greek pronoun is not gender specific (*cf.* 1 Tim. 6:3, 5).

In 21st century English, *tis* is best translated as "anyone," meaning "either a man or a woman." This is how, for example, the NIV translates *tis* in 1 Timothy 3:1*b*. It uses the word "anyone."

But other translations still use the word "man." According to modern word usage, by using the word "man" these two translations appear to exclude women from oversight (or serving as elder, bishop or senior pastor) in the church.

The politically correct KJV translation of 1 Timothy 3:1*b*, and the modern translations that follow it, subtly influence the thinking of many English-speaking Christians. These people find it difficult to readjust their understanding of 3:1*b* from "a man" to "anyone (male or female) who aspires to oversight."

The antecedent of the pronoun "anyone" is found in the verses in 1 Timothy 2. "Anyone" refers to the corrected errant women and misbehaving men who were aspiring afresh to proper oversight. Paul wholeheartedly encourages them, telling them at the end of 3:1*b* that they desire "a good work."

1 Timothy 3 is full of surprises. Because of these difficulties in translation in verse 1, many mistakenly suppose that the verses in 1 Timothy 3:2-7 must be teaching that *only* males may serve as overseers. But, as in 3:1, the Greek text of these verses is inclusive of both female and male overseers!

1 Timothy 3:1*b*-7. Candidates for oversight.

In 1 Timothy 1:16, Paul notes that he had been appointed for service *that he might be an example* for others. Not everyone would live exactly as Paul, but in every way that is applicable, Paul was a role model. In 1 Timothy 3:1*b*-7, he lists a number of traits that should be present in anyone who aspires to oversight in the church.

This list is not final or complete. For example, it refers to individuals who are married, but neither Paul, nor Timothy, nor Jesus, were married. The list outlines the kinds of behavior one must exhibit when an item applies to them.

Philip Payne ("1 Timothy 2:11-3:13 Reconsidered," *JH* 4, 19-21, 193-194) points out the seamless continuation of 1 Timothy 2 into 1 Timothy 3. He writes,

> The description … is a listing of qualifications which would apply to women as well as to men. In fact, parallels to each of these requirements are mentioned in 1 Timothy specifically regarding women, over half using identical terminology.

At the very time Paul wrote 1 Timothy each of these overseer descriptions not only could, but in fact did, apply to women. It is virtually impossible that so many of these infrequently used expressions describing overseers just happen to occur in nearly identical terminology in the verses of 1 Timothy dealing exclusively with women.

The long list of 12 qualifications in 1 Timothy 3:2-7 is not a complete checklist.... Candidates for resuming service will need to meet the qualifications that apply to their situation. These verses weed out those who do not qualify.

The work and character of overseers. A description of the *work* of overseers can be distilled from 1 Timothy 2:8-3:7.

- Leads in public worship and prayer (2:8).
- Preaches (2:10) in both word and deed.
- Teaches students of either gender (2:11-12, 3:2).
- Is hospitable (3:2).

The *character* expected of overseers can be distilled too.

- Holy (2:15*b*).
- Not disputatious but self-controlled (2:8, 15*b*).
- Full of faith (2:15).
- Makes wise use of wealth in personal dress (2:9).

Qualifications for overseers (3:2-7). People who are naïve usually don't realize that they are missing important facts. In verse 2, Paul uses a compound Greek word to state an important fact of life that applies to all overseers.

A naïve person might list a dozen qualifications for an overseer in the church without mentioning what Paul puts in first place. But Paul isn't naïve. He writes that overseers must be "above-reproach."

Rescue Mission. One summer, I was a student intern for an old-time evangelist who had grown up in a tough seaport town in the south of England. During the Roaring 20's he came to America to seek his fortune. When he arrived, he found hard liquor to be most to his liking and he became a raging alcoholic. But, at the age of 29, someone told him the good news of new life in Christ and he was wonderfully saved!

Bill Denton spent the rest of his life serving those he called, the "down-n-outers." He set up a Rescue Mission and preached there every evening. He roamed the streets late at night to find the homeless and the alcoholic and he brought them into his Mission to spend the night safe from danger and away from the elements. In the morning he gave them food, and clothing too, if necessary. He sought out help from doctors and dentists to aid his needy friends. He and his wife lived in a simple home and raised a family. He pioneered a live 30-minute nightly radio broadcast that continued for more than 50 years. At the end of each transmission he would end with, "Lost soul, get right with God!" On their 50th wedding anniversary, his wife surprised Bill with an anniversary ring. She had saved and saved over the years for this occasion. She loved him so much! It had a diamond in the middle. He was very touched by her gesture. But he never wore his ring in public.

Several times, I came to the house to drive him to his first call for the day. Before he left the house, he stopped just inside the door, took off his ring and placed it on a stand. When he came back to the house, he would put it on again.

He told me, "It wouldn't look right for a poor old preacher like me to wear a flashy thing like that out in public. What would people think I was doing with their money?" "But Bill," I argued, "It was a gift from your own wife!" "I know," he answered, "but I just wouldn't want anyone to get a bad idea in their head." He wanted to be sure he was "above reproach."

Being "above reproach" is the overarching character qualification Paul lists for overseers. All other qualifications are subordinate to it. This qualification is so important that Paul introduces it with the Greek phrase, "It is necessary...." According to J. N. D. White (in Earle, "1, 2 Timothy," p. 364), "above-reproach" describes "one against whom it is impossible to bring any charge of wrongdoing such as could stand impartial examination."

The list in verses 2-3. This first general qualification is "above reproach." It is followed by eleven more qualifications for overseers in verses 2 and 3.

1) "above reproach" the overarching requirement.
2) "faithful spouse" – as applicable. Some were single.
3) "temperate" – self-controlled (*cf.* Titus 2:2, 5).
4) "sensible" or "sober" – found here and in 2:9*a*, 15*b*.
5) "orderly" – also used in 2:9*a*, 15*b*.
6) "hospitable" – a wordless ministry (1 Peter 4:9-11).
7) "apt-at-teaching" – ministry of the word (2 Tim. 2:24).
8) "not excessive drinker" – "not quarrelsome over wine."
9) "not a striker" or "not pugnacious or a bully."
10) "forbearing" or "gentle" (Philippians 4:5).
11) "uncontentious" or "not a brawler" (Titus 3:2).
12) "not-avaricious" or "no lover of money" (Heb. 13:5).

Stumbling Blocks Due to Mistranslation

"Faithful spouse" (3:2). Qualification number two deals with the overseer's married life. The Greek words used to make this point are *unique*. Later in 1 Timothy 3 and elsewhere, Paul uses a phrase that is *different* in Greek, which says "husband of one wife." But in 3:2, the Greek is unique and more compact – "one wife/husband."

Careful research has shown that this qualification means that whether one is *a husband or a wife*, it is important to be a "faithful spouse." It requires an overseer, if married to be faithful and be "a one-spouse kind of person."

**Whether one is *a husband or a wife*, an overseer,
if married, is to be "a one-spouse kind of person."**

According to Lucien Deiss (notes to the French Bible, the *TOB*, Edition Intégrale, p. 646, note a), this Greek phrase was used in Asia Minor, on both Jewish and pagan gravestone inscriptions, to designate a woman *or* a man, who was faithful to his *or* her spouse in a way characterized by "a particularly fervent conjugal love."

**This Greek phrase was used on gravestone inscriptions
to designate *either* a woman *or* a man who was a faithful spouse.**

When I read Deiss' comment how this phrase was used on inscriptions in Turkey, where Paul and Timothy ministered, I confirmed it with him myself, reaching him by telephone in Vaucresson, France.

This insight into 1 Timothy 3:2 is at variance with modern versions of the Bible which translate this Greek phrase as if it were like the longer phrases used elsewhere – "*husband* of one wife." They indicate no difference with what is written in verse 2.

Their translations make this qualification appear to be restricted to men only! Instead, rightly understood, this qualification is about faithfulness in marriage by a Christian spouse. It is *not* saying that oversight is "for men only."

**This qualification is about "faithfulness in marriage by a Christian spouse."
It is *not* saying that oversight is "for men only."**

Is it surprising that this mistranslation has caused confusion in the churches? While instructions in the Bible apply to all people in all cultures, the misinterpretation of this characteristic has led to contradictory interpretations. I have come across three different, distinct and mutually exclusive interpretations of 3:2, none of which square with the colloquial meaning of this phrase:

In the **United States** I heard:
> No divorced and *remarried* man may be an overseer – one may have only "one wife."

In **France** I heard:
> *Bachelors* may not be overseers because they are not "husbands" and do not have "one wife."

In **Congo** I heard:
> No *polygamist* may be an overseer because one must have only "one wife," not many.

When the original meaning of verse 2 is understood as a comment on being a "faithful spouse" of either gender, it applies to *all* marriage situations whether one may live in the U.S., France or Congo. If married, either a husband or a wife may be an overseer, but in married life one must be a "faithful spouse."

"Family manager" (3:4-5). In addition to the twelve characteristics listed in verses 2-3, Paul adds several more in verses 4-7. Perhaps because the meaning of Paul's words in verse 2 have been misunderstood, verses 4-5 usually are translated in a way that excludes women from what Paul originally wrote. In 1 Timothy 3:4-5 and following, the pronouns should *not* be translated as "he" and "his." Instead they should be translated as "his or her," as in:

> [4]ruling *his or her* own household well …
> [5]… manage *his or her* own family …

The point is not that husbands should manage the family unit, but every overseer should manage his-*or*-her own household well.

The point in these verses is not that a particular spouse should manage the family unit, but rather that an overseer should be able to manage his-or-her own household well. Payne (*Surrejoinder*, p. 96) comments on 1 Timothy 3:2 and the related references in verses 4-5, as follows:

The [verses] describing the overseer in 3:2, 4-5 must not be interpreted as requiring that the overseer be male, married, and have children.... Common sense tells us that these phrases are intended *only to exclude* those who are not faithful ... or managing their children badly....

The other qualifications Paul lists in verses 4-7 are personal qualities reflecting spiritual maturity. This is one reason why he writes, in verse 6, that new believers should not hastily assume responsibility. Over time, a person's fitness for ministry would become apparent.

Here is a proper paraphrase of 1 Timothy 3:1-7:

[1]"Faithful is the Word," so if anyone aspires to oversight, that person desires a good work.
[2]Here is a partial list of important practices and traits one must display:
An overseer must be without reproach –
a faithful spouse, temperate, serious, modest, hospitable, a good teacher, [3]not an excessive drinker or pugnacious, but patient, uncontentious, and not avaricious,
[4]ruling his or her own household well, having one's children in subjection, [5](for if someone doesn't know how to manage his or her own household, how can that one take care of the church of God?)
[6]not a recent convert, so as to avoid the danger of being puffed up with pride, and falling into the same condemnation as the devil received. [7]It is important to have a good testimony from outsiders, so as not to fall into disgrace and the devil's snare.

A word about deacons, 8-13. Paul begins verse 8 with these two Greek words, "Deacons, similarly...." Similar to whom?
Verses 8, and following, refer back to the men and women of 1 Timothy 2 who were made fit for service by "the faithful Word." Just as the ones who aspired to oversight could be made worthy, *similarly*, "the faithful Word" could equip men and women for faithful service as deacons.
In Philippians 1:1 Paul refers to two groups: (1) the "overseers," and (2) the "servants" or deacons. Paul has these two distinct groups in view in 1 Timothy 3:2-13 as well. The main difference between overseers and deacons is being "apt to teach" (3:2). This qualification is not in the list for deacons.
The list for the deacons is not exhaustive nor restrictive. An obvious exception to it was Stephen, the martyr, who was also teacher (Acts 6).

In 1 Timothy 3:8-10, Paul refers both to men and women "deacons." In the early church, there were no "deaconesses." The characteristics required of men and women deacons were as follows: grave, not double-tongued, not given to much wine, not pursuing dishonest gain, having a clear conscience, having passed approval.

While verses 8-10 concerned both men and women deacons, verse 11 had specific advice for women deacons and verse 12 was specific to male deacons. As for women deacons, Paul instructed them to be worthy of respect, not slanderers, self-controlled, and faithful in all things. As for the men deacons, he exhorted them to work at being faithful husbands and to be responsible at home.

Structure communicates meaning. The organizational pattern of Paul's thoughts in the long passage of 1 Timothy 2:8 through 3:12 becomes evident as it draws to a close. Paul has organized his comments into a chiastic (or mirror) pattern! This ancient way of organizing one's thoughts usually placed the most important idea in the center section. Paul built the central section of his chiasm on the life changing power of "the faithful Word" (3:1*a*).

This can be diagramed as follows:

A Men (2:8)

B Women (2:9-15)

("Faithful is the *Logos*")   **C** Men and Women (3:1-10)

B' Women (3:11)

A' Men (3:12)

Difficulties of serving were not to dampen their enthusiasm, for there would be rewards for those who serve faithfully. For the men and women who would go on to fruitful ministries, Paul wrote in verse 13: "Those who have served well gain an excellent standing and great assurance in their faith in Christ Jesus."

Theological Implications. In 1 Timothy 2:8-15, Paul recommended appropriate discipline for injurious behavior. His recommendations took into account not only the sin committed, but also the heart motivation of the offender. In 1 Timothy 3:1-12 the women and men leaders who had been disciplined were encouraged to aspire to, and to resume, ministry in the church.

In these verses, Paul did not teach any doctrine of "authority-of-a-husband," or "leadership-by-men" in the church. Instead, he drew a picture of various Christian men and women actively serving Christ, having been made faithful by Jesus, the Word!

Heresy alert!

Paul did not teach about:
- "authority-of-a-husband," or
- "leadership-by-men" in church.

Overview of 1 Timothy 3

(v.1) **1) aspiring <u>overseers</u> must be**
    (vv.2-3) **a** - 1. blameless   2. a faithful spouse
                3. temperate   4. sensible
                5. orderly   6. hospitable
                7. apt at teaching   8. not a drinker
                9. not a striker   10. forbearing
                11. uncontentious   12. not avaricious
    (vv.4-5) **b** - faithful at home
    (vv.6-7) **a'** - not a novice/having a good record

(vv. 8-13) **2) aspiring <u>deacons</u> must be**
    (v. 8-10) **a** - 1. grave 2. not double-tongued 3. not a drinker 4. not greedy
                  5. pure of conscience 6. proven 7. irreproachable in serving
    (v. 11) **b** - female deacons: grave, not slanderers, sober, faithful
    (v. 12) **c** - male deacons: faithful husbands, faithful at home
    (v. 13)   closing encouragement

(vv. 14-16) **3) encouragement addressed to <u>Timothy</u>**
        a - reason for writing
        b - benediction

Conclusion

Paul addresses the third Section of the letter to Timothy himself, in the last three chapters of the letter. This Section of 1 Timothy is also based on "Faithful is the *Logos*."

Here are the three Sections of 1 Timothy:

(1) 1:1-17   **Paul** made worthy by "the faithful *Logos*."
(2) 1:18-3:16   **Leaders** guilty of Paul's three sins made worthy by "the faithful *Logos*."
(3) 4:1-6:21   **Timothy** made worthy by "the faithful *Logos*

Timothy's situation was different in several ways from that of Paul and that of the errant church leaders. He had not lived a life of sin, nor gone astray.

But, the Spirit warned that troubles were ahead. More would fall away (4:1-3). Timothy would need to be well disciplined in his ministry (4:6-8). But, "the faithful Word" (4:9) would sustain him in his struggle to minister faithfully.

In addition, Timothy was to stay away from favoritism (5:21) and was to test individuals before setting them apart for service (5:22, compare 3:10).

Paul even gives Timothy some medical advice in 5:23. Finally, Paul tells Timothy to keep a watch over himself and be on guard against opposition and any wandering away from the faith (6:20-21).

Revelation 2:2, written by John, after Paul's death, recorded that the church at Ephesus remained faithful to all that Paul and Timothy had taught. In the midst of a very corrupt and pagan society, the work of "the faithful *Logos*" had been fruitful!

Think Again!

"*Trust me – not God*" was the first "leadership" heresy in Eden. All teachers in one way or another ask their students for their trust. But some of the leaders in Ephesus were false teachers. Paul left Timothy to correct those who were spreading false doctrine and disrupting the church.

Should *you* believe every teacher in church? The people at Berea (Acts 17:11) received Paul's message, then checked it with Scripture to see if what he was teaching was correct. So should we.

1. Who are some false teachers of today?

2. Are there any doctrines you have taught that need correcting?

134

135

PART II

The "Headship" Heresies

Chapter 4

"Leadership" Heresies and the Weaker Spouse
... an inside look at 1 Peter 3:1-7

Chapter Contents:

- Paraphrase of 1 Peter 3:1-7

- Giving 1st Peter a "Glance"

- Wives Witnessing Wordlessly (3:1-6)

- Unequally-Yoked Husbands (3:7)

1 Peter 3:1-7

Advice to witnessing wives
[1]You unequally-yoked wives, be submitting yourselves to your own husbands so that even though they do not yet believe the Word, through your conduct without using a word, they may be won to faith in Christ, [2]when they observe your God-fearing, pure conduct
  - [3]not outward adorning or special coiffure, or the wearing of gold, jewelry and fine clothes [4]but the inner adorning of the heart by your incorruptible meek and quiet spirit which is of great value before God
  - [5]for indeed this is how the holy women of old, who kept hoping in God, adorned themselves as they submitted themselves to their own husbands.
    [6]Sarah, for example, trusted in God and submitted to Abraham her husband after the angel came. You are now her daughters by your well doing and your fearlessness of any disappointment.

Advice to witnessing husbands
[7]Likewise you unequally-yoked husbands, use good sense as you dwell with your unsaved wife while she is the weaker partner, treating her with dignity as a fellow human being, so that your prayers might not be hindered.

Familiar "Leadership" Heresies Uncovered   by Bruce C. E. Fleming
www.ThinkAgainAboutTheBible.com

138

Giving 1ˢᵗ Peter a "Glance"

The telephone rang. It was Myrl, my wife's aunt. She and Uncle Bob had been the first family members to fly out to visit us in Africa when Christy was a newborn. Now that we were back in the U.S., she had a question. "I keep wondering about 1 Peter 3:1-7. What do you think it means?" She was intense and persistent. I devoted my next studies to these verses that were bothering her. I soon learned they were a problem for others as well.

It was good to spend time with Peter, the raw-knuckled Galilean. I began to review what I knew about him.

Peter had been a full-time fisherman on the Sea of Galilee. After Jesus called him, he walked with Jesus for three years. He saw, heard and did many remarkable things:

- Peter walked on the waters of the Sea of Galilee.
- Peter heard God's voice and saw Christ transfigured.
- Peter rushed right into the empty tomb.
- Peter had breakfast on the shore with Jesus before the ascension.
- Peter boldly preached to thousands on Pentecost.
- Peter received the rooftop vision about the Gentiles.
- Peter saw the Roman Centurion added to the church.
- Peter became the Apostle to the Jews.
- Peter traveled extensively among the churches.
- Late in life, he wrote the letters: 1 Peter and 2 Peter.

The "second prayer"
The two neighbors got along well. One was a Christian. The other was a nice guy, but was not a Christian, and he knew it.

This second neighbor, sensing his need to give his life to Christ, asked his Christian neighbor to come over to tell him how to do it. As soon as the gospel message was explained to him, he prayed and asked Jesus to forgive his sins and become his Lord.

When he stopped praying, there was a new joy in his heart and a deep smile on his face that the older Christian had seen before when others had prayed to receive Christ. The new Christian asked if he could pray a second prayer. "Of course you can," came the reply.

Here is the second prayer the new Christian prayed, "Lord, help my wife become a Christian too."

How wonderful it was to be forgiven! How marvelous it was to have Jesus as his Lord! But the new Christian discovered he had a pounding new concern. As a child rushes to share great news with a parent, just so the new Christian wanted to tell the world – and especially his spouse – about his new Savior.

It is a sad and distressing experience to find that a spouse is closed, or even hostile, to the good news about Jesus. It is hard for a new believer to realize that just because one of them now has and understands new life in Christ, that the other may not yet be ready to believe!

Peter wrote the first seven verses of 1 Peter 3 to married believers who were the first spouse in their family to come to Christ. "The second prayer" for their spouse's salvation was predictable. But a positive answer to that prayer might come only after demonstrating the inward change that had taken place in them.

In verses 1-7, Peter told these Christians how to get their message across, even if they found themselves prevented from speaking a single word! First he addressed Christian wives with unsaved husbands, and then he wrote to Christian husbands in the same situation.

"Unequally yoked" meant these spouses were joined together in marriage but both were not pulling their full weight in the spiritual realm. One was alive in Christ. The other, as yet, was not.

The "10-minute glance" is a hunter's technique I learned as a boy on land that had belonged to my family for generations in the wooded hills of Western Pennsylvania. The "10-minute glance" improves one's observation. It can be described in two steps. (1) When arriving at the edge of a clearing, stop and become perfectly still. Then, (2) listen and look for ten minutes. It is a simple but surprisingly effective technique.

In the first seconds of a "10-minute glance," certain sights and sounds tend to stand out. For a while, they appear to be all there is to see and hear.

After holding still for five minutes, however, one begins to hear different noises and see different sights. The wind whispers in the leaves. A bird cries far off. Moisture drips from a rock and a cloud passes by. These new observations only point to more to come.

After five more minutes, one is surprised to notice a clear claw mark on the bark of a nearby tree. A flash of color high on a branch reveals the mate of the distant bird that had cried out. Finally, one's own breathing and heartbeat become loud in the silence. Pausing for a "10 minute glance" as a family, we have discovered many things a hurried look would have passed over.

A variation of this technique helps in studying a Bible passage. It is good first to "glance" deeply at a passage. After noticing the words, the verses and the surrounding context, we can then make practical application of the discovered truths.

Peter's unique voice. When we were professors in Africa, we lived on campus, next door to the seminary president. They had four children in the family ranging in age from four to ten years old. Some people were concerned because the youngest child did not speak until she was three and a half years old. Her father was unconcerned. "Children have their own ways of talking," he said. "She simply waited until she needed to say something out loud." While there are thousands of words in every language, each individual chooses certain ones to use. Some people have large vocabularies. Others use only 400 words or so. The way we use our words is unique to each one of us. It forms our unique "voice" that others recognize even if we only write down our words instead of speaking them out loud.

A person reading the New Testament straight through, starting with the four Gospels, soon reaches the many letters of Paul. Paul's "voice" was very recognizable. He had a very large vocabulary and a sophisticated way of using his words. From Galatians to 2 Timothy, the reader (in Greek) soon gets used to Paul's way of adding meaning to his words in long and complex sentences.

Peter's "voice" is very different from Paul's. His thoughts tumble onto the written page. Peter used many of the same Greek words that Paul used, but Peter used them in ways that were very unlike Paul's. Often a word found in Peter's sentences meant something different from the same word when used by Paul!

Peter spit out his words, using them in ways *he* chose, without bothering to add context or further definition. This is not surprising. It is typical of the straightforward way he did everything in life. As for Paul's fancy words and shades of meaning, Peter found some "hard to understand" (2 Peter 3:16).

For example, the following illustration contains Greek words used by both Peter and Paul. The words were defined so differently by them, that even though these passages sound similar, they are completely different.

Key word: "lord"

At first, these words seem the same in Peter and Paul:
    "lord"   **(1 Peter 3:6)**
    "Lord"   **(Ephesians 5:17-22; 6:1, 4, 5, 7-9)**

but closer inspection shows they mean different things:
    "husband" **(1 Peter 3:6)**
    "God"   **(Ephesians 5:17-22; 6:1, 4, 5, 7-9).**

Peter used "lord" in a reference to Sarah (Genesis 18:10-12) who, at a certain moment while standing in the doorway of her tent, talked to herself about Abraham her "lord," or "husband." Paul, on the other hand, frequently used the word "Lord" to refer to "God." These were very different meanings for the same Greek word! There are other, more profound examples.

To describe God's unique love, early Christians took one of several existing Greek words for "love" (*agape*) and filled it with the meaning that is now known as "God's agape love." Paul did something similar with a Greek verb in Ephesians 5:21-22. He redefined "submit yourself" so that it applied to Christians who "submitted themselves one to another." But Peter used that same Greek verb without redefining it. In 1 Peter 2:13-25, he used the verb "submit yourself" in the ordinary, non-Christian sense of "one person who submits to another person." Peter used this verb to tell Christian servants to submit themselves to their masters out of their own free will. In that way, they first served God while also serving their masters. Paul and Peter taught different lessons using the same Greek verb to mean different things! When similar-seeming words like these are used differently, great caution should be used before doing any cross-referencing. For example, Paul's verses that use this verb should not be compared to Peter's. It would be like comparing apples and oranges. It makes good fruit salad but poor theology!

Moving from subject to subject. Paul frequently strung together his ideas by using long and complex sentences, with many subdivisions, asides and lists, and he garnished them with additional, well-developed dependent clauses (like this sentence!). But Peter could move suddenly from one subject to quite another.

Peter was known for doing and saying things abruptly. Take, for example:

- His contradiction of Jesus (Mt 16:22-23)
- His "all or nothing" words at the Last Supper (Jn 13:6-9)
- His boast that he would not deny Jesus (Mt 26:33-35).

It should not be surprising to find that in chapter 2 he wrote about Christian servants in difficult circumstances, but then in chapter 3 he moved on to write about Christian spouses in different, but difficult circumstances.

Where does the passage begin and end? Suppose translators inserted a chapter break in the middle of the Ten Commandments making, in effect, two groups of five commandments each! People might wonder: "Which group of five commandments was the more important? The first group or the second group?" They might ask: "Why was one commandment placed in one group and not in the other?" All sorts of speculation might arise, just because the complete group of Ten Commandments was not shown together as one unit.

Familiar "Leadership" Heresies Uncovered   by Bruce C. E. Fleming
www.ThinkAgainAboutTheBible.com

In the same way, it is important to notice where the passage in 1 Peter 3 begins and ends. It *begins* in verse 3:1 with a new subject – a group of Christian spouses who found themselves in a difficult situation. It *continues* through verse 7 and ends there. In Greek, verse 7 begins with the word "Likewise." This indicates that verse 7 is a continuation from the earlier six verses. The seven verses form one unit.

The seven verses form one unit.

Another clue that these verses belong together is that Peter used the word "Likewise" at the start of his advice to unequally yoked spouses in verse 1. This "likewise" was yoked to the second "likewise" in verse 7. Together, they formed a parallel reference indicating the two related parts of the passage.

Then, Peter started verse 8 with Greek words that signaled grammatically a major break in thought. Starting with verse 8, Peter moved on from his advice to this group of spouses to a new subject.

Small but important. It is possible for a reader to notice that these seven verses stand together as one unit of thought, yet still misunderstand this passage. This can happen by missing which kind of "if" was used by Peter in verse 1. In English, "if" is not a complicated word. But it is in Greek!

In Greek, the little word "if" can mean three very different things. These are called: "3rd class, 2nd class and 1st class conditional clauses using if."

It is helpful to note how each conditional clause works:

- (3rd class). A third-class conditional "if" is very "iffy." Someone could say, "*If* I walk out the door now, *then* a meteor might strike me." It could happen, but this outcome is **highly unlikely**.
- (2nd class). A second-class conditional "if" is **more likely**. A person could say, "*If* I take a walk in the rain, *then* I might slip and fall." It could happen. This is an "iffy" proposal. This is the kind of "if" that is widely used in English.
- (1st class). A first-class conditional "if" is not "iffy" at all. It means "if, as is the case." It might be said as if it were unlikely, but everyone would know it was not. In English, a similar use of "if" would be like saying, "*If, as is the case,* falling out of an airplane in flight is dangerous, then don't open the exit." This isn't "iffy." It is **a sure thing**.

In commenting on 1 Peter 3, the book *Linguistic Key to the New Testament,* (Rienecker/Rogers, p. 756), points out that in verse 1 – "*if* any obey not the word" – is a 1st class conditional clause. As for the husbands in verse 1 it says: "The indicative is used in a 1st class conditional clause which assumes the reality of the condition."

Thus, for these husbands one should "assume the reality of the condition" that they "did not obey the word." In other words, they were unbelievers. Another way of saying the same thing would be to remark that each of these believing women was *unequally yoked* to an unbeliever! If this had been a 3rd or a 2nd class conditional clause, it would have meant that none, or maybe only some, of these husbands were unbelievers who did not "obey the word."

Here is how the passage looks in English when the 1st class conditional "if-clause" is clearly stated:

> [1]You unequally-yoked wives, be submitting yourselves to your own husbands so that even though they do not yet believe the Word, through your conduct without using a word, they may be won to faith in Christ...

I came across this important insight on the word "if" during my preliminary "glance" at 1 Peter. It helped bring into focus the elements of 1 Peter 3 that were troubling Aunt Myrl. I was now ready to look at the passage verse by verse.

Wives Witnessing Wordlessly (3:1-6)

Advice to Witnessing Wives

[1] ... through your conduct without using a word, they may be won to faith in Christ, [2]when they observe your God-fearing, pure conduct [3]not outward adorning or special coiffure, or the wearing of gold, jewelry and fine clothes [4] but the inner adorning of the heart by your incorruptible meek and quiet spirit which is of great value before God

[5] for indeed this is how the holy women of old, who kept hoping in God, adorned themselves as they submitted themselves to their own husbands.

[6] Sarah, for example, trusted in God and submitted to Abraham her husband after the angel came. You are now her daughters by your well doing and your fearlessness of any disappointment.

Verses 1-6: Unsaved husbands. The word "won," near the end of verse 1, is "a missionary word." This was the goal of the wives described in verses 1-6. These husbands did not know the Lord. They needed to be "won" to Christ!

In these verses, Peter dealt with wives whose everyday lives had been transformed because of their own salvation. As new Christians they felt a natural urgency to see their spouses won to Christ. "Wouldn't it be wonderful," they perceived, "to live each day as believers *together*, to pray *together*, and to interact with others as Christians *together!*"

For those who look forward to this, and pray about it for some time with no noticeable change in their spouse, a certain suffering begins to build.

- Why is God waiting?

- What else can I do to speed up this process?

- Will my spouse ever be won to Christ?

The church had been growing a number of years by the time Peter wrote his letter. Likely, there was a sizeable number of Christian spouses who wanted advice for their situation. Peter gave them hope. He told them how best to live in order to lead their spouse to Christ!

Temporary behavior. 1 Peter 3:1-6 addressed how wives ought to act during the temporary situation where one spouse in the marriage was a believer but the other was *not yet* a Christian. It did not address ongoing normal relations between a pair of believing spouses.

Peter wrote to wives who found themselves in the worst of situations, where they could not even speak with their husbands about Christ! They had to do all their "talking" through their actions.

When I worked for Youth for Christ as a college student, I often counseled teenagers who had just become Christians. I learned to remind them that, "Actions speak louder than words." I found that instinctively most of them wanted to go home, tell their parents about their own salvation and immediately instruct their parents on how to become Christians too. But this was not taken well by many of their parents.

I counseled these teenagers: "First, go home and be the best son or daughter you can be. Let the love of Christ flow through your actions and wait for your opportunity to tell your parents about Christ – once you have won the right to be heard. If the change *in you* is real, your parents will notice, and when you explain, they will believe your explanation."

In various cultures around the world today, wives find themselves in similar awkward situations where they are not able to speak to their husbands about

Christ. Waiting to witness is not easy. New converts need encouragement to bear up under their culture-imposed silence. This is what Peter was doing.

Verses 2-4: Witnessing through action. Peter's readers were Christians (1 Peter 1:1). He had advised them to grow in their spiritual lives (1 Peter 2:1-3). The unequally yoked wives had already taken the most important step they could take toward being effective "advertisements" for Christ – they themselves had been won by Christ.

Peter wanted the behavior of these Christian wives to catch their husband's attention. Elements that would stand out to them would be "purity," "reverence" and inner beauty.

Of all the people in the Bible, perhaps Peter understood impatience the best! Even as he counseled these wives to live chaste and pure lives, he knew some of their unsaved husbands seemed as if they would be forever blind to their actions.

At the close of verse 4, Peter reassured these waiting wives that all was not in vain. God was watching and approving. The life of a witnessing wife was "of great worth in God's sight." That was sufficient reward for anyone.

Verses 5-6: A cruel joke? On occasion, I have seen a dog owner tease his pet by dangling a tasty morsel just out of reach of his hungry dog. The dog leaps high in the air with jaws ready to snap on the prize. Up goes the dog. Up goes the arm of the human too! The jaws snap shut on air as the dog falls earthward.

God is not a tease. He does not place the cry "Save my spouse!" in the heart of a new believer just to deny answering that prayer. In verses 5-6, Peter encouraged waiting, witnessing wives to be patient and believe in, what to them may have come to seem an impossibility, the salvation of their unsaved husbands (see 2 Peter 3:1, 9).

Profiles in courage. Peter compared the difficult situation of these unequally yoked women to that of the holy women of old in various situations who placed their trust in God. Many of the women in the Old Testament found themselves in seemingly hopeless spots. In verses 5-6, Peter picked the specific example of Sarah.

Sarah's marriage was not like that of the women in 1 Peter 3. She had married a believer. But to Peter, Sarah was a supreme example of the kind of person he had in mind, a "holy woman of old." Both a waiting witnessing wife, and the barren and aged Sarah, could safely place before God their seemingly impossible prayer requests.

Sarah's request was for the fulfillment of God's promise – that she should have a child. Years had passed and she and her husband were past their childbearing years. Her case seemed hopeless, yet God answered her prayers! To Peter, holding fast to a similar faith as a witnessing wife was a way of believing in God as a spiritual "daughter of Sarah."

Married life as a Christian couple was **not covered** in these six verses. In verses 1-6 Peter gave advice that needed to be followed as long as the spouses were spiritually unequal. As soon as the second spouse was won to Christ and both spouses were believers, a full Christian home life could be enjoyed by both members of the couple! Biblical advice on that subject would have to be found in a different passage. Not here.

Unequally-Yoked Husbands (3:7)

Advice to Witnessing Husbands

[7]Likewise you unequally-yoked husbands, use good sense as you dwell with your unsaved wife while she is the weaker partner, treating her with dignity as a fellow human being so that your prayers for her salvation might not be hindered.

The other way around. After he advised Christian wives with unsaved husbands in verses 1-6, Peter turned to Christian husbands who found themselves in the same situation. Often, a wife leads the way in accepting Christ. But because sometimes it is the husband who first believes, Peter dedicated verse 7 to these men.

Verse 7 is packed full of meaning. In context, this verse provides the best practical advice in the Bible for husbands whose wives are unsaved. Peter's advice is that unequally-yoked husbands – Christian men married to unbelieving women – should be model husbands.

Peter's advice is that Christian men married to unbelieving women, should be model husbands.

Heresy alert! Often, parts of this verse are taken out of context. As always, whenever any verse is taken out of context, the resulting opinions on what it teaches can go far astray. This is true of 1 Peter 3:7.

The following ideas are based on study of the words in verse 7 in their context. The Greek word order of verse seven contains six distinct ideas.

It is helpful to look at each element one by one:

1. Likewise, husbands

2. Dwell-together according to knowledge

3. As with a weaker vessel

4. Assigning honor

5. As co-heirs of the grace of life

6. That your prayers be not hindered.

1. "Likewise, husbands." In 1 Peter 3:7, Peter begins with the word "likewise." This links up with the "likewise" he used to introduce verse 1.

What did it mean when groups of unequally yoked Christian wives and Christian husbands were in a "likewise" situation? How was the situation of the husbands in verse 7 like that of the witnessing wives of verses 1-6? Their spouses were unsaved too, and needed to be won to Christ.

Most modern English translations don't show that Peter used the same Greek word at the beginning of verses 1 and 7. It would be helpful if they were clearly shown. By repeating "likewise" in Greek at the start of each verse, Peter yoked these verses into coordinated advice to those Christian wives and Christian husbands who – "likewise" – found themselves in similar positions.

Heresy alert! Those, whose Bibles do not show the parallelism in these verses, often end up trying to make a backward link from the "likewise" in 3:1 to something referred to in 1 Peter 2.

This effort results in futility and confusion. 1 Peter 2 deals with glorifying God through suffering. It is not about winning people to Christ. Some people latch on to "submit" in chapter 2, which is used in the context of all citizens (2:13) and slaves (2:18).

When they try to link these two verses with the word "submit" in chapter 3:1 and 5 they run into trouble because Peter, the Big Fisherman, had moved on to another topic. If they persist, they develop non-Bible based theories that link wives with slaves! The results can be catastrophic.

This is a prime example of the value of implementing the Seven *Think Again* Bible Study Steps. Studying the progress of thought in 1 Peter, and determining the limits of the pericope in 1 Peter 3:1-7, protects the reader from attempting to draw erroneous links and make heretical conclusions.

If Peter's words, either to the husbands, or to the wives are studied out of context, his insights on the topic of these seven verses are lost, because each "likewise" section is necessary to help define the other.

2. "Dwell together according to knowledge." Peter recommended that these husbands be especially thoughtful with their wives. They were to "dwell together according to knowledge."

Among other things, this meant that they were to continue "dwelling together." They were not to separate. This squared with Paul's recommendation that a saved spouse should not abandon an unsaved one except under a limited number of specific exceptions.

Peter exhorted Christian husbands to demonstrate "knowledge" or "understanding." Reinecker (p. 757) suggested this meant that they had to use "Christian insight and tact." A conscious effort was required on the husband's part. He needed to stop and think before speaking and acting in order to let his understanding show through to his wife.

3. "As with a weaker vessel." The term "vessel" stands for a wife. Paul used the same word in 1 Thessalonians 4:4 to address a different aspect of marriage.

An important question is, "What is meant by weaker?" In this passage, the weaker vessel was the unsaved, and therefore spiritually weaker spouse.

Heresy alert! Some have strayed from the topic and speculated on *other* ways they think a wife might be "weaker." Obviously, as soon as they start to wander from the subject of 1 Peter 3:7 they deviate from the intent of Peter's words!

Some people speculate on how women in general might be "weaker" than men in general. Their speculations can be quite absurd:

- How do you propose that women are *physically* weaker than men? In many countries they are the ones who do the heavy labor. What about the fact that women live longer than men in western societies, where death in childbirth has been greatly reduced?

- How do you propose that women are weaker than men *intellectually*? Most American high schools and universities have greater numbers of women graduates than they do men.

- How do you propose women are weaker than men *spiritually*? Our studies (above) have shown that woman was not the Temptress nor even the more guilty of the two sinners in the Garden of Eden. They are called by God to fulfill the Great Commission and are gifted by the Holy Spirit as are male believers.

Nevertheless, many people say that "women are weaker" in one or all of these ways. They organize life in their church and life at home as if women really were "weaker." These ideas are wholly extraneous to this passage. They are not supported elsewhere in Peter or anywhere else in Scripture. These heresies must be identified, rejected and corrected.

If you believe that a woman is spiritually weaker *as long as she is the unsaved spouse* of the household, you are supported by Peters words of 1 Peter 3:7. If you hold to any of the erroneous views cited above, *think again!*

4. "Assigning honor." Why would Peter instruct these Christian husbands to "assign honor" to their wives? Was this advice they needed to hear? Were these unequally yoked husbands treating their unsaved wives as less than worthy of honor? Perhaps.

Peter's instructed these Christian husbands to be wise and enlightened in how they lived with their unsaved spouses. While his wife was unsaved, a Christian husband needed to live an exemplary life before her. If he did so, and accorded her "honor," his testimony for Christ would be all the more attractive.

This word "honor" was the same one used in the Greek Old Testament where children were told to "honor" their father and their mother. Peter's advice was for a husband to treat his unsaved wife with as much honor as was required in the Ten Commandments of a child who respectfully honored a parent!

5. "As co-heirs of the grace of life." These words provide the reason for assigning such honor. Many have read the words "co-heirs of the grace of life" as if they had been written by Paul, and as if they indicated that these Christian husbands had Christian wives. They take the phrase "co-heirs of the grace of life" to mean that both spouses were believers. But a closer look at Peter's use of these words shows otherwise, because Peter did not use his words as did Paul.

Peter did not use words the same way as Paul.

Peter did not use the words "grace," or "gift" or "heir," elsewhere in his letters in any technical or theological sense. Nor did he use the word "life" in a theological manner. In the two other occasions where Peter used the word "life" (1 Peter 3:10 and 2 Peter 1:3) he did not have in mind "eternal life." In these occurrences, his meaning is simply earthly life.

The words "grace of life" were used together in one short phrase in 1 Peter 3:7. They sounded very much like a typical description of a Christian. But these words were not used together anywhere else, by anyone else, in the New Testament.

This was not Peter's way of describing those who had received the gift of eternal life. It was his way of describing the grace of earthly life. A Christian man's unsaved wife was to be assigned honor as a human being, deserving of all the rights and respect due any other adult. In many ways this advice was quite revolutionary. It would also be quite powerful in communicating the power of Christ who had changed the life of a husband. New life in Christ would become attractive and believable to the wife of such a man who treated her well.

6. "That your prayers be not hindered." What prayers? These are not prayers about any and all subjects. In a household made up of unequally yoked spouses, one can assume that this prayer refers to "the second prayer" of a Christian spouse for the salvation of the other spouse.

What could "hinder" the answering of such prayers? A wife could be offended, put off or even be embittered by the actions of a clumsy offensive husband. Peter's advice to witnessing husbands was virtually the same that he gave to witnessing wives. Each one was to wisely and lovingly dwell with his or her respective spouse in such a way as to be a good example of the Christian life. In this way the unsaved spouse could be won to Christ in answer to heartfelt prayer. Then, together they could live the blessed life of a Christian couple.

Think Again!

1. Are you troubled that many have missed the evangelistic nature of 1 Peter 3?

2. Do you see the hope Peter offers to spiritually unequally-yoked spouses? Is there anyone you know who needs to see this passage in order to learn how to deal with their marriage situation?

3. Unequally yoked Christians can persevere in the hope of prayer answers yet to come. How would you counsel them by pointing them to this passage?

Chapter 5

"Leadership" Heresies and Submission
... an inside look at Ephesians 5:15-6:9 (with a focus on 5:21)

Chapter Contents:

154

155

Outline of Ephesians 5:15-6:9 (from the Greek)

5:15-21. *Therefore walk* **circumspectly being filled with the Spirit**
The 4 "-ing" ways to "walk" in the Spirit

┌─ 1) Speak*ing*

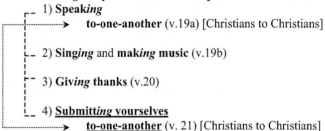
    ────➤ **to-one-another** (v.19a) [Christians to Christians]

└─ 2) Sing*ing* and mak*ing* music (v.19b)

┌─ 3) Giv*ing* thanks (v.20)

└─ 4) <u>Submitt*ing* yourselves</u>
    ────➤ **to-one-another** (v. 21) [Christians to Christians]

5:22-6:9. <u>Submitting yourselves</u>
      <u>**to-one-another**</u> [Christians to Christians]

Two illustrations on "verse-21 Christian submission"
┌─ **A. Christ and the church 5:22-32**

  ⤷ 1) **As Christ** is Savior of **the church** (v.23, 22-24)

  ⤷ 2) Just **as Christ** loved **the church** (v.25, 25-27)

  ⤷ 3) Just **as Christ** cares for **the church** (v.29, 28-32)

└─ **B. Members in the household 5:33-6:9**

  ⤷ 1) **Between** Christian spouses (5:33)

  ⤷ 2) **Between** Christian children and parents (6:1-4)

  ⤷ 3) **Between** Christian servants and masters (6:5-9)

Introduction

"**I heard your words** but I really didn't understand until I saw for myself."
He was talking about a ministry in the inner city. His visit to the neighborhood
changed his vague ideas into a consuming passion.

Familiar "Leadership" Heresies Uncovered by Bruce C. E. Fleming
www.ThinkAgainAboutTheBible.com

156

Two hundred miles north of the city lived an elderly woman. She heard about the ministry too. She had never been to the neighborhood, but through her daughter's words she came to understand. She became a donor and a prayer supporter for the ministry.

The Apostle Paul started churches in many cities and towns throughout Asia Minor. Some of the new believers in one town visited other churches started earlier by Paul. There they saw Christians in action and learned by observing. In Ephesians, helps his readers understand spiritual unity. He uses the word picture of the church and Christ united in one body.

In Ephesians, Paul explains what it means to be "in Christ Jesus" (1:1). He describes the new ways people interact with each other when they are "alive with Christ" (2:5). And he puts into words how Christians practice a new behavior, that of "submitting themselves to one another" (5:21).

"Christian submission" is such an important truth that it is worth taking time to revisit Paul's Letter to the Ephesians as it was first written down in Greek. It is time to *think again* about submission in the body of Christ.

Two Key Concepts – "Body" and "Walk"

The "body" is an important image used by Paul in Ephesians. He introduces it in chapter 3, develops it further in chapter 4 and refers to it extensively in chapter 5.

In 3:3-6, Paul explains that each believer is **joined** together with every other believer. Three times he adds the Greek prefix which stands for "**joint-**". In the second of these instances Paul uses the word picture of a "**joint-body.**"

> In reading this, then, you will be able to understand my insight
> … that the Gentiles should be joint-heirs (along with Israel)
> and a **joint-body** and joint-sharers of the promise in Christ
> Jesus through the Gospel. (Eph. 3:4, 6)

In Ephesians 4, Paul further develops the picture of a **joint-body**. Jesus himself is joined with all believers in this body:

> But speaking the truth in love, we may grow into him in all
> respects who is the head, Christ, of whom **all the body being
> brought together** by every supporting ligament, grows and
> builds itself up in love, as each part does its work. (Eph 4:15-16)

To picture this joint-body, it is helpful to consider an ant. It has a three-part joint-body. No one part can function by itself. Each part works with the others.

Familiar "Leadership" Heresies Uncovered   by Bruce C. E. Fleming
www.ThinkAgainAboutTheBible.com

Ant body? No.

Ant body? No.

Ant body? No.

ONE PHYSICAL JOINT-BODY?   YES!

The human body has two distinct parts. They are the head and the torso. No one part exists by itself. As the whole body prospers, its parts prosper.

In Paul's imagery, **Christ is the** "**head part**" and **believers are the** "**torso part**" of a two-part spiritual body. This **one joint-body** consists of the sum of its parts (see 1 Corinthians 12:20).

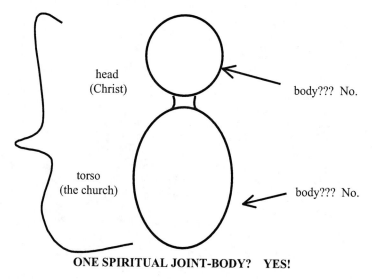

head
(Christ)

body??? No.

torso
(the church)

body??? No.

ONE SPIRITUAL JOINT-BODY?   YES!

Familiar "Leadership" Heresies Uncovered   by Bruce C. E. Fleming
www.ThinkAgainAboutTheBible.com

The "walk"

Another important word picture Paul uses in Ephesians is the Christian "walk." He develops this concept in six sections in chapters 4-6.

The Apostle Paul uses the Greek word for "walk" (Eph 5:15), to refer to how a person "walks" through life. Translations deal variously with "walk."

NASB. "Therefore be careful how you *walk*..."

NIV. "Be very careful, then, how you *live*...."

NKJV. "See then that you *walk* circumspectly..."

Most people agree that the first three chapters of Ephesians are mainly about *theology*. And the last three chapters are mainly about *practical theology* or *application* of the truths found in the first three chapters of the book.

Paul repeatedly uses together the words "therefore" and "walk" to introduce new sections in chapters 4-6. These sections deal with six practical recommendations on how to live the Christian life. At the end of his letter, Paul changes "walk" to "stand." Christians stand as they engage in spiritual warfare.

The six parts of Ephesians 4-6 (set off by *"therefore"* plus *"walk,"* or a variation on these words, in Greek) are as follows:

1) 4:1-16   *therefore walk* worthy
2) 4:17-32   *therefore walk* not in vanity
3) 5:1-6   *therefore walk* in love
4) 5:7-14   *therefore walk* as children of light
5) 5:15-6:9 *therefore walk* very carefully
6) 6:10-20   *therefore stand* against the devil

1) *Therefore walk* worthy (4:1-16). "Let someone else do it," is often murmured in church. It has been estimated that 80 per cent of the work in church is accomplished by only 20 per cent of its people. This is how society in general does things. But it is not the *Christian* way to "walk."

Paul uses "walk" to describe how one progresses in everyday life. He begins with an appeal to live worthily in daily life, "I ... beg you to walk worthy of the calling you have received" (4:1). This "walk" means being humble and gentle, being patient and bearing with one another in love. Every Christian is called to live this way (4:3).

Paul explains that some Christians have the work of building up the other Christians. These serve as apostles, prophets, evangelists, and pastor-teachers (4:11). The other believers, in turn, work to build up the whole body of believers into a mature unity (4:12-14).

2) *Therefore walk* **not in vanity (4:17-32)**. Gentile (or non-Jewish) influences were infiltrating the church in and around Ephesus. Paul describes the behavior of unbelieving Gentiles as follows:

Walking in vanity. In futility of thinking. Having their understanding darkened. Alienated from the life of God. Ignorance within them. Hardening their hearts. Being past feeling. Having given themselves over. Licentious. Working all uncleanness with greediness.

Paul teaches that Christians must *not* walk this way. Everything old must be left behind (verse 22). Christians should practice the virtues listed in verses 25-32 which include practicing kindness and compassion toward one another, and forgiving one another.

3) *Therefore walk* **in love (5:1-6)**. Believers are deeply loved children of God. Like little children who mimic the ways of a parent, believers are to imitate God and live in a way fitting for persons made holy by God.

During my teen years, not long after I became a Christian, I needed help walking as a child of God. I like to laugh and I have always enjoyed a good joke, especially one with a clever play on words. This is where I had trouble. Along with the guys at our school lunch table, I began to tell dirty jokes. As Paul describes it, I was participating in "foolish talking" and in "coarse jesting."

One weekend, I attended a retreat for Christian teens. The speaker opened with a joke that made us all groan. I liked him right away! But then, while we were off guard, he warned us about coarse language. He encouraged us to start memorizing as many clean jokes as we could. "When it's your turn in a group," he said, "you tell a joke too, but make it a clean one."

With a serious face he confided in us that the night before, all night long, he had dreamt he was a Midas muffler. There he was, under a car driving down a wet roadway. For endless hours he steamed and hissed as the car drove through puddle after puddle. And that morning, when he awoke – he felt *exhausted* – of course! I couldn't wait to tell the muffler joke to our sixth-period lunch bunch. They groaned. I learned to be ready for my turn with a clean joke – and I tried to make it last as long as possible, so we wouldn't have much time to listen to anyone tell a dirty joke.

The speaker's advice worked! Our bunch stayed together and the tone of our group changed. Two of my lunch buddies have since become believers!

4) *Therefore walk* **as children of light (5:7-14)**. Christians are to counteract acts of darkness as they participate in the ministry of Christ.

Believers should walk as children of the light and not like those who are full of darkness (see Matthew 6:23).

5) *Therefore walk* **carefully (5:15-6:9).** This is the most serious introduction to all the "walk" sections. For some reason special care will be needed to walk this way. This long section is composed of an exhortation in verses 15-21, plus the addition of two sets of examples that help explain the meaning of the new verb Paul uses in verse 21. (These verses will be looked at in detail in the following pages.)

6) *Therefore stand* **against the devil (6:10-20).** Paul starts the final section once more with the Greek word "therefore." But this time he uses the verb "to stand." In spiritual warfare Christians must *stand* their ground against the devil. Paul lists the items that make up the defensive armor of a Christian, as well as their two offensive weapons – the Bible and prayer.

How to walk carefully (Eph 5:15-6:9)

Paul reveals a "mystery" in the fifth "walk" section in Ephesians. For Paul, a "mystery" is not something "mysterious" in the modern sense of the word. For him, a "mystery" refers to something that *once* was hidden *but now* is understood.

In Ephesians, a "mystery" is something *made known*. In Ephesians 1:9, the "mystery" that has been made known is *God's will*. God's will is no longer "mysterious." It is clearly stated and understood. God's will is "that he might gather together in one all things in Christ" (1:10).

A "mystery" in the New Testament is *no longer* mysterious!
It is something *made known*.

In Ephesians 3:9-10, Paul refers to his ministry, which is "to bring to light … the mystery which … has been hidden…." In Ephesians 6:19, he writes that his task is to "make known the mystery of the gospel." There are no hidden meanings in Ephesians. Every "mystery" is clearly spelled out.

After exhorting his readers to take care to live a life filled with the Spirit (5:15-19), Paul lists four actions that spring from a Spirit-filled life (19-21). He then develops at length the last aspect, listed in verse 21. These details reveal the relationship ("mystery") of Christ and the church (32).

Exhortation in four imperatives: (5:15-21). An exclamation point is used to indicate an imperative verb. Imperative verbs call for action: Jump! Clap! Cheer! Stop!

In verses 17-18, Paul uses four of them in a row:

1. *Don't be foolish!*
2. *Understand* what the will of the Lord is!
3. *Don't be drunk* with wine!
4. <u>*Be filled*</u> with the Spirit!

The last of these four verbs is different from the others. It is a passive verb. It means, "*allow yourself* to be filled!" People cannot fill themselves with the Spirit of God. But they can allow themselves to be filled by God's Spirit.

Paul describes what a life filled with the Spirit looks like in verses 19-21. He uses four "-ing" verbs (or participles). Sometimes these verbs indicate an imperative verb, but not in the case of these four.

These verbs describe the ongoing activity of Christians who are filled with the Spirit:

1. *Speaking* to one another in psalms and hymns and spiritual songs
2. *Singing* and *making* music in your heart to the Lord
3. *Giving thanks* always to God the Father for everything, in the name of our Lord Jesus Christ
4. <u>*Submitting yourselves*</u> to one another in the fear of Christ

The last of these four "–ing" verbs is different from the first three in four ways. In addition, it is so important to understand this behavior that Paul attaches to it a string of verses down to the end of this "walk" section.

Life in Christ is a group activity. To make it perfectly clear that the Christian life involves other Christians, Paul adds one Greek word "to-one-another" to the first and last verb phrases in verses 19 and 21.

- Christians are to *speak* "to-one-another." (19)
- Christians are to *submit reciprocally* "to-one-another." (21)

At one time or another, Joy and I have lived and worshiped with Christians on five different continents and in many different languages. Every time we do, we encounter two factors that make us feel right at home as members of the body of Christ – (1) the joy of praising God together, and (2) the joy of serving one another in Christ.

A cleaver under my pillow. During our first year as missionaries in Africa, thieves slipped into our house one evening. We were in the back of the house putting our baby daughter to bed. They took a number of important items, including our house keys, a metal file box with my doctoral papers from France, some toys, and our garden machete.

Instantly, we felt vulnerable. Faceless intruders had been inside our home. We were open to further invasion. And it was a terrible setback for my research.

We had no way to change our locks. We were unsure whether we were personally in danger or not. That night I slept with a meat cleaver under my pillow. Most important of all, we prayed and trusted ourselves to Christ's care.

The next afternoon, two local Christian women came to our house. They had walked all the way across town to come and "sit" with us. They had heard of our trouble and this was the typical African way to grieve with someone.

One of the women took Joy's hand and looked deeply into her face with loving and comforting eyes. We discussed promises in Scripture. We made small talk. We laughed together. Then we prayed. When we opened our eyes nightfall had come. They had comforted us and made the time fly.

There was no moon. Both were barefoot and there were the dangers of serpents and ankle twisting ruts on their return path. We offered them a kerosene lantern to use and bid them goodbye with hearts filled with encouragement.

Only later did we learn (she hadn't mentioned it), that one of these two dear comforters in Christ had been the victim of a burglary herself just the week before. While she was away in the rain forest working in her jungle garden, thieves had broken in and cleared out *every* item she owned in the world! All she had left was what she had with her when she returned. *Her* loss was much greater than ours, and yet this sister in Christ comforted *us* during our time of vulnerability and grief! What an example of caring for one another in Christ.

After exhorting his readers to live a life filled with the Spirit, Paul described the uniquely Christian behavior of *reciprocally submitting* to-one-another in Christ. Most Christians have experienced this "one-another care" at various times in their Christian lives. But Paul presents it as something that is as regular as singing and making music in our hearts, and giving thanks to God.

Paul uses a typically hierarchical verb to describe this reciprocal care. This care was part of Christian behavior and Paul had been preaching about it wherever he went. The care of Christians for one another was a known behavior.

Yet, it was still difficult to picture and often more difficult to do. So Paul devotes verses 5:22 through 6:9 to illustrate this behavior and to encourage Christians that in Christ such mutual care is indeed possible, whether in the church or in the home. He points out what he is doing in 5:32: "This is a great mystery. I speak about Christ and the church."

Paul uses two three-part sets of examples to illustrate Christian reciprocating submitting:

Illustration 1 – examples 1-3: verses 22-31

Illustration 2 – examples 4-6: verses 33-6:9.

The diagram of the first part of this passage is worth reviewing as follows:

5:15-21. *Therefore walk* circumspectly being filled with the Spirit
The 4 "-ing" ways to "walk" in the Spirit

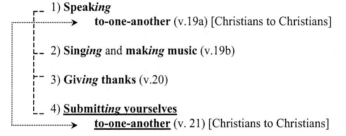

1) **Speak*ing***
  ➤ **to-one-another** (v.19a) [Christians to Christians]

2) **Sing*ing*** and **mak*ing* music** (v.19b)

3) **Giv*ing* thanks** (v.20)

4) **Submit*ting* yourselves**
  ➤ **to-one-another** (v. 21) [Christians to Christians]

"Submitting Reciprocally in Christ" (Ephesians 5:21)

Telling a new truth in verse 21
In verse 21, when Paul wants to add a fourth and final verb to complete his description of how Spirit-filled Christians should act, no available Greek word fits what he wants to describe. So he does the next best thing. He takes a common Greek verb, which everyone knows means one thing, and he modifies it so that it means a *new* thing – a Christian way of acting. Here are several ways to explain how Paul accomplishes this.

> **Paul takes a common Greek verb, which everyone knows means one thing, and he modifies it to mean a *new* thing, a Christian way of acting.**

Paul takes the verb "to submit" (a "vertical" verb) and turns it into "mutually submitting" (a "horizontal" verb). Grammatically speaking, he makes the verb "to submit" into a participial, or "-ing", verb, and then he makes the verb reflexive. This kind of submission is something one does of his, or her, own accord – "submitting oneself."

To this, Paul adds the reciprocal pronoun "to-one-another." Each one must intentionally behave this way toward others.

This is quite plainly a verb with a new meaning. It is helpful to note the steps Paul took in making the new verb: "*Submitting yourselves* to-one-another"

- First, he makes the verb a *participle*, or an "*-ing*" verb, like the three previous verbs. These four are all lifestyle verbs – something that Christians are doing continuously, being filled with the Spirit.

- Second, he makes the verb *reflexive*. This means that it is an action taken because one chooses to do it, as in "I am submitting myself."

- Third, the verb is a *plural* reflexive participle, meaning "*we* are submitting *ourselves*." Thus each Christian is choosing to submit to every other Christian. Making this is a plural verb means this behavior is a reciprocal one. As Foulkes describes it (*Ephesians*, Eerdmans, 154), "There must be a willingness in the Christian fellowship to serve any, to learn from any, to be corrected by any, regardless of age, sex, class or any other division."

- Fourth, Paul modifies this verb with a *reciprocal pronoun*. The reciprocal meaning is already included in the reflexive participle, but Paul makes this explicit by adding the pronoun. This pronoun is one word in Greek but is usually translated into English using three words, "to-one-another." (Hyphens show these words originally come from *one* Greek word.)

In this way, to describe the reality of the Christian life, Paul creates a new verb with a uniquely Christian meaning. It is breathtaking in the way it redefines any and all previously defined relationships in society!

Paul's uniquely Christian verb is breathtaking.

It redefines any and all previously defined relationships in society!

The result of this kind of submission seems at first to be a no-win situation. In practice, however, it turns out to be a wonderful win-win behavior! This unique action may be shown as follows:

Life in the body of Christ

       While I am **submitting myself**   to you

       and you are **submitting yourself**   to me

       we are **submitting ourselves, one to the other**

New Testament scholar, Dr. Gilbert Bilezikian describes how Paul remakes the common verb "to submit" to give it its new Christian meaning in Ephesians 5:21 (*Beyond*, 154-156):

> The word ... "submit" means to make oneself subordinate to the authority of a higher power, to be dependent for direction on the desires and orders of a superior in rank or position, to yield to rulership. ... This is the natural meaning of "submit" whenever the word appears in the New Testament, *except where its meaning is deliberately changed by a modifier such as in verse 21 of our text.* ...

> "Being subject to one another" is a very different relationship from "being subject to the other." ... Being subject to one another is only possible among equals. ... Mutual subjection is a horizontal relationship among equals. Subjection is a vertical relationship between ruler and subject. ...

> ... It is precisely because the church is not the army, nor a business corporation, nor a political empire, that mutual subjection is enjoined by the Word of God as the normal pattern of relationships among Christians. The church thrives on mutual subjection. ...

> We conclude that mutual subjection as defined on the basis of Ephesians 5:18-21 refers to relationships of reciprocal servanthood under ... Christ, and that the reciprocity of such relationships renders hierarchical distinctions irrelevant within the Christian communities of church and family.

Familiar "Leadership" Heresies Uncovered   by Bruce C. E. Fleming
www.ThinkAgainAboutTheBible.com

166

> ... to yield to rulership. ... is the natural meaning of "submit" ...
>
> *except where its meaning is deliberately changed by a modifier ...*

Christian submission is not hierarchical. In ordinary language, when one person is submitting to another person, normally the *other* person ends up "on top," or "in charge," or imposing their will on the person who submits. The person who submits ends up being "on the bottom," as "a follower," and implementing the will of the other.

But the kind of Christian submitting described in verse 21 is the action of two (or more) persons who are each submitting themselves to the other, at the same time the other person is simultaneously submitting to them! The resulting exercise of submitting to the other comes to a balanced stop only when each is fully serving the other and both are agreed, each with the other.

> **Christian reciprocating submission is not hierarchical**

To reinforce the point that this "reciprocating submission" is a uniquely Christian behavior, Paul adds the final phrase of verse 21. Here again he is forced to improvise. Paul takes the common biblical phrase – "in the fear of God" – and turns it into – "in the fear of *Christ*." This is the only place in the New Testament this expression is used. It is God who gives us the will to interact in this way: "*submitting-yourselves* to-one-another." Christians are able to do this because they are empowered by the indwelling Spirit of Christ (5:18*b*).

Thus, this behavior is not only

1) a willing *self*-submission (the reflexive verb)

2) a *mutual* behavior (the reciprocal pronoun),

3) it is also a *Christian* action (the final phrase).

How does it work?
Paul successfully describes this Christian action in verse 21. But, it was another thing for his readers to grasp the implications of this new kind of behavior. To illustrate his meaning, Paul adds two strings of examples, which complete the rest of this "walk" section. All of these verses (25:2-6:9) are subordinate to verse 21 and serve as a commentary on it. Scholars have pointed this out in various ways.

- [Verse 21] functions as a heading for the entire section, 5:22-6:9.... (Sampley, p. 10).

- The unique message of Ephesians is silenced whenever the dominant position of verse 21 ... and the peculiarly startling content of this verse are neglected. (Markus Barth, p. 608, 610)

The 1st three-part illustration – "as Christ" (22-31)

Before writing Ephesians, Paul had preached the gospel to many people and started churches in many locations. Then, much of his time was spent in teaching the new believers in these churches.

As he describes *submitting reciprocally* in 5:22-6:9, he builds on feedback he has received over time on this very subject. He knows some people were likely to misunderstand this kind of submission. He also could predict that some would be tempted to reject it altogether.

Every church has its own mix of people. To some, *submitting reciprocally* to each and every other believer in church is too difficult to picture. "Can Paul have *every* person in mind?" "What about the ones who are ...?"

But *submitting reciprocally* is indeed possible *for* every believer *to* every other believer. Christ modeled it himself. It can be practiced in the Christian church. It can be practiced in the Christian home.

What does it look like? In verses 22-31, Paul presents the example of Christ's submission three different times. He introduces Christ's example each time with an introduction from everyday life. Then, in Ephesians 5:33-6:9 he gives three examples of *submitting reciprocally* in the Christian household. Christ's example holds us in awe. Paul's descriptions for family life can only be lived out by Spirit-filled individuals. *Submitting reciprocally in Christ* revolutionizes relationships in the household.

The three examples are based on Christ's relationship with the church:

- In the first example (22-24), *Christ submits* as Savior of the church, to which he is joined in one joint-body. Christ's example is presented in the context of mutually submissive spouses who are one in Christ.

- In the second example (25-27), *Christ gives himself* for the church. His example is introduced by an order to husbands to love their wives with *agape*, self-sacrificing, love.

- In the third (28-31), *Christ cares* for the church. His example is presented in the context of the care people give to their bodies.

Thus, (1) Christ submits, (2) Christ gives himself, and (3) Christ cares. He does these three things for the church. This is how Christians should care for one another.

The three introductions are based on examples from everyday life:

- In the first introduction (22-24), *submitting reciprocally* is found in the example of the intimate relationship Christian couple. It is mutually supportive. In verses 22 and 24, Paul focuses on the example of the Christian wife. (In the next introduction he will focus on the Christian husband.) Thus, Christ's example is presented in the context of mutually submissive spouses.

- In the second introduction (25-27), *submitting reciprocally* is found in the example of the Christian husband who loves his wife with the same love that Christ loves the church. At this point Paul uses the imperative verb, "Husbands, love your wives!" Christ's example is introduced by an order to husbands to love their wives with *agape*, self-sacrificing, love.

- In the third introduction (28-31), *submitting reciprocally* is found in the example of the intimate care a person gives to his or her own body. Christ's example is presented in the context of this kind of detailed and regular care.

Thus, (1) as Christian wives are *submitting reciprocally* for their part to their own husbands, Christ submits, (2) as husbands are submitting reciprocally to their own wives by loving them with Godly love, Christ gives himself, and (3) as a person intimately and consistently cares for his or her own body, even so

Christ cares. Christ is our example of *submitting reciprocally* as he does these three things for the church. Christians should care for one another as well. **Heresy alert!** Somehow, in these verses Paul's three-fold emphasis on *Christ's* exemplary, self-sacrificing care for the church is missed! People wrongly focus on the introductory examples Paul uses to supplement his illustrations on *submitting reciprocally*. Focus must be on the main point in each example, on Christ, and not the introductory information in these verses. In each case *Christ's example* is remarkable by contrast in its depth and its completeness.

Three Introductory Ideas	Christ's Example
Wife (and husband) submit reciprocally (21-22, 24)	**As Christ** is savior of the church / his body (23)
Husband loves (25*a*)	**As Christ** gave himself for the church (25*b*-27)
Person cares for body (28, 31)	**As Christ** nourishes and cherishes the church/his body (29-30)

A Detailed Look at Verses 22-31.

One evening, I found myself sitting in the open with the village chief and several villagers looking up at the African night sky. A shooting star blazed across the sky and then burned itself out.

"Ah, someone in that direction will die tonight," one of the villagers pronounced. The chief turned to me under the starlit sky and asked, "What do your people say when you see a fiery streak at night?" I was challenged by his question. I wanted to answer simply and in a way he could verify. I knew he was judging the truth of things I had taught him from the Bible.

Was this a time for complex scientific explanations, or for ridicule of my neighbor's comment? No. It was a time for a simple answer. Since I could not take him with me to investigate the workings of a shooting star burning up as it raced into our atmosphere, I groped for a way to illustrate what had happened.

I began to rub together the palms of my hands in a rapid, noisy manner. I challenged the others to do so as well. "Do you feel that heat?" Yes, we all did. I asked a second question. "Have you ever felt wind against your cheek, even though you could not see what was touching you?" We all had.

"Well," I explained, "the space between us and the fire we saw in the sky is not empty, it is full of air. What we just saw was a rock coming from far away into the air around the earth and rubbing the air. It rubbed through it so fast that it heated up until it burst into flames and then burnt out." The example was simple, but it was enough to begin to explain the truth.

Example #1: *As Christ* **is head of the church, savior of the body**
Paul's first example is simple as well. In Ephesians 5:22-24, Christ's example is the main focus. It is introduced by a Christian wife, in a relationship with her Christian husband, as they are *submitting reciprocally* to-one-another.

However, the way the ideas in these verses are assembled makes it difficult for modern readers to understand what point is being made. These verses are not written in *one, two, three* order, but in the order of a chiasm. In this chiasm, the main idea is in the middle, and it is surrounded by parallel subordinate ideas.

This way of organizing ideas was used both in Hebrew (it could be very long) and in Greek literature (usually much shorter). It made memorizing easier. Since most people were illiterate, memorization of what was read aloud was very important.

In verses 22-24, Christ's example is placed at the center and serves as the main point. The words wrapped around it, point to Christ and his example. A Greek reader would have known the middle of the chiasm was the best part.

5:23b – The middle of the chiasm. The example of Christ's relationship with the church is at the center of these verses. Christ is the best model of this submitting. In it, Paul uses the image of Christ and the church **in one body**.

This imagery was used earlier in Ephesians 3:6 and 4:15-16. In 5:23, the parts of the body, the "head" and the "torso," stand for the single unity of the "body." Jesus and the church, together, make up one spiritual body. Here is another look at the joint-body diagram:

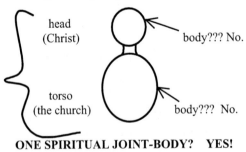

ONE SPIRITUAL JOINT-BODY?   YES!

Familiar "Leadership" Heresies Uncovered   by Bruce C. E. Fleming
www.ThinkAgainAboutTheBible.com

Christ and the church function together as *one spiritual joint-body.* And because all parts of a body work together for the good of the body, Paul is able to point to Christ's relationship with the church as the ideal example of a *reciprocating* one. Christ gives himself for the church, and the church gives itself back to Christ.

This putting of oneself on the level of others, and then serving them, is found in other places in the New Testament. Christ served his disciples by washing their feet (John 13:15). Paul paid his own way making tents while he spread the Gospel in Corinth (Acts 18:3-4).

This attitude is also found in the many *"one another"* passages of the New Testament. Here are several examples:

- "be devoted to *one another*" (Rom 12:10)
- "serve *one another*" (Gal 5:13)
- "carry *one another's* burdens" (Gal 6:2).

Heresy alert. Some people skip over the joint-body imagery in verse 23. They look for something more abstract in Paul's words. Then, they search for a theological meaning to their abstract ideas. They ask questions such as "What does it mean for Christ to be *a head?*" and "What does it mean for a husband to be *a head?*"

We now know the "head" is part of "a whole" body. It means the head forms a unity with whatever forms the other part of the body.

But these searches for "deeper" meanings take place because one, or more, of the basic steps in the interpretation process has not been taken. These are:

1. To interpret a word or phrase, first see if it can be taken *literally.*

2. If the literal sense cannot be the intended sense, then move to the *simplest level* of abstraction.

3. If that sense makes no sense and cannot be the intended sense, then, and only then, consider a *more abstract* level of meaning.

Only after living several years in Central Africa did I begin to see the simplest meaning of Paul's teaching on the spiritual joint-body. This came about as I became familiar with the way my African colleagues, students and friends were used to picturing things.

Many Africans express concepts in a *concrete-relational* way. This is in contrast to the Western way that expresses concepts in a *philosophical* way, such as saying, "There are four principles at work here."

172

For example, the African may use an object to express a concept, as in the following example.

The Bible trees.

- Some people are like a *tree* struck by lightning during a storm. This tree is stripped of its bark and is leafless. It stands stark and bleached in the sun. All who pass know that it is dead.
- Another *tree* looks grand and lush on the outside. But inside it is filled with insects that have turned its core to a soft pulp. This tree is also dead. Even though it looks healthy to others, it will be blown over in the next storm.
- Some people are like a young fruit *tree*. Though this sapling is healthy and strong it needs water and care. If it is not protected from passing animals, they might rub against its trunk and damage its bark. Careless children must be taught that it is too weak to climb. Their weight would be too much and its branches would be broken off.
- The last *tree* is like a giant baobab tree. Its roots go deep. It spreads it branches wide giving shade to a full acre of ground. It did not grow to be this large overnight.

Sinners are like these first two Bible trees. Some are dead and it is obvious for all to see. Others look fine on the outside but inside they are rotten to the core. Bible trees teach us about Christians too. Some new Christians are like the sapling fruit tree. They must be nurtured and cared for in order to grow and be fruitful. Mature Christians are like the giant tree. They prosper even during the harshest season and they help many others by their sheltering care.

In this example, theological lessons are presented using concrete examples, and pointing out the relationship each tree has to a certain type of person.

The simplest abstraction of verse 23. Paul uses concrete-relational words to describe the concept of "the unity of Christ with all believers." In his example, the *literal* use of the word "head" must be ruled out. It makes no sense.

The simplest level of abstraction expressed in a concrete-relational way does make sense! At this concrete level of abstraction, the word "head" stands for "one of two parts that together make up a joint-body." This is the point in 5:23 – Jesus (the "head") and the church (the torso) are united in one body.

In the first part of verse 23, Paul refers to *spouses* who form a *joint-body*. This familiar imagery has been used since the Beginning (Gen 2:24) – a husband and wife form one body. Thus, in Ephesians 5:23, Paul takes the imagery of *unity* in one joint-body, as in the case of a husband and wife, and adds it to *Christ and the church – united* in one *joint-body*.

At the end of verse 23, Paul adds the insight that Christ is "Savior of the body." Christ gave himself up for the church as Savior. He submitted for the rest of the body, the church. In this way, Christ modeled "verse 21 submission."

Resolving the meaning of verse 23 helps us understand the parallel verses on either side of it, verses 22 and 24.

Verse 22. The first thing calling for attention in verse 22 is that in the Greek text *there is no verb*! Here is a transliteration that corresponds to the Greek word order of verse 22 (the brackets show where the verb should be):

> [22] *e.g.* wives [   ] to their own husbands, as to the Lord.

To the Greeks, this was not a problem. In Greek writing, if a verb is omitted, the reader is supposed to look back, find the preceding verb, bring it down and insert it as the "understood" verb in the new sentence.

In this case, the preceding verb is the redefined Christian verb – *submitting reciprocally*. This verb should be brought down to fill the gap in verse 22.

**The uniquely Christian verb of verse 21
is supposed to fill the gap in verse 22.**

Here is verse 22 with the verb from verse 21 properly placed in the gap:

The special reciprocating Christian verb of verse 21 is:

> [21]*Submitting yourselves* (or *reciprocally submitting*) to-one-another
> [Christians to Christians]

> ↓   **This is the intended verb for verse 22**

> [22]Wives (insert verb from above) to your own husbands
> [Christian spouse to Christian spouse]

The result in verse 22 is

> [22]Wives [are] *submitting reciprocally* to your own husbands
> [Christian spouse to Christian spouse]

A pair of unbelieving spouses cannot be expected to behave in this way for they are not filled with the Spirit. However, Ephesians is a letter written to Christians. They are empowered to live this very way, as they carefully "walk" filled with the Spirit of Christ. Married Christian wives and husbands would represent this to-one-another behavior in a one to one equation, in marriage.

Christian husbands are not mentioned specifically in verse 22, but they are included as well, for it takes two to submit *reciprocally*. In verse 24, which mirrors verse 22, Paul mentions *both* husbands and wives.

Thus these three verses exemplify this new Christian way of acting. It is the behavior of believers in Christ who act "as to the Lord" (22), "in everything" (24). Paul's thought in verses 21-24 may be illustrated as follows:

---

[21] Submitting yourselves to one another in the fear of Christ

(A) [22]... e.g. Christian **wives** (*submitting reciprocally*)
to their own Christian husbands
as to the Lord

(B) [23]for a husband is head of the wife [joint-body]
as Christ is head of the church [joint-body]
himself, Savior of the body

(A') [24]as the church is *submitting reciprocally* to Christ,
so Christian **wives** (*submitting reciprocally*)
to their own Christian husbands

Heresy alert! A major problem can be found in English translations of verse 22. Even though the redefined verb of verse 21 should be brought down to fit into the gap in verse 22, many translations instead have inserted a different verb. They insert the unmodified, everyday "vertical" sense of the verb "to subject." Their translations convey none of the meaning of "Christian reciprocity" that Paul so carefully crafted into the verb in verse 21!

The use of the common meaning of "to submit" makes it look as if there is a break in meaning between verse 21 and verse 22. The rest of the passage can then be translated *as if there really were* a shift in meaning from one verse to the next.

Furthermore, publishers often lay out the page putting verse 22 into a new paragraph, so that it seems all the more disconnected from verse 21. This makes it very difficult, if not impossible, for their readers to discern the connection between the redefined verb of verse 21 and the verses that follow!

When the verb is made out to convey the meaning, "submit to someone who is *over* you," this turns the chiasm of verses 22-24 on its head and makes it look as if Paul is writing about the subjection of wives, and the subjection of the church! No wonder people puzzle over many aspects of these verses in English. Translators into other languages make this inexcusable meaning change as well. The mistranslation of the Greek in this text has not gone unnoticed. The French commentator, Alphonse Maillot (*Marie*, p. 142) states flatly that translators change the verb in verse 22 from what is found in verse 21:

'Submitting yourselves' is changed ... to 'you are to be subject' ....

The chiasm of verses 22-24 is a tightly knit unit. If the wrong sense of the verb is inserted into verse 22, it distorts the meaning of all three verses!

Since verses 22 and following are all "for example" verses, commentator Marcus Barth (*Ephesians 4-6*, p. 610) has suggested beginning verse 22 in a way that clearly shows its "for example" connection with verse 21. He uses *e.g.*

"...[e.g.] wives to your husbands."

Barth explained what goes wrong when this verse is translated incorrectly:

... translations obfuscate the fact that a wife's subordination to her husband is commanded only within the frame of mutual subordination; they support masculine superiority complexes that are supposedly grounded in Pauline ethics.

Wrong "head." Matters become further complicated, when an extremely abstract meaning of the word "head" in verse 23 is sought. If one bypasses the simple meaning used in the "head/torso metaphor," any number of meanings can be inserted.

One can inject foreign ideas into the text, such as the military and corporate meaning of "head-as-leader." Many people commonly assume that this passage teaches that "a husband is the leader in marriage." But this passage does not teach that. If Christ were "head" of the church in that way, one would expect Paul to have said in verse 23 that Christ was "*Lord over* the church." But Paul said Christ was "*Savior* of the *body.*"

**Many people wrongly assume this passage teaches
"a husband is the leader in marriage."
Instead, a husband and wife are *submitting reciprocally.***

Example #2: *As Christ* **gave himself for the church**

Ephesians 5:25-27 focuses on the example of Christ's love for the church, introduced by an earthly example:

25*a*   Husbands commanded to *love* their wives

25*b*-27   Christ's love for the church (described at length)

In verse 25*a*, Paul introduces Christ's example with another example from everyday life. Apart from the first five Greek words in this section, the rest are dedicated to describing Christ's self-sacrificing love for the church.

> **Apart from the first five Greek words in this section,**
> **the rest are dedicated to describing**
> **Christ's self-sacrificing love for the church.**

In verse 25*a*, Paul uses an imperative verb, "Husbands, *love* your wives!" This is not the only imperative verb in the passage. As already noted, the passage began in 5:15 with a string of imperative verbs. But Paul, in passing, takes the occasion to stress to husbands the depth with which they must love their wives. They must love their wives with God's own pure love.

The details, in this second example about Christ's love, come after the first five words. In 25*b* Paul writes,

"Christ loved the church and gave himself up for it."

Then, in verses 26-27, Paul adds three Greek *hina* clauses (*hina* means "in-order-that"). These three clauses focus on the impact of Jesus' self-sacrificing love on the church. This is always true of selfless submission. It focuses on the one being served, not on the one doing the serving.

> **Self-sacrificing love involves selfless submission.**
> **It focuses on the one being served, not on the one doing the serving.**

In three ways, Christ's loving care makes the church better:

"In order that"
- he might sanctify it, cleansing it ... (26)
- he might present ... the church glorious (27*a*)
- it might be holy and unblemished (27*b*)

A three-fold repetition is a Hebrew way of showing emphasis. By using three *hina* clauses, Paul, the former Pharisee and Jewish scholar, emphasizes the complete and full result Christ's love has on the church.

(Paul also uses a three-fold repetition in regards to husbands. Three times, he tells husbands to love their wives in an *agape* self-sacrificing way, in verses 25*a*, 28, and 31.)

Christ demonstrated his *agape* love for the church when he "gave himself" for it. To behave *like Christ* does not mean to "lord it over" or "be king over." His *agape* love was shown in seeking the best for the church.

Heresy alert! Those who think that *marriage*, not Christ, is the main topic of these verses have difficulty dealing with verse 27. The verse makes good sense as a description of Christ's example. But how can one apply this verse to marriage?

Husbands are not told to enter the skin care business to deal with their wives' literal "spots," "wrinkles" and "blemishes." But Christ, himself the perfect and spotless sacrifice, did give himself for the church in order to make her a perfect offering fit for a king – Christ himself!

The example of Christ's love for the church, not of a husband's love for his wife, is described in verses 25*b*-27. Christ's love is another lesson on how "to submit" in the Christian way of verse 21.

Example #3: *As Christ* cares for his body

In Ephesians 5:28-31, Paul organizes his thoughts into another chiasm. Here too, as in the first ABA' chiasm (22-24), Paul's readers would have been in a hurry to get to the center of this chiasm to see the best part.

The center of this chiasm is found in verses 29-30. Here Paul uses a different type of parallelism. It is the familiar two-line parallelism that is so often found in Proverbs.

In Proverbs, the idea in one line is repeated in a second line. In the second line the idea is usually worded differently. The second line typically adds depth to the first line. In this case Paul writes parallel lines about a person's love for his own body.

Everyone understands this kind of love. It is a natural and dependable kind of love. Paul began verse 29*b* with the Greek words "... just as Christ." Here at the center of the chiasm, Paul points to Christ, the supreme example.

In a startling theological declaration he draws a parallel between the care
one provides for the body with Christ's love for the church. In doing so, Paul
leaves no room for doubt about the steadfast love Christ has for the church.
In verse 30, Paul puts into words the rest of the startling truth, "because *we*
are members of his body." No Christian who understands the deity of Christ and
the power of God can ever again harbor an inferiority complex after realizing
the amazing position gained by a believer in Christ. Christ would no sooner
cease to love and care for any member of the church than a person would cease
to love and care for any part of his or her own body! Furthermore, this natural
sort of care, elevated to the level of agape love, is for believers to practice on
their own level, to-one-another.

Just in case someone doubted whether this kind of close knittedness could
ever be lived out on the human level, Paul repeats the first idea in his chiasm.
The best example humans have of such intimate care is in marriage.

Marriage defined. Paul returns to the Garden of Eden to find a biblical
reference to marriage. To those who knew their Bible well, this reference to
Genesis 2:24 brought to mind three levels of commitment.

First, the marriage commitment surpasses all family ties – the man "leaves."
Similarly, the believer "leaves" father and mother and transfers primary
allegiance to Christ.

Second, the unity of marriage is one of the heart and mind. This unity was
indicated by the second verb in Genesis 2:24, "to cleave." This same verb was
used to describe Ruth in the Old Testament who "cleaved" to Naomi. Ruth made
a ringing confession of such a close-knittedness: "Your people shall be my
people, and your God, my God" (Ruth 1:16). The Christian is knitted together
with other believers. The Spirit in each Christian testifies to the Spirit in every
other believer that all are one in Christ (Romans 8:15-17).

Third, as a husband and wife unite intimately as one flesh and heart, so new
believers in Christ are united with all other believers in the body of Christ.

The chiastic parallel of verses 28-31 can be illustrated as follows:

Eph 5:28-31: a mirror passage on love for the body

(A)   [28]so ought Christian husbands to love (*agape*)
their own Christian wives
the one who loves **himself**, loves **his wife**

(B) [29a]no man hates **his flesh**/but cares for it
[29b]just **as Christ** the church [30]we are members of **his body**

(A')   [31]for this reason
a man shall leave his father and mother
and will be united (cleave) to his wife
and the two will become **one flesh**

Somehow, many people still picture Christ as separate from the church, disembodied in some way. But according to verse 30 the opposite is true, "for we are members of his body." Christ is not pictured as standing beside the church. Christ and the church form one body.

Many picture Christ as disembodied from the church.
But the opposite is true, "for we are members of his body."
Christ does not stand *beside* the church. He and the church form *one* body.

This unity of believers in one body with Christ, is the main idea illustrated in the three examples of Ephesians 5:22-31. This is the foundation for walking in the Spirit, *submitting reciprocally* to-one-another.

In verse 32, Paul confirms this in an "all of the above" statement. What was once a mystery, formerly unknown, has been clarified by verses 22-31.

All of the above. In verse 32 Paul writes,

This is a profound mystery, that I have revealed,
about Christ and the church.

Although many claim that the last half of Ephesians 5 is not about the church but is all about marriage, the clear summary statement of verse 32 should redirect them onto the right track. Ephesians 5:22-31 is about believers caring for one another, *submitting reciprocally*, in the church of Christ.

To Paul, this life was akin to life before the Fall in Genesis 3. His three introductions reveal he has the events of Genesis 2 on his mind. In Genesis 2 God made the man's body from the dust. He breathed life into his nostrils and he became a living soul. All was not good until God created woman and the husband and wife walked with God. No wonder Paul quotes from Genesis 2 in Ephesians 5.

What do we regain from Genesis in the church?

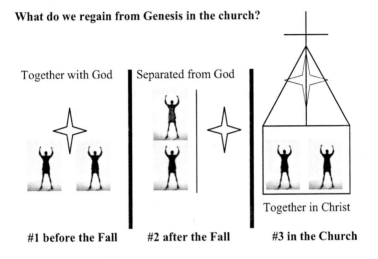

Together with God   Separated from God

Together in Christ

#1 before the Fall   #2 after the Fall   #3 in the Church

Heresy alert! While some people focus their attention on the word "head," Paul focused instead on the concept of the "body." As early as Ephesians 1:22-23, Paul referred to the church as "the *body* of Christ."

Some commentators confuse other metaphors used in Ephesians. In Ephesians 1:20-23, Paul said that Christ was raised from the dead by God to sit at God's right hand. Jesus was far above and over all things. In these same verses Paul also said that Jesus and the church were related to each other, as a head and body. There is nothing said about this head being "over" this body in some way.

But some assert that Christ is "over" the church, and that the church is just one of the things over which Christ towers. Paul did not teach this in Ephesians! As we have seen, to attribute such a meaning to "head" requires moving to an unnecessary level of abstraction for the word "head" (*cf.* Zerwick and Grosvenor, *Grammatical Analysis*, p. 580).

Parallel imagery. Paul also used the word "head" in Colossians 2:10, in an extended series of verses. Some people think he used the word differently there from in Ephesians. But in Colossians the ideas are the same. Appended to the "head" are "fullness" (verse 9, compare Eph 1:23) and "completeness" (verse 10). These ideas round out the image of "body"

In Colossians 2:12-13, Paul listed a remarkable series of descriptors about Christ. These applied *with him* to members in the church! Christians are,

> "*co*-buried with him" (verse 12)
> "*co*-raised" (verse 12)
> "*co*-quickened with him" (verse 13).

In Colossians 2, Paul did not view the church *apart from* Christ. He incorporated the church *along with* Christ, in all of Christ's spiritual triumphs and honor. As in Ephesians, Paul stressed wholeness in the united functioning of the parts of the body.

Thus, for Paul, the body was made up of *both* Christ *and* the church. In speaking of "the body of Christ," the body and the head are intimately connected and inseparable in Paul's theology.

Heresy alert! Many have called this part of Ephesians 5, "the longest single passage in the Bible on marriage." This is incorrect! 1 Corinthians 7 wins this title in the New Testament. In the Old Testament it is Genesis 2. Ephesians 5:21-6:9 is the longest passage in the Bible on walking in the Spirit with other Christians in mutual Christlike submission.

There are many teachings on marriage that incorrectly claim to be biblically based. For example, "To love, honor and obey," is an old and familiar phrase. But, it is not a biblically correct statement. It is correct to say that a child is to obey a parent, a servant is to obey a master, and a person is to obey God. But wives are *not* told "to obey" their husbands.

"To obey" dates back to the Catholic notion that a woman remained a minor "child" and never reached "majority" during her lifetime. As a "child," she could neither own land nor make important decisions. When she was little, the female child was under the tutelage of a male guardian. When grown, she was "given away" to her husband who legally became her new guardian whom she was bound to obey as a child obeys an adult. This is still the official teaching of Roman Catholic dogma.

Sadly, this teaching was not corrected. Partly this was due to the Reformation theologians' faulty view of Creation and the Fall:

- They incorrectly thought woman was a secondary creation, even though when *she* was created all was finally "very good."

- They wrongly thought *she* was the temptress. Somehow, at the same time, they despised her as disposed to being more easily tempted – even though she never sinned on purpose but only after being deceived by the real Tempter.

- They falsely thought she was cursed (the Jewish *Babylonian Talmud* taught she was "cursed ten-times over"). But in Genesis 3, neither the man nor the woman was cursed. The word "curse" was used only in relation to the serpent and the soil.

- They incorrectly thought God subjugated her to be ruled by the man – whereas instead God praised her for her continuing love and warned her of the fallen man's intent to rule over her.

Reformation theologians could have returned to the Bible and found that from Creation, both were adults, designed and installed to rule the earth:

- Both were responsible to God.
- Both became mortal as a result of sin and died.
- Each was called on to believe anew in God's promised salvation.

The 2ⁿᵈ three-part illustration – at Home (5:33-6:9)

As Paul's readers digested what he had just written in verses 22-31, they were coming to an understanding that Christ was the perfect example of *submitting reciprocally.* Christians in the church were to be *submitting reciprocally* one to another in the fear of Christ, verse 32. But was it possible to practice this behavior away from church, in the home?

In 5:33-6:9, Paul touches on every aspect of typical home life. *Submitting reciprocally* was exactly how a Christian carefully walking in the Spirit was to behave at home! Paul considers the three basic relationships that could occur in a household of believers. He discusses each category in turn:

1. married adults (5:33)

2. children and parents (6:1-4)

3. servants and masters (6:5-9)

It is important to remember that Paul wrote this section on "walking" carefully in the Spirit hundreds of years before chapter breaks and verse numbers were added to his writings. There were no chapter and verse breaks when Paul wrote Ephesians.

Paul subdivided his own writing by placing verse 32 in between his two sets of examples. The first set of examples (5:22-31) and the second set of examples (5:33-6:9) both had to do with "Christ and the church" (5:32). And all pointed back to 5:21. Ideally, chapter 6 should not start until the end of verse 9, at the end of this entire "walking" section.

To reconnect with verse 21, Paul uses the word "fear" in 5:33 at the start of his second three-part illustration. This is the word that was left hanging when Paul inserted his first three examples on how to live as Christians who are *submitting reciprocally.*

To reconnect with verse 21, Paul uses the word "fear" in 5:33 at the start of his second three-part illustration.

The word "fear" ties together all three pairs of relationships in 5:33-6:9. In verse 33, Paul uses the Greek word "fear" (or "reverence") in reference to husbands and wives. In 6:1-4, an implied reference to "fear" is present in the verses that are addressed to parents and children. (According to Leviticus 19:3, children were to "fear" their parents). Lastly, "fear" is part of the servant-master relationship (6:5).

Verse 33 deals with the example of believing adults united in marriage. Theirs is a reciprocal relationship.

The other two examples are different. In 6:1-4 and 5-9, Paul focuses on relationships in which the individuals were temporarily in a position of inequality – as child and parent, and as servant and master.

With the passage of time children grow up, and at some point in time a servant may be set free. At that point the reciprocity in their relationships may become totally unhindered. Yet, in these last two pairings, *submitting reciprocally* among believers could be practiced even when social structures dictated they should be unequal.

Submission by the members of the Christian household:

1. **Spouses** treat one another as mature believers (5:33)

2. **Children** are exhorted to obey "in the Lord" (6:1-3)
   Parents are to act in a balanced way in the Lord (6:4)

3. **Servants** are urged to obey "from the heart" (6:5-8)
   Masters are to act in the same way (6:9)

It is helpful at this point to review an important rule in studying the Bible: "For detailed answers go to the most detailed passage."

For example, a person may learn some details about life in the early church by reading the words addressed to the seven churches of Asia Minor in Revelation 2-3. But many more details can be learned about the early church by reading the 28 chapters of the Book of Acts.

In the same way, there are many passages in the Bible that contain a reference to "love." But the most detailed description of love is found in 1 Corinthians 13. To learn about love in detail, 1 Corinthians 13 is the best passage to consult. After informing oneself from the verses in 1 Corinthians 13, a person can turn to other passages on love for additional details.

The verses in Ephesians 5:33-6:9 are more detailed than the parallel passage in Colossians 3:18-4:1. Barth (*Ephesians*, p. 609) pointed out that "only the Ephesian version opens with a call to mutual subordination." Therefore, it is important first to study the detailed verses in Ephesians. Keeping them in mind, one can then turn to the passage in Colossians for a summary of the more detailed version.

One illustration ends; a new one starts.

In English, verse 33 seems awkward. This perceived awkwardness disappears when one keeps in mind that verse 33 is a direct continuation of verse 21, even though verses 21 and 33 are separated by a long digression in thought.

The perceived awkwardness in verse 33 is mostly a problem for modern readers. This is because English is a much more rigid language than Greek (Weir, *Greek Grammar*, p. 672). Weir describes how an intervening parenthetical statement (or anacolouthon), as verses 22-32, doesn't disturb a developing flow of thought in Greek.

Anacolouthon is caused… by the intrusion of some explanation requiring a parenthesis of such an extent that the connection is obscured or the continuation of the original structure made difficult. In this case the beginning may be repeated, or what has already been said may be summed up in a different grammatical form….

In verse 33, Paul picks up the thought of verse 21 and illustrats it with an example from the household about spouses. This is the first in his next series of examples. He signals that there is a connection with verse 21 by beginning verse 33 with the Greek word "nevertheless" and ending with "fear."

Marcus Barth was concerned that modern translations give a false impression to readers because they make verse 33 look more like a reference to verse 22 with its incorrect meaning of "to submit" (pp. 608-610, 648). He saw an additional grammatical reason why translations should point to verse 21:

[All] are called to the "fear" [or reverence] of Christ (5:21). Such resumption of a motif from the beginning of a hymn or discourse has been called a ring-composition or an *inclusio*.

The new element Paul introduces in verses 5:33-6:9 is that of *submitting reciprocally* in a Christian household. This was important for Paul to address because readers of ancient literature were used to asking, "How does this apply to life in the household?"

A number of lists on "how to" organize a household were in circulation. They reflected the value systems of the religions of the day and were called "domestic codes" (or *Haustafeln*, in German).

Paul met his readers' expectations by providing them with something like a domestic code of his own, except that he modifies the typical literary forms and their content to fit his own needs. This has frustrated a number of scholars who have tried to squeeze this section of Ephesians into one or another outline typical of ancient domestic codes.

A close study of these codes shows that Paul breaks *almost every rule* in the existing patterns. He reverses the usual order in the way he names the members of the family and he advises them to relate to one another in ways that are quite revolutionary when compared to the established patterns of his day. Here, once again, Paul takes what was at hand and turns it to his purposes as he describes the new Christian way of life.

Verse 5:33. What about Christian spouses? Verse 33 applies *submitting reciprocally* to the Christian couple. If every Christian is supposed to love every other Christian in the body of Christ out of "respect" (or "fear") for Christ, then certainly two Christians, married to each other, should treat each other in this new way within their marriage.

Of all relationships found within the church, Ephesians 5:21 is to be lived out first and foremost between Christian spouses. They can be excellent models of *submitting reciprocally* (they had already been used as models along with Christ in 5:22-31).

By living carefully together in the Spirit and *submitting reciprocally* to one another, the Christian wife "respects" her husband and the Christian husband "loves" his wife with *agape* love. Thus, in verse 33, Paul picks up the thoughts from verse 21 and applies it to spouses at home. In this way a Christian couple puts into practice the Prophet's observation (Amos 3:3): "for two persons to walk together they must be agreed."

Verses 6:1-9. Christians in unequal positions. Starting with Ephesians 6:1, temporal distinctions enter the picture. For Paul, there are relationships within a Christian household where obedience is appropriate: child/parent and slave/master.

These unequal relationships can be limited in duration. They exist only as long as the child is obligated to obey, and only as long as the servant (or slave) is obligated to serve. In some cases a servant was freed from service after seven years. In other cases, the slave might be set free by the master at any time (*cf.* Philemon 1:1-25).

"Obedience" was not an element of the illustrations mentioned in Ephesians 5:22-31. It was not required of one Christian to another, nor was it required of one spouse to the other. The word "submission" was not used as a synonym for "obedience" in any way.

According to Ephesians 4, all believers exercise their gifts for the good of the body. No hierarchy is present and no obedience is required, except to God and his word. Those who would be great must become servants of all.

Some people, who have strayed into the interpretative dead ends already mentioned, have thought there is a hierarchy among believers, between spouses, or both. Nothing could be farther from the Biblical truth in these passages.

Children and parents. In Ephesians 6:1-3, Paul exhorts children to obey their parents. In verse 4, he addresses their parents. His comments apply to individuals living in a *Christian* household. Paul specifies this in verse 1 and 4 by adding the words, "in the Lord" and "of the Lord."

In verses 1-3, four reasons are given for children to be obedient. Paul makes his appeal in terms that are appropriate to children who already know the Lord. The four reasons are instructive and encouraging. Children are to obey because:

- They are "in the Lord"
- They are expected to do what is "right"
- They have a "commandment" of God
- They are given a "promise"

In verses 2-3, Paul quotes the Fifth Commandment of Deuteronomy 5:16: "Children, obey your parents in the Lord, for this is right." To this familiar commandment, the Jewish mind was trained to associate the parallel statement in Leviticus 19:3, "Ye shall *fear* every man his mother and his father ..." (KJV). The phrase "in the Lord" is reminiscent of Ephesians 5:21. And the idea of "fearing" also refers back to 5:21. Thus, believing children actively and fully enjoy all the rights and privileges of *reciprocally submitting* members of the body of Christ.

Christian children are, nevertheless, called on to obey. Obedience to parents is not something taken lightly by Paul.

J. A. Robinson (*Ephesians*, p. 177) noted:

> In characterizing the Gentiles of whom he thrice says that 'God gave them up', the Apostle notes among other signs of their depravity that they were 'disobedient to parents' (Rom 1:30). Similarly the evil men of 'the last days' are described as 'disobedient to parents' and 'without natural affection' (2 Tim 3:2).

In verse 4, Paul turns from Christian children to their Christian parents. The Greek word he uses to refer to them is *pateres*, a word frequently translated as "fathers" in English Bibles. However, *pateres* should be translated "parents." It is like the biblical term "brothers" which Paul frequently uses to include all Christians of *both* genders.

The Greek word *pateres* in 6:4 should be translated "parents."
It is like the biblical term "brothers" which Paul frequently uses to include all Christians of *both* genders.

In old English, one could say "brethren" and everyone knew it meant "brothers and sisters." If there were such a word, the word in verse 4 would be the equivalent of "fathren" – meaning both "mothers and fathers." Confusion can easily be avoided by simply translating the term into English as "parents."

188

In Ephesians 6:1-2, *both* parents are specifically named. In the reference to Leviticus 19:3, mothers *and* fathers are both mentioned. Mothers are mentioned first. There is no preferential treatment given to fathers by Paul in Ephesians 6:4, as if in some special way he is writing to them to the exclusion of mothers. The Greek word for "parents" used in Ephesians 6:4 is the same Greek word used in Hebrews 11:23. There, it designates the "parents" of Moses who hid him for three months.

In his commentary on Ephesians, F. F. Bruce (Revell, p. 122) held that Ephesians 6:4 denoted not just fathers, but both parents. He pointed out how this fit with the parallel passage in Colossians 3:20-21.

In a similar way, Paul often referred to all believers, both male and female, as "brothers." Galatians 1:2, is an example of this.

Thus, in verse 4, Paul forbids both Christian parents from "embittering" or "provoking to wrath" their children. Both parents are to be respectful in their dealings with their children. In Christ, their children are members together with them in the same spiritual joint-body.

Similarly, according to the Greek of verse 4, both parents are responsible for their children, to "nurture them in the discipline and admonition of the Lord." "Nurturing" is an important responsibility. The verb, "to nurture," is used only one other time in the New Testament, Ephesians 5:29. There it means "to nourish," as in "to nourish and cherish one's own flesh, as Christ does the church."

Paul teaches that nurturing children includes both "discipline" and "admonition." "Discipline" is a general term and means "discipline in general" (as used in 2 Timothy 3:16, and Hebrews 12:5). "Admonition" means "special admonition" as in Titus 3:10. The NIV translates this into English as "the training and instruction of the Lord."

Thus, honorable parents, worthy of obedience, are to model righteous and measured living. Both the mother and the father are to instruct their children in biblical doctrines, clarifying for their children the motivation behind their acts as parents. In this way their children will come to know that the loving care and discipline they receive from their parents is the outflow of the will of their loving God, who inspired the commandments they and their parents are putting into practice.

Servants and masters. In the household of Paul's day, often there were many servants. It has been estimated that in some of the cities and towns where Paul preached up to 80 per cent of the population was either enslaved or worked as servants. What word does Paul have for these Christians? What equivalent truth does he have for modern workers?

In verses 5-9, Paul illustrates how, even in the context of the obedience required in the servant-master relationship, *submitting reciprocally* can still be practiced in everyday life, especially in the context of Christian households. In verse 5, Paul again uses the words "fear" and "as to Christ," reminding readers of the connection with 5:21. Paul cautions servants against serving only when someone is watching.

In life, the distinction made between servants and masters is not a spiritual distinction. It is only a social and a temporary one. Paul exhorts servants to be thoroughly Christian in all they did (verse 5). They are to work "as servants of Christ" (verse 6) and serve "as to the Lord" (verse 7) because their ultimate master is the Lord (verse 8).

It is from the Lord that payment would come. In this way, vertical relationships of servants with their earthly masters are overlaid with the priority of spiritual relationships. This being the case, Paul makes a bold application to Christian masters in verse 9. He tells them to act as do their servants!

In addition, they are to hold themselves back from threatening, remembering that they too share a master in heaven. Their heavenly master is no respecter of person or rank.

Completing the "walk." In sum, according to the two three-part strings of illustrations that Paul uses to explain the meaning of Christian submission in Ephesians 5:21, "walking circumspectly in the Spirit" means every believer is to be *submitting reciprocally* to all other members in the body of Christ. Christ sets the example for us to follow.

This kind of behavior is possible in church and at home. Each one is to practice this reciprocal submitting to other believers at church. And where the case applies, each Christian is to practice this reciprocal submitting to others in the household, whether as spouses, as children and parents, and even as servants and masters.

What this passage does *not* say

In Ephesians 5:15-6:9, Paul explains how to walk carefully in the Spirit of Christ. In verses 15 through 21 he sums up in broad strokes how this happens. In verses 21 through 32, he gives three examples from Christ on how to practice *submitting reciprocally* in the church. In 5:33-6:9, he gives three more examples based on life within the household unit.

This passage, from 5:15-6:9, does not center around the question, "Is the man the 'head' of the woman?" It does not teach, "The man is 'head' of the house."

No part of this passage teaches that a husband is held ultimately responsible for the spiritual health of a wife. Nor does it teach that a father is more responsible than a mother for the upbringing of their children. Such ideas are "leadership" heresies based on misunderstandings of the passage.

This entire passage is about *walking carefully as Christians filled with the Spirit*. From verse 21 on this passage is *not* primarily about marriage. Being a married member of a human family is subordinate to being a member of Christ's one-another spiritual family.

An individual may know Christ yet never marry. Or, an individual might know Christ before marrying, during marriage, and even after the death of a spouse. Through it all, a person's relationship to Christ is the most important one of all.

Ephesians 5:15-6:9 (three translation elements outlined)

Key Verse 5:21 "Submitting yourselves one to another
in the fear of Christ"

Paul redefines the ordinary verb "to submit"
He makes the verb reflexive—*submitting yourselves*
He adds a reciprocal pronoun—*to one another*
He adds the unique phrase—in the *fear of Christ*.

Members of the Christian church.
First part of 2-part illustration:

1. **Christ's example** - context of submissive spouses
2. **Christ's example** - context of husbands and wives
3. **Christ's example** - context of care given to one's body

Hinge Verse and Interpretive Key (5:32)
"I am talking about Christ and the church"

Members of the Christian household.
Second part of 2-part illustration:

1. **Christian spouses** treat each other as mature believers.
2. **Children** are exhorted to "obey." Parents to act "in the Lord."
3. **Slaves** urged to "obey." Masters to be mindful of their Lord.

Ephesians 5:22-24: a mirror passage (main point is in center)

(A) v. 22... e.g. wives (*submitting reciprocally*) to their own Christian husbands
as to the Lord

(B) v. 23   for a husband is head of the wife (as one)
as Christ is head of the church (as one)
himself, Savior **of the body**

(A') v. 24   as the church is *submitting reciprocally*
so are Christian wives and husbands

Think again!

It is helpful to pause and think again. If it turns out that the Bible does not support a certain theological point, then it can safely be relegated to the filing drawer of "human opinion only." Erroneous human opinion elevated to the authority of God-breathed Truth (2 Timothy 3:16) can do great harm.

Familiar "Leadership" Heresies Uncovered   by Bruce C. E. Fleming
www.ThinkAgainAboutTheBible.com

PART III:

The "Legalist" Heresies

Chapter 6

"Leadership" Heresies and Authority in Church
… an inside look at 1 Corinthians 11:2-16 (with a focus on verse 10)

Chapter Contents:

Familiar "Leadership" Heresies Uncovered   by Bruce C. E. Fleming
www.ThinkAgainAboutTheBible.com

1 Corinthians 11:2-16 (paraphrase in outline form)

Introduction and praise [2]Now I praise you, brothers and sisters, that you remember me in all things and keep the traditions just as I delivered them to you

Principle of unity established

> [3]I want you to know that the head of every man is Christ
> > the head of a wife is a husband,
> > > the head of Christ is God.

Quotation of legalists in Corinth

> [4]"Every man who prays or prophesies with his head covered dishonors his head.
> [5]"But every woman who prays or prophesies with her head uncovered dishonors her head – it is the same as having her head shaved. [6]For if a woman does not cover her head, she might as well have her hair cut off; but if it is a disgrace for a woman to have her hair cut off or her head shaved, then she should cover her head."

Paul corrects their incomplete view

> [7]Indeed a man ought not to cover his head,
> > since he is the image and glory of God;
> and a woman is the glory of man.
> [8]For man did not come from woman, but woman from man
> [9]neither was man created for woman, but woman for man.

Application for Christian women

[10]Therefore, a woman has authority over her own head, as she will over angels.

Theological basis for unity

> [11]Nevertheless, neither is man independent of woman,
> > nor woman independent of man,
> > > in the Lord.
> [12]For, as woman came from man,
> > even so man also comes through woman;
> > > but all things come from God.

Appeal to non-Jewish Christians

> [13]Among yourselves judge this. It is proper for a woman to pray to God with her head uncovered.
> [14]Not even Nature itself teaches you that a man is dishonored by long hair, [15]nor if a woman wears her hair long it is her glory because long hair has been given to her instead of a covering.

Conclusion [16]But if anyone wants to be contentious, we have no such custom, nor do the churches of God.

198

Introduction.

"Why must women sit only on the left side of the church with the men on the right? Is there a verse in the Bible that we follow when we do that?"

"I can't think of any verse," he replied after a few moments' reflection. "But we've always done it that way." Then, President Mopepe smiled.

I was a new missionary, visiting with the African church president in his office. It was a friendly, but serious conversation. Neither of us was joking. I was being oriented to the work in his denomination and had noticed this seating pattern. Thus, the question. And his answer.

I smiled back.

When most people first hear someone explain 1 Corinthians 11:10, they usually have to smile and respond in the same way. In verse 10, it is clear that Paul is saying something about women. But to most people this verse doesn't make sense.

This interpretation of this passage in 1 Corinthians 11 has a direct impact on more than half of all the people in church – women. Verse 10 should make sense, but the explanations of it are contradictory and difficult to understand.

What is Paul saying? Did this verse originally make sense?

There are other "difficult" verses in this passage. Will applying the Seven *Think Again* Bible Study Steps help us out of the confusion?

Step 1. *Think Again* about what the Bible says. Step 2. *Think Again* about the context of your passage. Step 3. *Think Again* about the content of your passage. Step 4. *Think Again* about the key image and/or idea. Step 5. *Think Again* about the target verse(s). Step 6. *Think Again* about the points of application. Step 7. *Think Again* about what the Bible does *not* say.

Yes! And coming to understand Paul's interaction with the Corinthians throughout the letter will build up all who read, understand and practice what he advises in 1 Corinthians 11:2-16.

A Church in a Seaport City

The city of Corinth was a port city, filled with sailors from many nations on shore leave. They came to town for provisions and a "good time." It was a bustling center of activity.

There was a large market and the trappings of commerce. There were many pagan temples. And there was a synagogue. In this city, Paul founded a church.

At this point in his second missionary journey, Paul had gone on ahead of his missionary team (Acts 18) and was alone when he first arrived in Corinth. While waiting for Timothy and the others, he set up business as a tentmaker along with two other tentmakers he met. These two were a Jewish married couple, recently expelled from Rome by the Emperor Claudius along with all the other Jews in the capital. Their names were Priscilla and Aquila.

Together with Paul they attended the synagogue in town. The locals in the synagogue invited Paul to lead them during teaching times because he was a well-trained Pharisee, a student of Gamaliel, the greatest Rabbi of that day.

From Paul, they heard the good news of salvation through grace by faith in Christ. Many Jews believed! Others, known as God-fearers, who were non-Jewish attendees at the synagogue, also believed. Soon a number of believers in Christ, both Jews and non-Jews, were meeting together in Corinth.

A number of believers in Christ, both Jews *and* non-Jews, were meeting together in Corinth.

The other members of Paul's ministry team finally arrived and took over his other duties. This freed Paul to minister full-time. Perhaps the increased frequency of Paul's teaching grated on the hard-line Jewish legalists in the synagogue who had not yet believed in Christ. They actively opposed Paul.

After warning them of the consequences of their unbelief, Paul left them to their legalism and moved his lessons out of the synagogue and into the building next door. There, he kept on teaching. Sad to say, some of the new believers also tended toward legalism.

As time passed, more and more people spent their time next door where Paul was teaching. The church grew day by day. It was filled with Jews and non-Jews, some who had a deep knowledge of the Old Testament, and some who had none. Some had been believers longer and had progressed faster. Others were beginners in Christ. Eventually Paul moved on to other cities. After he left, he wrote the church with more advice.

Paul learned how they received that advice when visitors from Corinth brought him news (1 Co 1:11). He learned more through a letter he received from Corinth (1 Co 7:1). This news prompts Paul as he writes much of 1 Corinthians.

The letter is co-signed by Sosthenes, likely the converted ruler of the synagogue at Corinth. This letter is unlike any other in the New Testament, as

point-by-point Paul responds to the news and questions received from his
spiritual children in Christ in Corinth.

Band camp. When I began my years in high school, I signed up to play in
the marching band. A week before school began, every band member attended
band camp. There I encountered the "torture pits."

The Band Director strung thin kite string across a portion of the marching
field in parallel rows, at eighteen-inch intervals and eight inches high. This
height taught us to step high and keep our toes pointed down as we marched
down the field.

Each string was stretched taut as a wire. In groups of four we marched
briskly through the strings. If anyone's toe touched a string it would snap and all
four of us would have to march through it again until we got it right.

It was hard enough to march and blow into my mouthpiece at the same
time! Doing all that, while marching four in a row, was torture for the first year
band members. The Director taught us a whole new way of playing, along with a
whole new way of stepping high.

On Wednesday at camp, the Director added marching in formation. We
marched backwards in a line. We criss-crossed in lines, threading between
groups moving in different directions. No one person could see "the why" of our
motions because the large formations were only visible to the Director from high
in his platform.

Through it all, we were worked into a great marching band! The pageantry
was grand, our ranks were precise and our music was stirring. As year followed
year, the veterans marched through the pits with relative ease. But the new
students always struggled.

In a way, Paul was the Director for the new band of Christians in Corinth.
1 Corinthians was his letter to his spiritual band members. In his letter known as
1 Corinthians, he responded to proposals that came from factions among the
believers.

On some points he commended them for their behavior and their proposals.
On other points he reasoned with them and corrected them.

Sadly, across the centuries, the reasons behind some of these statements
have dimmed. Paul didn't need to spell out all the details to his first readers who
knew these situations well. Thus, modern readers must try to reconstruct the
situation from what we know of Paul and Corinth.

Praise for Proper Practice (11:2-16)

²**Now I praise you**, brothers and sisters, that you remember me in all things and keep the traditions just as I delivered them to you. ...

¹⁰Therefore, a woman should have authority over her own head ...

¹⁶But if anyone thinks of being contentious, we have no other custom, nor do the churches of God.

¹⁷**Now I do not praise you** in giving these next instructions since you come together not for the better but for the worse. ...

After Paul moved on in his missionary journeys, the church he had founded in Corinth continued the practices he had taught them. They followed what he had taught them about women and men ministering to the congregation. God raised up both women and men to lead the congregation in worship and to teach God's Word.

Apparently there were grumblers who tried to restrict some people from leading the group. They wanted their old religious traditions to be followed and grew contentious about it. But the rest of the congregation maintained the course on which Paul had set them and earned his praise for this.

Paul wanted them to continue what they had started together in Corinth. In every church he started, this was the way he wanted the believers to worship and teach.

Incomplete or incorrect? Paul learned from the visitors from Corinth (1:11) that the church had developed four distinct factions. Some people purported to be "of Paul," others "of Peter," and still others "of Apollos" or "of Jesus."

In spite of all this, Paul was still their unquestioned spiritual parent, the one who first planted their church. Divisions of opinion had arisen among them on practical issues dealing with marriage (7:1) and idolatry (8:1; 10:14). Some wanted the church to follow the rules and regulations found in the Jewish oral law (14:34-35).

In 1 Corinthians 11:2-16, Paul addresses those in the church at Corinth who wanted to limit the ways women were participating in ministry. Had Paul really meant that women should pray and prophesy along with men? Shouldn't the women have to submit to some extra regulations? Jewish tradition overflowed with restrictions on women. Shouldn't women have to follow these too?

In verses 2-16, Paul affirms that women are full members of the body of Christ and are fully gifted by the Holy Spirit to minister in the name of Jesus. Paul appeals to Genesis, and to reason, to restate his case. He is firm. There is no room for dissension on this point of doctrine and practice.

Five keys to understanding. A number of people find 1 Corinthians 11:2-16 difficult to understand. Whenever a passage seems difficult, it is important to look at the surrounding context of the passage to see if some tips to its meaning may be found. In this case, the *immediate context* will give us two helpful keys to unlocking the meaning of the passage: **praise** (key #1), and Paul's **three-fold focus** (key #2).

To unlock the meaning of a passage it is also helpful to look for *internal key words* that give insight into the historical context. In this case there are key words in the last and first verses of the passage: **"contentious"** (key #3 in verse 16), and **"traditions"** (key #4 in verse 2).

The most basic key to understanding the meaning of a Bible verse is a clear translation from the original language into modern language. It will be especially helpful to make **a fresh translation** from the Greek of the key action verse in this passage, verse 10 (key #5).

Key #1: Praise.

Paul praised the Corinthians in verse 2:

> [2]I praise you, brothers and sisters, that you remember me in all things and keep the traditions just as I delivered them to you. ...

Apparently there was difficulty for them in doing this because, in verse 16, he refers to some who were "contentious." In spite of these contentious ones, the church at Corinth had remembered what Paul had taught them to do and they had done it.

He did not always praise them. In the next section of his letter he gave them some energetic criticism:

> [17]I do not praise you in giving these instructions since you come together not for the better but for the worse. ...

What were the Corinthians doing that earned them the praise or the criticism of Paul? In verses 17 and following it is clear that they were criticized for not conducting themselves properly when they celebrated the Lord's Supper.

As for verses 2-16, what they were doing that was praiseworthy is often misunderstood.

This is where a basic rule of interpretation is helpful:

Whenever you see the word *therefore* in a passage, check to see what it is *there for.*

In this case, a "therefore" occurs at the beginning of verse 10:

^{10}therefore, a woman ought to have authority ...

Apparently, the verses leading up to verse 10 argued in favor of what he affirmed in verse 10. Paul had taught, and most of the Corinthians had agreed with him, that a woman *ought to* have authority.
Some people in Corinth had been contentious about this. Paul praised the rest (Key #1) and encouraged them to keep following what he had taught them.

Key #2: Three-fold focus.
Immediately before writing the words of chapter 11, Paul wrote, "Do not cause anyone to stumble, whether Jews, Greeks or the church of God..." (1 Corinthians 10:32). It is helpful to note that Paul was sensitive to the needs of these three overlapping groups:

1. Jews
2. Non-Jews (also called Greeks or Gentiles)
3. All Christians without regard to their background

In 1 Corinthians 11:2-16, Paul focused parts of the passage on each of these three groups in the church:

- Verses 3-9: converted **Jews**.
- Verses 11-12: everyone in **church**.
- Verses 13-15: converted **non-Jews**.

In these three sections, there are details appropriate to each group. Paul's appeal to Nature, in verse 14, is a case in point. The non-Jews would have related to an appeal to Nature, but not the Jews. Paul had to appeal to the Jews on other grounds.
In the verses not addressed to any specific group – verses 2, 10 and 16 – Paul deals with the real business of the passage. He praises the Corinthian Christians (verse 2). He gives instructions on how to behave (verse 10). He dismisses any who wanted to be contentious (verse 16).

Key #3: Contention.

A third key to understanding this passage has to do with Paul's reference in verse 16 to those who had been "contentious." The ones who were the most contentious about Paul, his teaching and his practice were *those who promoted Jewish legalism.*

As the early church spread across the Roman Empire there was confusion as to whether Christianity was something new, or whether it was just a sub-sect of Judaism. This confusion was understandable since the promises of a coming Messiah had been given to the Jews. Jesus was a Jew. And the first converts were Jews.

When non-Jews began believing in Jesus as their savior it seemed logical to the Jews who had become Christians that the new Gentile believers should become practicing Jews as well. But there were two main reasons why this logic was incorrect.

First, many of the practices required of Jews in the Old Testament served to represent spiritual truths that only pointed to the promised Messiah. The blood sacrifices of spotless animals in the Temple pointed to the ultimate blood sacrifice that would be made by the sinless Messiah. The regulations that guided the behavior of the priests on duty all worked to keep the symbolism of the future spotless Lamb of God perfectly clear.

These practices and these rules were made obsolete with the sacrifice of Christ on the cross. The early church dealt with these regulations and discarded them early on. They were famously discussed in depth in the meeting of the church in Jerusalem described in Acts 15:1-29.

Second, there were other lesser regulations and rules that had been built up during the 400 years that passed between the ministry of the last Old Testament prophet, Malachi, and the coming of John the Baptist and Jesus.

This system of case law and regulations obscured the message of the Old Testament. At times it contradicted it altogether. Jews at the time of Jesus, including Paul, practiced these legalistic regulations to a greater or lesser degree in their daily lives. Known as the oral law, these regulations were scrupulously followed by the Pharisees. The Scribes were teachers of this law.

One of the things that the oral law required was the covering of the head both by women and men. This covering symbolized that sin caused an ongoing separation of the worshipper from God.

Jesus fought against this form of Judaism during his earthly ministry. He confounded self-righteous sinners who followed rules of this Jewish oral law.

In his Sermon on the Mount, Jesus identified and rejected its regulations. Six times he said: "You have heard it said, …, but I say to you …." (Matthew 5:21, 27, 31, 33, 38, 43).

Familiar "Leadership" Heresies Uncovered   by Bruce C. E. Fleming
www.ThinkAgainAboutTheBible.com

As a Pharisee, Paul had been a scrupulous follower of the Jewish oral law. But as a Christian, Paul left behind those empty practices. Jesus the Messiah had fulfilled the Old Testament Law and gave each and every believer full status as a child of God (see Galatians 2:14).

During the years following his conversion, Paul became skilled at discerning and discarding the dry husks of legalism. He excelled in teaching truths straight from the Old Testament, especially how Jesus fulfilled the prophesies of the coming Messiah.

After Paul's first missionary journey, legalists came and tried to impose Jewish regulations on the converted Gentiles. Paul opposed their teachings.

Acts 15 records that the church in Jerusalem supported Paul in his work and agreed that Christians did not have to convert to Judaism. Nevertheless, Paul continued to face direct opposition from Jews outside the church and frequent contradiction from legalistic Judaizers inside the church.

A number of times, Jews *outside* the church opposed Paul and denounced him publicly. This resulted in beatings, stonings and imprisonments. At other times, Judaizers *within* the church visited places Paul had ministered. They contradicted his teachings to modify them to fit more or less with the oral law.

Here is Paul's own description of the havoc wreaked by unbelieving Jews who were hostile to the Christians in Thessalonica. This was the church Paul planted in northern Greece before he started the church at Corinth:

> [14]For you, brothers, became imitators of God's churches in Judea, which are in Christ Jesus. You suffered from your own countrymen the same things those churches suffered from the Jews, [15]who killed the Lord Jesus and the prophets and also drove us out. These displease God and are hostile to all men [16]in their effort to keep us from speaking to the Gentiles so that they may be saved.... Thessalonians 2:14-16 NIV)

Key #4: Traditions.

If some of the Corinthians were "contentious," as Paul said in verse 16, what were they contending for and what were they challenging? Verse 2 tells us. They challenged "the traditions" Paul had taught the Corinthian believers.

What might they have wanted to change? Since, in verse 10, Paul focuses on women, it can be assumed that they were challenging Paul on what he had taught about the status and ministry of Christian women.

There were numerous regulations in the *Jewish oral law* that applied to women *in the synagogue*. These regulations implied, or said outright, that the nature and status of the women was not on a par with the men.

Much like modern Islamic regulations require women to cover their heads differently from men, so the ancient Jewish regulations required women to cover their heads in a way different from men. While the Jewish oral law said that men and women both had to cover their heads, there were *many more reasons* given for why women had to cover their heads.

Paul never passed on such legalism to his spiritual children in Christ. If the Jews had their reasons for restricting women, Paul had his for ensuring their full participation in ministry. No wonder people flocked to hear Paul's teaching! He presented a vibrant counterpoint to the dead legalism of his day.

Paul never passed on Jewish legalism to his spiritual children in Christ.

As the following pages show, Paul's words in verse 10 confronted those who wanted to impose regulations on women believers. Both men and women believers had the right to discard any covering hinting at sin. No one had the right to tell them to do otherwise and it was obviously wrong to do so.

Key #5: Translations.
In 1 Corinthians 11:10, Paul restated his position. A look at the Greek words in which the New Testament was written makes this quite clear. But modern translations of this passage make it look as if Paul is saying something here *opposite* to what he originally wrote!

Before taking a look at what Paul said these in 13 Greek words, here is a sampling of what translations present verse 10 as saying:

CEV. And so, because of this, and also because of the angels, a woman ought to wear something on her head, as a sign of her authority. (26 words)

TEV. On account of the angels, then, a woman should have a covering over her head to show that she is under her husband's authority. (24 words)

LB: So a woman should wear a covering on her head as a sign that she is under man's authority, a fact for all the angels to notice and rejoice in. (30 words)

NIV. For this reason, and because of the angels, the woman ought to have a sign of authority on her head. (20 words)

NKJV: For this reason the woman ought to have a symbol of authority on her head, because of the angels (19 words).

However, in Greek, verse 10 is made up of just thirteen easy words. The following is a word-for-word transliteration of the Greek of 1 Corinthians 11:10:

1. "therefore" or "for"
2. "this" ("reason")
3. "ought"
4. "the"
5. "woman"
6. "authority"
7. "to-have"
8. "over"
9. "the" ("her")
10. "head"
11. "because-of"
12. "the"
13. "angels."

Thus, the verse can be translated literally as follows:

Therefore, the woman ought to have authority over her head, because of the angels.

Although it has rearranged the words, one modern version translates clearly the original Greek text. It is *Today's New International Version* (TNIV):

For this reason, and because of the angels, the woman ought to have authority over her own head.

Thus, Paul affirms that a woman is in charge of her own head. How this meaning fits with the verses around it is the topic of the following pages.

Getting a "Head" Start (11:3)

Principle of unity established
[3]I want you to know that
the head of *every* man is Christ;
the head of a wife is a husband,
the head of Christ is God.

The church at Corinth had compiled a letter to Paul spelling out specific questions and points of dispute among them. He responded to each one in turn starting at the beginning of 1 Corinthians chapter 7:

[1]Now for the matters you wrote about... (NIV)

To the Jews. When, in 1 Corinthians 11:2-16, Paul addresses the issue of regulations concerning the covering of a woman's head, he begins by addressing the converted Jews at Corinth in verses 3-9. Were the Jewish legalists at Corinth concerned with "men" and "women" and the covering of their physical "heads"? Paul takes their words and uses them to make his own points.

First, he reminds his Jewish readers, who are monotheists, of the importance of *unity*. Three times he points to independent elements that together make up one *unit*. The image he uses is that of the parts of the body that, united, make up one whole body:

- Believers-and-Christ united in one spiritual body
- A wife-and-husband united in one flesh
- Son-and-Father united in the Godhead.

Second, he states his main idea in the first line of verse 3, and then adds two subordinate parallel images to illustrate it. In his reference to the parts that make up the body Paul challenges the reader to answer the question, Just *who* is "every man"?

"Every man" is every *believer* – every man and every woman who is a Christian. This image is parallel to the one Paul uses in Ephesians 5:23: "Christ is the head of *the church*."

1 Corinthians 11:3:   Christ is the head of **every man**
Ephesians 5:23*b*:   Christ is the head of **the church**

An extraordinary response. Paul begins his response to those who did not hold to the tradition he had taught the Corinthians with some word play. Usually a "play on words" has an *extra* element in it that draws attention to the fact that something extraordinary is being said, even though ordinary words may be used.

Here is an example:

"I am going out into the refrigerator."

This phrase uses simple words, in a seemingly straightforward way. Refrigerators keep things cold. At first glance, the sentence seems to mean that someone is about to go into a refrigerator.

But no one literally climbs into a refrigerator! So that sense of these words must be ruled out immediately. It is nonsense.

There is an indicator that a "play on words" is being made. It is the word "out" – "I am going *out* into the refrigerator."

Those who live in wintry climates know that when someone *goes out* in the winter, they go outside where the temperature is as cold as it is inside a refrigerator. The person who said, "I am going out into the refrigerator," used a "play on words" to mean "I am going outside, into the cold." There was never any intention of climbing into a real refrigerator.

In 11:3, just as "going *out* into the refrigerator" has an extra word that indicates to the reader that something out of the ordinary is meant, there is an extra word in verse 3 in the phrase: "the head of every man is Christ." The extra word is: "*every*."

> [3]I want you to know the head of *every* man is Christ

The word "every" indicates that Paul is making a "play on words." The word play occurs in the very next word, man, which is used by Paul in a special way.

> [3]I want you to know the head of every *man* is Christ

Paul could have used his image of multiple units forming a unity by writing, "the head of every *person* is Christ." But Paul uses the word "man" in a special way to make a more precise point.

By first saying *every* man, Paul leaves no room for exceptions. *Every* member of the body of Christ is set free from all extraneous regulations. Then, by using the word, "man," Paul highlights the issue of gender in the body of Christ. Is a woman to be included in the scope of meaning of the words "every *man*"?

Those in the World War II Generation often used the English word "man" generically. To them, "man" could mean "person" and often included women.

When the Liberation Generation of the 1960s and 1970s came along, the generic use of the word "man" began to fall out of use. People made an effort to be more precise in their use of words to denote gender. This process is ongoing.

In Paul's time a situation existed that was similar to how the World War II generation used the word "man." In his day most people read the Old Testament in the Greek translation known as the Septuagint. In that version it was common to use the Greek word "man" to mean "person" and not just "men."

"Man" means "person." We get an insight into this in Romans 4:6.

- Just before quoting from King David's words in the Psalms, Paul first paraphrases David's comments. In his paraphrase, Paul uses the Greek word *anthropos*, the word generally used for "mankind" or "humanity," including both males and females.

- Then, in verses 7-8, he quotes Psalm 32:1-2 following the Septuagint version. In rendering David's comments the Septuagint used the Greek word *andros*, the word most commonly used to mean a "male" or "a man." Paul understood that the word "man" in the Septuagint also stood for "person."

Familiar "Leadership" Heresies Uncovered   by Bruce C. E. Fleming
www.ThinkAgainAboutTheBible.com

In the succeeding verses in Romans 4, Paul never elaborates on his interchange of the words for "man" and "person." He never explains it or excuses it to his readers. He doesn't need to, because it was acceptable to interchange these words in Greek.

Paul could use "every *man*" in Greek to stand for "every *person* – male or female" in 1 Corinthians 11:3 and not worry about being misunderstood. Writing "every man" he made a gentle play on words to make a point:

Do some of you want to focus only on what a *man* is free to do in Christ? Not I. I will focus on *every* man in Christ because I want you to focus on what every *person* – male or female – is free to do in Christ!

Heresy alert. There are some people who are perhaps unaware of the Septuagint's easy use of the Greek word *andros* to stand for people. At any rate, those who assume that Paul is speaking only of "males" here start their interpretation of the whole passage with a false impression. Incorrect interpretations have resulted from this.

"The body." The United States Marine Corps by its very name means the "body" (*corps*) of Marines. Every Marine, and all Marines, make up the one "body" of the Marine Corps.

Each and every new believer is incorporated into the body of Christ. This "body" image is used neither in the Gospels, nor in the other letters. It is Paul's unique way of expressing how, together, all believers and Christ are united into one spiritual body. Paul speaks of the "body of Christ," because Jesus is in this body, and so are all believers.

In verse 3, Paul makes figurative use of the word "head" to evoke the image of a joint-body:

³I want you to know
the head of *every* man is Christ;
the head of a wife is a husband,
the head of Christ is God.

First, he uses the image of a joint-body to illustrate the spiritual body, which is made up of Christ united with all believers, regardless of gender. Then he gives two subordinate images of joint-bodies help to illustrate the first:

- A husband and wife are "one flesh" (Genesis 2:24). Together, they form one joint-body.

- God and Christ form one joint-body in the Godhead, or Trinity.

Here are diagrams of the images in verse 3:

Main Principle

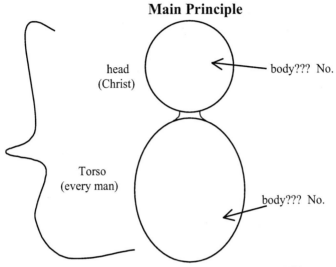

head
(Christ)

body??? No.

Torso
(every man)

body??? No.

ONE SPIRITUAL JOINT-BODY? YES!

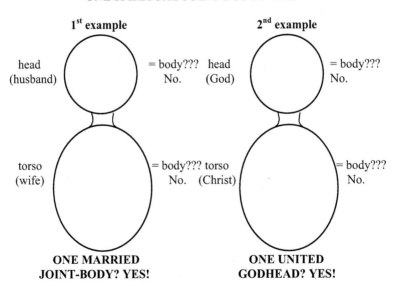

1ˢᵗ example

head
(husband)

= body??? No.

torso
(wife)

= body??? No.

**ONE MARRIED
JOINT-BODY? YES!**

2ⁿᵈ example

head
(God)

= body??? No.

torso
(Christ)

= body??? No.

**ONE UNITED
GODHEAD? YES!**

Familiar "Leadership" Heresies Uncovered   by Bruce C. E. Fleming
www.ThinkAgainAboutTheBible.com

The unity of believers and Christ is much like the unity of the Godhead, which is one entity but is made up of three Persons. The unity of believers and Christ is also like the union of a man and a woman who form one flesh in marriage.

Verse 3 is Paul's compact explanation of these truths. All believers – men *and* women – are united with Christ in one body. They are just as much *one* in Christ, as a husband and wife are *one* flesh, and Christ and the Father are *one* God.

Literal or figurative? It is best first to take a word literally. If the literal sense makes no sense, then a figurative sense must be intended. The literal meaning of believers being joined in one body with Christ is not possible. Therefore a figurative meaning has to be sought.

When trying to determine the meaning of the figurative sense of a word, it is best to start with the simplest level of abstraction. In this case, the first level of abstraction works well – the "head" is one part of a body.

If this meaning had made no sense, then it would have been necessary to move to a *more* abstract level to find the meaning of the word "head." But it is not necessary.

As was discussed in our chapter on Ephesians, this can be illustrated by diagramming the body of an ant. It has a three-part joint-body. No one part by itself is the body.

A dog has two parts to its body, the head and the rest. In much the same way, the human body has two parts that form one body. They are the head and the trunk, or torso. Neither part can exist by itself.

As the whole prospers, each part prospers. In Paul's spiritual joint-body imagery, Christ is the "head" of the body, and all believers together form the "other part." The whole *joint-body* united is of ultimate importance.

These illustrations are examples of "concrete-relational thinking." The Western world does not favor this way of thinking. It tends to use philosophical categories of thought. Perhaps this is why it is popular in the West to interpret verse 3 in a non concrete-relational way. There, great attention is focused on various abstract meanings of the word "head."

Some suggest "head" means "source." Others propose that "head" means "authority" or "priority" in some way. But, since the simplest level of abstraction makes perfectly good sense in this case, it is not necessary to occupy oneself with other more abstract possibilities.

I was born and raised in the West, so I first was attracted to the more abstract and philosophical interpretations of the word "head." As mentioned before, only after a number of years working in Africa and speaking an African dialect, did I begin to see that Paul's head/torso metaphor functions on the concrete-relational level. That should be no surprise. It is typical of the culture of the Old Testament.

Words from the Legalists (11:4-6)

Introduction
> [2]Now I praise you, brothers and sisters, that you remember me in all things and keep the traditions just as I delivered them to you.

Paul establishes principle of unity
> [3]I want you to know that the head of every man is Christ;
>> the head of a wife is a husband
>> the head of Christ is God.

Paul inserts quote from the legalists in Corinth
> [4]"Every man who prays or prophesies with his head covered dishonors his head.
> [5]"But every woman who prays or prophesies with her head uncovered dishonors her head – it is the same as having her head shaved. [6]For if a woman does not cover her head, she might as well have her hair cut off; but if it is a disgrace for a woman to have her hair cut off or her head shaved, then she should cover her head."

The Bible was written using more than 11,000 Hebrew, Aramaic and Greek words. The average modern translation into English uses 6,000 words. Studying the words used in the original languages can be helpful because in translations there is inevitably some loss of nuance and subtlety.

The original languages of the Bible were written without punctuation marks. Translators try to discern where they would have been placed. Then they add them to their translations because modern readers rely on punctuation marks.

Bible publishers often insert other things as well. Each new version contains headings and explanatory notes that are inserted between verses by publishers at their own discretion. These were not in the original texts of the Bible.

Placing punctuation. The New International Version of 1973 placed quotation marks around Paul's words in 1 Corinthians 10:23-26. Not every word in these verses was put in quotes. The translators noted that Paul was dialoguing with his readers in a brisk give and take. They showed this by adding quotation marks, dashes, and a paragraph break to his comments. They added these even though no punctuation marks were used in Paul's original letter.

Here is how the NIV punctuated 1 Corinthians 10:23-26. The words placed in quotation marks by the NIV are highlighted:

> [23]*"Everything is permissible"* – but not everything is beneficial. *"Everything is permissible"* – but not everything is constructive. [24] Nobody should seek his own good, but the good of others.
>
> [25] Eat anything sold in the meat market without raising questions of conscience, [26]for, *"The earth is the Lord's and everything in it."*

The proposals from Corinth are set apart by the quotation marks and the punctuation added by the NIV. This passage immediately precedes the verses on women and angels in 1 Corinthians 11:2-16.

Heresy alert. Modern readers would be confused if translations did not add punctuation marks. Nevertheless most translators and editors have not placed quotation marks around verses 4-6.

The reader who does not realize that 1 Corinthians 11:4-6 are a quotation finds the rest of the passage impossible to decipher. By omitting this punctuation translators make it look like Paul is advocating these legalistic ideas! Reasoning in circular fashion, some scholars have even accused Paul of "reverting to his pre-Christian roots as a Pharisee in verses 4-6."

In order to continue the thought of verses 4-6, major modifications have been made in the translations (some of which we have noted in verse 10). Commentators have gone to great lengths to try to make sense of the passage as a whole. But *none of this is necessary* if one places verses 4-6 in quotation marks.

Good doctrine. "Praying and prophesying," in verse 4, occurred when the church gathered together. In 1 Corinthians 12:27-28, Paul mentioned those in the body of Christ who were "prophets." In the Bible, more than ninety per cent of the activity of "prophets" was forth-telling the truth of God. Today we call that "teaching" or "preaching."

According to Acts 13:1, Paul himself was a prophet and almost all of his prophesying described in the Book of Acts consisted of vigorous teaching and preaching. Paul served as a model for the men in Corinth. He was a man who did not cover his head when he prayed and prophesied. Paul laid aside the practices of Jewish legalism in his ministry as Apostle to the Gentiles.

The proposal from Corinth. Anyone who wishes to be persuasive soon learns that to win over someone it is helpful first to find common ground. Building on established common ground, one can then introduce new or difficult ideas.

Those who wanted to convince Paul to change his policy on women in the church started their argument with words Paul could accept. After siding with Paul to a limited extent in verse 4, the legalists then proposed the legalistic restrictions they wanted to impose on women in verses 5-6.

First, they agreed with Paul in verse 4:

> "Every man who prays or prophesies with his head covered dishonors his head."

The implied action from this was that, as Paul had taught, Christian men should not cover their heads. This view was contrary to the Jewish oral law that required men to cover their heads when they prayed. But the legalists apparently were willing to concede this much to Paul. They would agree that other *men* like them could lead worship and teach with their heads uncovered.

The tradition Paul had taught them was that any Christian could freely enter into the presence of God without restriction. The Temple curtain covering the Holy of Holies, which separated God from the people, had been torn apart upon Christ's sacrifice. Every believer now was part of the new royal priesthood (*cf.* 1 Peter 2:9). Each had full access to God's throne (*cf.* Eph 3:12).

According to verse 4, these advocates for legalistic restrictions had accepted this much of Paul's teaching for men. They were "praying and prophesying" without covering their heads.

(Note: The word "head" could not be taken literally in verse 3, but the literal sense of "head" fits for every other occurrence in the passage.)

Their words. The noted nineteenth century archaeologist, Sir William Ramsay wrote that in Paul's letters one could usually tell Paul had inserted a quote from someone else into his letter "...whenever there was a sudden change in subject, in vocabulary, style, or a combination of these." In many ways verses 4-6, and especially 5-6, fit this description.

Verses 5-6 veer off in a radically different direction as soon as women become the subject. Some legalists even may have been willing to accept women leading the congregation, but they would not agree to women doing so with their heads uncovered.

Why? Perhaps it was because the Jews had so many more reasons for restricting women's participation in worship! Thus, they made their counter-proposal from verse 5 on.

[4]"Every man who prays or prophesies with his head covered dishonors his head. [5]"But every woman who prays or prophesies with her head uncovered dishonors her head – it is the same as having her head shaved. [6]For if a woman does not cover her head, she might as well have her hair cut off; but if it is a disgrace for a woman to have her hair cut off or her head shaved, then she should cover her head."

This counter-proposal was filled with words and ideas typical of the Jewish oral law. For example, prostitutes were to have their heads "shaved," and covering a woman's head was required by many of the Jewish regulations. The Greek word for "disgrace" in verse 6 is harsh and vulgar. It is surprising to find it in the Bible. But is typical of the sentiments and vocabulary of the oral law.

How could words descriptive of Christian women and of prostitutes get mixed together? How could thoughts of raw disgrace be used in the context of women members in the body of Christ? This was not Paul's way of thinking!

Segregated synagogues. On a family visit to Jerusalem, Joy and I looked forward to showing our daughter and son the base of the Western Wall of the Temple in Jerusalem. Months in advance an appointment had been booked to enter the tunnel that had been excavated along the length of the foot of the original Temple wall. We arrived early and went over to the public prayer area.

As we four approached, Mark and I were handed white paper yarmulkes to cover our heads in accordance with their custom and then we were encouraged to head straight ahead to the wall. But Joy and Christy were waved away and directed to go off to the side where a "women's section" was set apart. We hurriedly glanced at each other before separating and agreed to meet together in time for our tunnel tour.

Our experiences at the Wall were very different. The "men only" side took up much more than half of the visible wall. The small "women's section" was crowded with worshippers at prayer. The men's side was almost empty.

As we stood looking at those walls that were there in the time of Jesus, a smiling man gently came up to us. "Would you like to visit the synagogue?" Would we! Joy's Ph.D. is in Old Testament theology. I knew she would appreciate the visit far more than I could. How wonderful it would be to visit a synagogue at the Wall!

The man took Mark's arm and led the way – to the left, away from the women's section and the barrier that separated us. Only the two of us would be allowed in. Leaving the glare of the high sun outside, we entered the synagogue. As our eyes adjusted to the shadows, we could pick out several scholars standing, several scholars sitting, and many empty places.

Our meeting time was near. I quickly glanced around, my heart saddening –
no place for women.

In Support of Women (7-9)

Paul corrects the legalists' incomplete view
[7]Indeed a man ought not to cover his head,
since he is the image and glory of God;
and a woman (ought not cover her head, since she is
the image and glory of God, *and* she) is the glory of man.
[8]Now man did not come from woman, but woman from man
[9]For indeed the man was not created for woman but woman for man.

In the course of 1 Corinthians, when Paul corrected proposals from the
letter from Corinth, his responses typically included the following points:
- He quoted their own words
- He corrected their proposal
- He applied the correct view

Paul followed this pattern in 1 Corinthians 11:2-16 as he corrected the
proposal from the legalists in Corinth:
- He quoted their own words (verses 4-6)
- He corrected their proposal (verses 7-9)
- He applied the correct view (verse 10)

A compact example of this pattern is found in 1 Corinthians 6:12:

Quote: "Everything is permissible for me"
Correction: But not everything is beneficial
Application: The body is not for sexual immorality …

Other quotations corrected by Paul in 1 Corinthians include the following:

"It is good for a man not to touch a woman" (7:1ff.)
"We know that we all possess knowledge" (8:1ff.)
"All things are lawful" (10:23ff.)

Responding to the Judaizers. The Jewish oral law required worshippers to cover their heads because they were considered sinners who were unfit to come uncovered into the presence of God, or without some sort of physical barrier between them and God. But Paul taught that *all* believers were counted spotless in Christ. This was equally true for Jewish believers and for non-Jewish believers. All had full access to the throne of grace (Ephesians 3:1-12)!

Using all his rhetorical skills, Paul defended what he had already taught the Corinthians (11:2) using puns (verse 3), irony (verse 3), quotation (verses 4-6) correction (verses 7-9), application (verse 10) and reference to Scripture (verses 11-12).

New Testament scholar, John Coolidge Hurd, Jr. (*Origins*, pp. 119-121, 183), describes Paul's method:

> Paul's counterstatements are evidence that the initial statements ... were not Paul's own composition here in 1 Corinthians, but were quotations which he used in order to modify them.

Verse 7a. The proposal from Corinth began, in verse 4, with words with which Paul could agree, so he picked up these words and made them the first part of his response:

7a*Indeed* a man ought not to cover his head...

But Paul believed that women also ought not cover their heads. He had laid the groundwork for a "more-than-males-only" theology with his word play in verse 3 on "*every* man." As commentator Leon Morris (*First Corinthians*, p. 150) pointed out: "*every man* ... plainly refers to mankind ...."

Verse 3 was Paul's verbal first strike at his opposition. It made their "males only" comments in verses 4-6 stand out awkwardly.

It is unlikely that any of Paul's readers in Corinth missed the point of his word play. This was a point under dispute in Corinth. Everyone wanted to see how Paul would resolve it.

When they read 1 Corinthians 11:2 they anticipated Paul's dialog to come. In verse 3, they were delighted with his clever play on words and wanted to see how he would respond to the words they had sent to him, that he quoted in verses 4-6. They anticipated what Paul would say next, after quoting their words.

But modern readers, far from the world of first century Corinth, can, and do, misunderstand this passage. This is especially true when they fail to understand Paul's words in context.

Missing the point. A classic example of this happened in Ethiopia during World War II. Missionaries had just begun work in the countryside when they were expelled for the duration of the war. They left behind a handful of new believers and a copy of the Bible. Years later, after the war, the missionaries returned wondering what they would find. They found that a great revival had taken place. Thousands of new believers welcomed them back to their villages! But the villages were strangely different. There were no dogs racing out to greet them. All their hunting dogs were gone! When the missionaries asked where the dogs were, the new believers told of finding a passage in Philippians 3:2 that said "Beware of the dogs." They had taken that verse literally and disposed of all their dogs!

Two reasons for men to uncover. Had the legalists tried to win over Paul by espousing part of his position in verse 4? Paul did the same thing to them in verse 7*a*. He echoed the part of their statement that was correct and then built on this truth by spelling out clearly two reasons why males leading worship should indeed keep their heads uncovered!

Paul argued that a Christian man reveals the "image" of God. This brings "glory" to God. These two points had not been made by the legalists in their proposal to him. But no doubt they agreed with him.

This can be diagrammed as follows:

Christian man

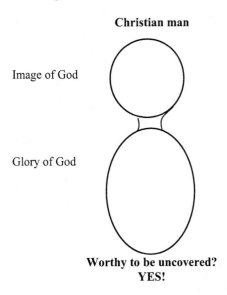

Image of God

Glory of God

Worthy to be uncovered?
YES!

Familiar "Leadership" Heresies Uncovered   by Bruce C. E. Fleming
www.ThinkAgainAboutTheBible.com

Paul says "Gotcha!" How long did it take them to realize that Paul's introductory words in verse 7*a* justified Paul's point of view but not theirs? These two points did not apply only to Christian men. They applied to Christian women as well! Genesis 1 records that *both* the man and the woman were created in the *image* of God:

> ²⁷So God created man **in his own image,**
> in the image of God he created him;
> **male** *and* **female** he created them.

Both the man and woman were God's delight ("glory" is not a reflection, but a source of light or even delight, *cf.* Hebrews 1:3-4):

> ²⁸God blessed **them** … ³¹God saw all that he had made, and it was **very good.**

If Christian men were free to lay aside the restrictions of the past because of the two reasons advanced by Paul in verse 7*a*, this was an equally strong argument for Christian women!

Three **reasons to uncover.** In verse 7*b*, Paul assumes the first two points as a given for women and adds a third point to ensure their equal treatment when they minister in church.

> ^{7*b*}*and* the woman is the glory of man.

In verses 8 and 9, Paul builds on what he meant by this.

> ⁸For man is not from woman, but woman from man.
> ⁹Nor was man created for the woman, but woman for the man.

He reminded his readers of how, according to Genesis, it was the man who was needy and alone in the Garden. God remedied this situation ("for the man") by creating the woman. God put the man to sleep and used part of his flesh ("from man") to make the first woman. When finally both were together in the Garden, the man rejoiced (Genesis 2:23).

Thus, in verse 7*a* Paul starts with *two* reasons that validate the high status of a man who is restored to a right relationship with God: "the *image* and *glory* of God." These two reasons also apply to a woman in Christ. In verse 7*b*, Paul adds that a woman has a *third* reason in her favor: "*and* the woman is the *glory* of man." Verses 8-9 point out that the man alone was in a sorry state until God chose to create the first woman.

This can be illustrated as follows:

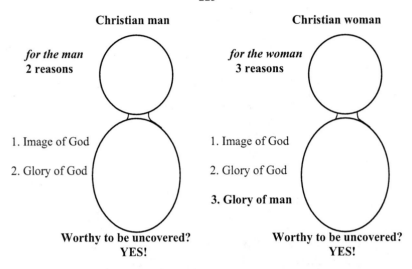

Christian man   Christian woman

for the man
2 reasons

for the woman
3 reasons

1. Image of God

2. Glory of God

1. Image of God

2. Glory of God

3. Glory of man

Worthy to be uncovered?
YES!

Worthy to be uncovered?
YES!

Heresy alert. Many modern writers, much like the legalists of Paul's day, look at the end of verse 7 and claim that Paul admitted *only* that "the woman is the glory of man." In *their* math, Paul listed two reasons unique to men and just one for women! They further suggest that the third reason signifies a *reduced* status for woman. This turns Paul's reasoning on its head. It makes woman the *reflection* of the *man's* glory as if Paul had said,

> The male is like the radiant sun;
> the female is the stony moon reflecting his rays from a distance.

This misses the mark. "Glory" is *glorious* for both of them. And "glory" is a positive point for the woman not just on one count, but on two. In the same way, Paul referred positively to the Thessalonians as his *"glory* and joy" (1 Th. 2:20). Thus, according to verse 7, the woman had three points in her favor. That she was "the glory of man" was a third attribute in her favor. These three attributes confirm the value and status of women who walk with God. The redeemed and restored woman is qualified to stand and serve Him without restriction.

Application and Theology (11:10-12)

Application of the principle for Christian women
[10]Therefore, a woman ought to have authority over her own head, because of the angels.

Theological basis of the principle of unity
¹¹Nevertheless,

        neither is man independent of woman,
        nor woman independent of man,
    in the Lord.
¹²For

        as woman came from man,
        even so man also comes through woman;
    but all come from God.

Prior to verse 10, Paul defended the principle that a Christian woman was a member of the body of Christ in every way. In verse 10, he applied this principle. He ended verse 10 by adding another principle that argued in favor of the full status of women in ministry (those who were "praying and prophesying," or preaching and teaching).

Then, in verses 11-12, he put the matter in perspective. Women and men share in reciprocal relationships and God is over all.

Running the Bases. At the beginning of my senior year in college, from September to Christmas, I did my student teacher service. At Roswell Kent Junior High School I was known as Mr. Fleming, ninth grade English teacher.

All day long I taught classrooms full of ninth grade students. Most of the day I taught advanced English classes. But at the end of each day I had a group of students for whom English was a chore. They had a background of poor grades in English. They were unhappy about that and they were sure they weren't going to like studying English in my ninth grade class.

To make things worse, my classroom was on the sunny side of the building and this group of students was assigned to a double-period class to give them enough time to soak up the subject matter. To them this seemed like a double sentence of doom. Most of these were kids wanted to be anywhere else but English class.

I was supposed to teach them grammar! I decided that the only way for all of us to survive was to use our time creatively. I had them do homework during the first period. The second, and last period of the day, we played "blackboard baseball."

Each row of students from front to back was a team. I drew a baseball diamond on the board and put up six columns off to one side to keep score for each of the six rows. I called on the first student in Row 1 to give the answer to the first homework question of the day.

A right answer equaled "a hit" and I drew a runner on first base. If the next student answered the next question correctly, I drew a second runner, one on first and one on second base. Enough right answers equaled "a run." A wrong answer equaled "an out." It took three outs before we moved on to the next row. The students got into the game answering their grammar questions. I had to close the door to the hall to keep the cheers and jeers from wafting down to the other classrooms.

If we had studied the grammar of 1 Corinthians 11, we would have noted the following developments in the passage:

- Verses 4-6 are a unit that should be set off with quotation marks
- Verse 7a is a thought by itself
- Verse 7b is a different thought followed by two verses that are subordinate to it and elaborate on it
- Verse 8 is subordinate to 7 – it is introduced by: "for"
- Verse 9 is subordinate to 7 as well – "for indeed"
- This structure is rare in the New Testament but is used six times in 1 Corinthians (pointing *this* out would be worth a "home run")
- Verse 10 is introduced in Greek by "therefore" and is the culmination of this series of thoughts
- The verb in verse 10, "ought" is the same one used in verse 7, where a man "ought not" cover his head (another home run observation)

Before dismissing class, these would have been my parting summary thoughts:

A Christian woman is as equally obligated and empowered as a Christian man to not cover her head when ministering in church.

"Because of the angels" The final Greek words of verse 10 pointed to the principle that showed why a Christian woman at Corinth had the authority to put into practice what she had learned from Paul.

[10]Therefore a woman ought to have authority over her head, *because of the angels.*

Paul's previous mention of angels came in 1 Corinthians 6. There he referred to the noteworthy authority all Christians will have in the future to judge the angels:

[6:1]If any of you has a dispute with another, dare you to take it before the ungodly for judgment instead of before God's people? [2]Or do you not know that God's people will judge the world? And if you are to judge the world, are you not competent to judge trivial cases? [3]Do you not know that we will judge angels? How much more the things of this life!

(TNIV)

One day a Christian woman, just like a Christian man, would judge angels. She certainly could judge what was best and follow Paul's instructions on removing head coverings!

Striking out. A survey of Bible commentators reveals that most find themselves at a loss to explain what "because of the angels" means. Some suggest it refers to angels "looking on women," and that a woman ought to put something on her head for their sake.

These ideas have made their way into translations of verse 10 – note the italicized words:

NEB. [10]And therefore it is woman's duty to have a sign of authority on her head, *out of regard for the angels.*

Phillips. [10]For this reason a woman ought to bear on her head an outward sign of man's authority *for all the angels to see.*

RSV. [10]That is why a woman ought to have a veil on her head, *because of the angels.*

Jerusalem. [10]That is the argument for women's covering their heads with a symbol of the authority over them, *out of respect for the angels.*

LB. [10]So a woman should wear a covering on her head as a sign that she is under man's authority, *a fact for all the angels to notice and rejoice in.*

Based on what these translations say, some people theorize that verse 10 teaches something about hierarchical "power structures" within the family and church regarding the two genders. But, properly understood, verse 10 says no such thing.

Basic Theology – verses 11-12.

In 1 Corinthians 10:32, Paul indicated that he had three groups in mind. In chapter 11, he addresses each group: Jewish Christians, the church as a whole, non-Jewish Christians. In verses 11-12, he addresses the second group, the church as a whole, and gave the foundational theology on which his teachings are built:

Nevertheless, neither is man independent of woman, nor woman independent of man, in the Lord. For as woman came from man, even so man also comes through woman; but all come from God.

In Greek, "nevertheless" (verse 11) typically concludes a discussion, while emphasizing what is essential. "For" (verse 12) introduces a parallel thought to the concluding idea.

In these verses, Paul taught that neither the Christian man nor the Christian woman stood aloof, on a different plane from the other. Together, they had the same point of reference for all things – God. Both were dependent on God. Verse 11 concluded with "in the Lord." Verse 12 ended with "all things are of God." What counted in church was God's point of view.

At the beginning of creation God was *over all*. Among women and men believers in the Lord, **this still is His place.**

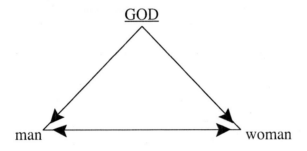

Appeal to Greek Opinion (13-15)

Appeal to non-Jewish Christians

[13]You yourselves judge: It is proper for a woman to pray to God with her head uncovered.

[14]Not even Nature itself teaches you that a man is dishonored by long hair,

[15]nor if a woman wears her hair long it is her glory because long hair has been given to her instead of a covering.

When Joy and I lived and ministered in Africa, we gained extensive experience among people who were non-Jewish.

These Christians had no great appreciation for Christmas. I discovered several reasons for this. In that part of Africa many children die before the age of five. Some children grow up to be sinners and bring shame on their family. Only at funeral could one rejoice over the good someone had actually done. When I explained the joyful prophecies that applied to the birth of Jesus they began to see how one could rejoice over His birthday.

They also were puzzled by what their translations of 1 Corinthians 11:13-15 said. Long hair does not naturally fall down in long tresses for the women in that part of Africa. What were these verses saying to them? The African women agreed with what the non-Jewish women in Corinth made of the legalistic claims by the Judaizers. The claims didn't make sense to them. They weren't moved by them. And this is what Paul said.

In verses 13-15, Paul argued, in the Greek text, that Nature did *not* support the proposals of verses 4-6. To the Jewish legalists, a Christian woman's uncovered head might have looked as bad as if it were shorn like a prostitute's. But was this the way the non-Jews saw these things? It was not!

Paul appeals to Nature to support his view. Such an appeal would have had no weight with the Jewish Christians. It would have been shocking! But verses 13-15 were directed at the *non*-Jewish Christians in the church. Appealing to Nature was meaningful for them.

More reasons. In verse 13 he encouraged the non-Jewish Corinthian Christians to judge this matter for themselves. In verses 14-15, he spelled out the argument so they could better make their decision.

In the Greek text these verses are straightforward affirmations made in declarative sentences. In most translations into English, however, these statements are turned into questions! The two senses are 180 degrees opposed to one another.

For example, the Greek is declarative in verse 14:

Not: "Does not Nature itself teach you ...?"

But: "Nature itself does *not* teach you ...."

When translating, first take a declarative sentence at face value. If the words make sense that way, there is no reason to take them in any other way.

Do the sentences in verses 14-15 make sense as they stand? Yes.

[14-15]Not even Nature itself teaches you that a man is dishonored by long hair, or if a woman wears her hair long it is her glory because long hair has been given to her instead of a covering.

Among the non-Jews at Corinth there was a variety of ways for men and women to wear their hair. Nearby to Corinth was the coastal town mentioned in Homer's *Odyssey* where he embarked with a number of brave "longhaired Achaeans." These Corinthian heroes wore long hair. Neither Nature nor style suggested they do otherwise!

Honest scholars admit what Walker observes in the *Journal of Biblical Literature* (94, p. 103). These three verses "actually imply rather strongly that women do not need any artificial head-covering."

Another way to test these verses is to see if the alternative way of translating them makes better sense. However, nothing but trouble arises when an attempt is made to turn these statements into questions.

Heresy alert. Having modified verse 10 to "clarify" its meanings, translators have modified these later verses as well. Here is a sample of several translations that make Paul's positive statements look like questions deserving negative answers:

KJV. [13]Judge in yourselves: is it comely that a woman pray unto God uncovered? [14]Doth not even nature itself teach you, that, if a man have long hair, it is a shame unto him?

LB. [13]What do you yourselves really think about this? Is it right for a woman to pray in public without covering her head? [14]Doesn't even instinct itself teach us … a man with long hair tends to be ashamed?

NIV. [13]Judge for yourselves: Is it proper for a woman to pray to God with her head uncovered? [14]Does not the very nature of things teach you that if a man has long hair, it is a disgrace to him…

No More Arguing Please (11:16)

Conclusion
> [16]But if anyone wants to be contentious, we have no such custom, nor do the churches of God.

Paul concluded his dialog with the knowledge that some might not be convinced. There would likely be individuals, genuinely converted to Christ, who would still want to pick a fight with others – or as Paul said, "be contentious."

Paul appealed to them on two more grounds:

> (1) his personal example

> (2) the example of other churches.

At least the legalists at Corinth should admit that Paul had not taught what they want him to adopt. Now, they needed to admit that he would not go along with them. The same would be true in the other churches. If they looked at what other churches were practicing, they would see that theirs was not the correct view.

Conclusions

1 Corinthians 11:2-16 is an application of the principle that one does not have to become a Jew in order to be a Christian. Jewish regulations were laid aside as having no relevance to Christians – non-Jews and Jews alike.

Prompted by the proposal from the Corinthians (embodied in the quotation in verses 4-6), Paul affirmed his previous teaching that both male and female believers should minister in church, praying and prophesying, leading worship and preaching, without being limited by any of the restrictions of the oral law.

In the 21st Century, Christians need to be mindful of Paul's battle to keep women fully involved in ministry. Few people today would refer to the Jewish oral law in an attempt to limit the freedom of women ministering in church. But, for their own reasons, many still try to draw a distinction between the service of Christian women and Christian men.

21st Century Christians need to be mindful of Paul's battle not to restrict women in preaching and teaching ministry.

If anyone wanted to be contentious about this, Paul had no such custom, nor did the early churches of God, nor should the churches of today.

Think Again!

According to Paul's comment in verse 11:2, did the Corinthians practice what he preached? If so, why bring up the subject in verse 10?

Chapter 7

"Leadership" Heresies and Silence in Church
... an inside look at 1 Corinthians 14:34-40 (with a focus on 34-35)

Chapter Contents:

1 Corinthians 14:34-40 in Context

Summation on ministry

^{26}What shall we say, brothers and sisters? When you come together, each of you has a hymn, or a teaching, a revelation, or an interpretation. Let all things be done for edification. ... ^{33}For God is not a God of disorder but of peace, as in all the congregations of the people of God.

The legalists propose restrictions

^{34}"Let the women keep silent in the churches, for it is not permitted for them to speak; but let them be subject, as also the law says. ^{35}And if they want to learn something, let them ask their own husbands at home; for it is a shame for women to speak in church."

Paul responds to the Jewish legalists

^{36}Did the word of God come from you? Was it you only that it reached? ^{37}If anyone claims to be a prophet, or spiritually gifted, let that one acknowledge that the things which *I* write to you are the Lord's command.

Practical application

^{38}If anyone ignores this, that one will be ignored.

Resumption of summation and conclusion

^{39}Therefore, my brothers and sisters, be eager to prophesy, and do not forbid speaking in tongues. ^{40}Let all things be done in a fitting and orderly way.

As I studied by the yellow light of a kerosene lantern in our jungle home on the Bible Institute campus in Congo, I came to 1 Corinthians 14:34-35. I had been reading through the book of 1 Corinthians as part of my class preparation. I had scaled the heights of the "Love Chapter" as I read through 1 Corinthians 13. As I continued to read, I was strengthened by Paul's description of the early church in 14:26-33.

But then, I hit the harsh words of verses 34-35. Where had these thoughts come from?

I reached for a helpful book I had found in the school library by the noted nineteenth century archaeologist, Sir William Ramsay. Just as was the case in 11:4-6, here too 14:34-35 perfectly fit the pattern of Ramsay's dictum.

He wrote that one could tell when Paul had inserted a quote:

> ... whenever there was a sudden change in subject, in vocabulary, style, or a combination of these.

Here, inserted in Paul's letter, were words that sounded just like the legalistic Jewish Scribes advocating the imposition of restrictions found in the Jewish oral law. Nowhere else did Paul advocate Jewish laws. If this was a quotation of the words of someone else, whose words could they be?

Paul had quoted the legalists at Corinth a number of times in 1 Corinthians. Likely, the words in verses 34-35 were quoted by Paul, in order to then give his own opinion of them. In my English Bible I have penciled in quotation marks around verses 34-35 to make the quote stand out clearly.

From chapter to chapter, through the length of 1 Corinthians, Paul strung together a series of replies in a written dialog with the church at Corinth. As he drew near to the end of 1 Corinthians 14, he had another proposal from Corinth to deal with.

It was an especially distasteful one. After quoting it, Paul then responded vigorously to it, and to those who had proposed it.

In 1 Corinthians 11:16, Paul had described as "contentious" those who were the source of the words he quoted in 1 Corinthians 11:4-6. Those who were behind the words he quotes in 14:34-35, he further identified (verses 36-37) as acting like the teachers of the Jewish oral law. Rejecting their proposals (verse 38), he advised the church to implement the teachings he himself had just given them in chapters 12-14.

Coming from deep within legalistic Judaism, Paul was especially skilled at spotting the influences of the Jewish legalists who had worked their way into the church and contradicted the teachings of Jesus. Over and over, Paul stood against anything that might dilute or change the Gospel (Acts 9:22; 29; 13:45-46).

And Paul would not voluntarily give up an inch of territory once it was won. He was a hand-to-hand combatant, who gained ground for Christ on two fronts:

- against heathenism
- against lifeless Jewish legalism.

Why write? 1 Corinthians was written to the church of Corinth in response to numerous questions and proposals that had been communicated to Paul by messenger and by letter. Here are some verses in 1 Corinthians that refer to how Paul gained his information about the Corinthians:

– News by messenger:

- "For I have been informed concerning you, my brothers and sisters, by Chloe's people…"(1:11).

- "It is actually reported that…" (5:1).

- "I rejoice over the coming of Stephanus and Fortunatus and Achaicus…" (16:17).

– News by letter:

- "Now concerning the things about which you wrote…" (7:1).

- "Now concerning things…" (8:1)

There were major divisions in the church at Corinth (1:12). Some had become arrogant and disputatious (4:18).

Throughout his letter, Paul systematically dealt with the issues that were percolating in Corinth. Paul usually introduced a new issue by inserting a quote from one of the proposals that had come to him from Corinth. He corrected each idea to the extent that it contained false doctrine, and reiterated correct doctrines to hold and right practices to implement.

From 11:2 to 14:40, Paul answered questions about "How to worship in church." In the last verses of 1 Corinthians 14, Paul encouraged *each and every* Corinthian believer:

"Let all things be done so that the church may be built up (14:26)."

He encouraged them to prophesy, "that all may learn and all may be encouraged" (verse 31). This was what he had done in the other churches (verse 33). He wanted this to be done in Corinth as well, as long as things were done "decently and in order" (verse 40).

Previous to this point in this lengthy section of three chapters (12-14), Paul had not inserted any quotations from the Corinthians. But at the end of this section he did, in 14:34-35.

In these two verses the subject, tone and vocabulary of the passage change noticeably. Then, in verses 36-38 comes a return to Paul's normal vocabulary and style with a strong rebuke to those who proposed the ideas contained in the previous two verses. Finally, in verses 39 and 40, the storm passes and earlier themes are picked up again.

According to the proposal in 1 Corinthians 14:34-35, some person or group wanted the Corinthian Christians to adopt legalistic limitations on who could, and who could not, use their gifts for the building up of the church. Specifically, the proposal excluded Christian women from speaking in church.

Quoting Their Distasteful Proposal (34-35)

The legalists propose restrictions on Christian women
[34]"Let the women keep silent in the churches, for it is not permitted for them to speak; but let them be subject, as also the law says. [35]And if they want to learn something, let them ask their own husbands at home; for it is a shame for women to speak in church."

Paul responds to the Jewish legalists
[36]What! Did the word of God come from you? Was it you only that it reached? [37]If anyone claims to be a prophet, or spiritually gifted, let that one acknowledge that the things which I write to you are the Lord's command.

Contentious claims.
The two-verse unit of 1 Corinthians 14:34-35 was a string of bad ideas that did not belong to Paul. Some group in the church in Corinth proposed restricting women from teaching and from learning God's word in church. These were *their* words.

They proposed that women should no longer speak publicly in church worship. (Obviously they had been speaking publicly all along.) Why should women not speak, or preach, publicly? Because they were "not permitted." By whom, or by what?

Women were also supposed to "be subject." Why? Because that's what their "law" *said.*

The words quoted in verses 34-35 proposed further restrictions and some small compromises. Namely, that women should no longer be learning God's word in church! If a Christian woman had a Christian husband who was informed enough to be able to instruct her, she would have to learn from him at home!

What law? People have suggested that the "law" referred to in verse 34 is a reference to Genesis 3:16. However, Genesis 3:16 says nothing about "speaking" or about "being silent." As we have seen earlier, that verse is not a curse, nor does God institute any change in her status. But the sinful man tried to do so.

Paul's teaching elsewhere in the New Testament was nothing like the proposal in 1 Corinthians 14:34-35:

> Paul ... states time and again that Christians are not under the law, but are free of it. ... "But now we are discharged from the law" (Rom. 7:6). Earlier, in 1 Corinthians Paul instructs the Gentile men of Corinth that they are free of the law and are, therefore, not required to be circumcised (1 Cor. 7:18-19). Elsewhere, too, Paul has rejected the claim that Gentile Christians should keep the Jewish dietary laws. (Odell-Scott, *BLT*, p. 14)

Those who made this proposal in 1 Corinthians 14:34-35 were espousing the ideas of the legalists, the sayings of Jewish teachers that were passed on orally and later written down in the Jewish oral law.

Philip Payne ("Libertarian Women" *Trin J* 1 NS, p. 187) points out how verse 34 indicates the source of these ideas:

> ... when Paul refers to the Old Testament, he usually does not write 'as the law *says*' (which often suggests *oral* tradition) but 'just as it is *written*'.

Payne also points out the elements in these verses that come from the milieu of the Jewish oral law:

> ... According to Jewish custom, the part of the synagogue given to the scribes' teaching was open only to males, as its name suggests: *andron*. ... Women were forbidden to teach....
> Their position in society was reflected in the common formula, "women, slaves, and children." In the home, too, the wife was not even to pronounce the benediction after a meal.

The "law" appealed to in 1 Corinthians 14:34-35 was the *oral* law. The words used in these verses (such as the Greek word for "shame" in verse 35) are typical of the rough language used in the oral law. They are not the kind of words Paul uses. These recommendations are an example of the segregationist practices of Jewish legalism seeping into the church.

To clarify that verse 34 refers to the "oral law," and not the Old Testament "Law" editors have removed the capitalization that was used in the NIV of 1971 to the TNIV of 2001. Instead of "Law," the verse now reads "law," as in "... as the law says."

Was Paul intimidated? In attempting to justify their position by a reference to the oral law, those who contended with Paul made a serious tactical error. Paul did not look with favor on the rules he had followed as a Pharisee before his conversion.

Those contending with Paul made a serious tactical error. He did not look with favor on the rules he had followed as a Pharisee before his conversion.

Paul had rebuked Peter for giving in to such influences (Galatians 2:11-14). He would not be swayed by a similar appeal coming to him from Corinth!

When the church at Jerusalem discussed the place of Jewish rules in the Christian church (Acts 15), Paul had been intimately involved at all levels of that discussion. Everyone agreed that Christians who were not Jews and did not practice all their rituals were still Christians.

This meant that Jewish and non-Jewish Christians alike were expected to continue freely participating in every type of ministry. This was the tradition Paul preached when he founded the church in Corinth.

Jesus set this example during His earthly ministry. Time and time again He stripped away all the non-inspired regulations that had been attached to the message of the Old Testament.

For example, Jesus restated the original intent of the Old Testament message in his Sermon on the Mount. Six times in a row (Matthew 5: 21, 27, 31, 33, 38, 43), Jesus corrected the prevailing traditions of the oral law. He introduced his corrections saying,

"You have heard it *said*... but I say unto you...."

Jesus said this whenever He encountered rabbinic regulations that had reversed the inspired teaching of the Old Testament. In his turn, Paul refused to accept the legalistic proposals of verses 34-35!

Why are there no quotation marks in my Bible? Some Bible translations never use quotation marks because they were not used in the original Greek text. The original readers of the Bible in Greek simply had to figure out on their own where the quotations were. But most translations insert them now because this is the way modern English is written.

Familiar "Leadership" Heresies Uncovered   by Bruce C. E. Fleming
www.ThinkAgainAboutTheBible.com

Though modern translations insert quotation marks for at least some of the quotations inserted by Paul earlier in 1 Corinthians, most don't indicate them around 1 Corinthians 14:34-35. Why not?

Some people argue that these verses are not a quotation to be refuted, but words that convey Paul's *own* ideas. This viewpoint has caused people to wander off in problematic directions. Here are some they propose:

1. "This is a contradiction." In these verses, Paul contradicts what he has written elsewhere.

2. "These verses are time-bound." This passage applied only in its original time and place, not today.

3. "These verses were not in the original letter." They were added later by Paul or someone else.

4. Some people try to modify the content of these verses by linking them with parts of the paragraphs before or after them: 33*b* attached to 34-35, or 36 attached to 34-35.

5. Unsure of the meaning of these verses, some try to explain what they mean by referring to the content of other verses instead, so-called cross-references. Too often they mistake the content of the cross references as well. The resulting tangle is very difficult to straighten out.

6. Other options. Some ignore these verses. They dismiss them because they don't like what they think they say.

A better way. It is only necessary to recognize that, here again, as at various points throughout his letter, Paul inserted a proposal from the Corinthians. These two verses were not an expression of his own ideas. His ideas came next. In verses 36-38, Paul unmasked and denounced the purveyors of this harmful legalism.

Paul Responds (36-38)

Paul responds to the Jewish legalists
[36]Did the word of God come from you? Was it you only that it reached? [37]If anyone claims to be a prophet, or spiritually gifted, let that one acknowledge that the things which I write to you are the Lord's command.
Practical application
[38]If anyone ignores this, that one will be ignored.

Fighting back

Paul maintained a lifelong struggle against Jewish legalists. Virtually his whole letter to the Galatians revealed his battle against them. Here is an excerpt:

> ... some false believers had infiltrated our ranks to spy on the freedom we have in Christ Jesus and to make us slaves. We did not give in to them for a moment.... (2:4-5 TNIV)

Elsewhere, Paul took a word the Jews sneeringly used for non-Jews, "dogs," and forcefully applied it to those Jews who wanted to require the Gentile Christians to follow their laws: "Watch out for those dogs, those who do evil..." (Philippians 3:2)!

Who **did Paul rebuke?** Paul's words in verses 36-38 were a sharp response to the words of 34-35. He accused the authors of the words in verses 34-35 of four things. These indicated either that these proposals came from those who were under the influence of the teachers of Jewish regulations, or that these proposals came from some of the Jewish teachers (the Scribes) themselves.

While I was studying in France, I came across a French edition of the book *Jerusalem in the Time of Jesus*. In a lengthy appendix at the back of the book, the author, Joachim Jeremias, included an article where he described the Scribes, the Jewish teachers of the law. He listed four outstanding characteristics of the Scribes. By the way, his comments were made in a context totally divorced from the passage at hand. I found the overlap to be, therefore, all the more informative.

According to Jeremias, the Scribes were not mere stenographers, who transcribed something. They were "teachers of the law" who claimed to be:

1. Individual sources of "inspiration"

2. Possessors of a special and private (esoteric) knowledge

3. On a par with the prophets of the Old Testament

4. Especially spiritual.

These are the same four markers that defined those whom Paul rebuked in verses 36-37!

Marker 1. *Individual sources of "inspiration."* The Scribes considered themselves sources of "inspiration," mouthpieces for God. What *they* said was supposed to be as authoritative, or even more so, than what the Old Testament prophets had written in the Bible.

There were many false prophets in Old Testament times. God showed the people which ones were true prophets by bringing something to pass within a relatively short period after one of their prophecies was made. In this way all their words were *verified* as true. If no prophecy of theirs came to pass, they would be stoned to death for being a false prophet.

But no one ever stoned a Scribe. This was, the Scribes claimed, because unlike the prophets, their words needed no verification. They taught that this showed that *their* words were *more* authoritative than those of the prophets!

When Paul began verse 36 by asking, "Did the word of God come from you?" he identified the persons behind verses 34-35 as those who claimed to have the prophetic authority to tell the Corinthians the word of God. But Paul knew God does not contradict Himself. Paul accepted no contradiction of the inspired teachings he had given the Corinthians.

Marker 2. *Possessors of a special and private (esoteric) knowledge.* The Scribes claimed to be the keepers of a "private and secret (esoteric) body of knowledge." They claimed that *they alone* had the inside track on God's revelations. Paul critiqued the authors of verses 34-35 for this attitude when he asked in verse 36: "Was it you only that the word of God reached?"

Marker 3. *On a par with the prophets of the Old Testament.* Jeremias pointed out that the Scribes demanded to be addressed in public by the title of "Prophet" and not of "Scribe." Paul took aim at those who thought of themselves in this way as "prophets." He certainly did not think of them in that way. He challenged them point blank: "Did any of them claim to be a prophet?"

Marker 4. *Especially spiritual.* In verse 37, Paul referred to those who considered themselves to be "spiritually gifted." The Scribes thought of themselves as superior to others in this very way. Paul challenged them: Did they think they were "spiritually gifted"?

A thunderous rebuke! In response to his four rhetorical questions, Paul affirmed in verse 37 that *his* word had divine authority, not theirs. He alone had been called by Jesus to be the apostle to the Gentiles (Galatians 2:7-8).

Those who rejected Paul's teaching were to be identified as ignorant of what God truly said to the church. Anything further that came from them was to be ignored by the church, verse 38.

A closer look. Paul started verse 36 with the one-letter Greek word ("*eta*") meaning, "What?" or "Indeed?" This word was often used in a diatribe, or the middle of a written "dialogue." The RSV translated verse 36 as follows:

What! Did the word of God originate with you,
or are you the only ones it has reached?

In 1 Corinthians 10:22, this *same* Greek word was used at the start of his reply to those Corinthians who were putting undue stress on the saying, "All things are lawful." There, Paul used it to introduce his vigorous response,

Indeed? Do we really get the better of the Lord?

Odell-Scott (p. 14) described the situation like this:

Verse 36 rejects the self-righteous assumptions of the men voiced in verses 34-35 who believe women should be silent.

What was Paul *not* saying?
Since many people take verses 34-35 as Paul's own ideas, it is important to realize how important it is to correctly identify these words as coming from other people – those influenced by the Scribes. Since these are not Paul's words – but ideas he vigorously rejected – it means that:

1. Paul did *not* say in any way that Christian women should be silent.

2. Paul did *not* say that women should "be subject."

3. Paul did *not* restrict women from learning the word of God.

4. Paul did *not* consider women's words to be shameful.

5. Paul did *not* respect, nor defer to, any "law" that taught any of this.

Summary and Application (39-40)

Resumption of summation and conclusion
[39]Therefore, my brothers and sisters, be eager to prophesy, and do not forbid speaking in tongues. [40]Let all things be done in a fitting and orderly way.

Moving on.
In verses 39-40, Paul left behind the diversion of the legalists. He picked up his train of thought, from the end of verse 33. His words harmonized with what preceded verses 34-38. It was as though verses 34-38 hadn't been written at all.

Women in public teaching ministry. The words in verses 34-35 were not Paul's words. He vigorously rebutted them not only in word but also in deed. Paul had many women co-laborers in public ministry. A third of those persons listed as ministering in Rome were women (Romans 16). In Corinth and Ephesus, Paul worked openly and fruitfully with Priscilla, an accomplished theologian, teacher and church planter. In no place did Paul restrict women from use of any spiritual gift in the church, in the home, or in society.

In order to shake out the cobwebs of the ideas proposed in verses 34-35, it is helpful to review what the Old and New Testaments teach about women in ministry.

Old Testament. In the Old Testament, a number of women were great judges, prophets and queens. Miriam was one of the three great leaders of Israel during the Exodus (Micah 6:4). She sang the great song of celebration after the defeat of Pharoah's army. The prophet Hulda's threefold "Thus says the Lord!" led to a great revival (2 Kings 22:13-20). Judge Deborah was a leader in Israel (Judges 4:4-5; 5:1-2).

Esther became queen for "such a time a this" (Esther 4:14). Her leadership resulted in many Gentiles coming to faith in God (8:17). She was recognized for her prudence and judgment and was vested with authority (9:11-12, 29-32).

Hebrew pronouns, which are more gender precise than they are in English, showed that women were told in the Psalms and in Isaiah to *proclaim* the Word (Kroeger and Kroeger, p. 13):

> The Lord gives the Word. Great is the host of women who proclaim it. (Psalm 68:11).

> O woman who is herald of good tidings in Zion, lift up your voice with strength, O woman who is herald of good tidings to Jerusalem, lift it up, fear not; say to the cities of Judah, 'Behold your God.'" (Isa 40:9).

During the Old Testament period only the few Israelites who were descendants of Levi were allowed to be priests (Exodus 29:9, 40:15). Even those who were Levites had to disqualify themselves if they had a blemish or open wound of any kind (Leviticus 21:17-24). This was part of the symbolism embodied in the sacrificial system of the Tabernacle.

Since women have regular menstrual periods, they were freed from duty as priests. This was in order to maintain the symbolism that the only blood in the Tabernacle or the Temple would be the blood of the sacrifice (Leviticus 15:31-33; cf. 16:1-4, 17; 10:1-3). This blood represented Christ's coming sacrifice in which His blood would cover sins (Romans 3:25). No other blood was allowed.

This restriction due to the symbolism of the blood of the lamb was similar to the restriction placed on fire because of the symbolic importance of the fire used to light the sacrifice on the altar. Aaron's eldest sons presented unacceptable fire to the Lord and were put to death (!) for doing so (Leviticus 9:23-10:2). All this was done to maintain the purity and the clarity of the spiritual meaning of these symbols.

New Testament. Jesus replaced the symbolism of the Old Testament period with the real thing. Instructive symbolism was no longer needed. The rituals that pointed to the sacrifice of Jesus were no longer needed. Instead people could clearly point to Jesus dying for our sins on the cross.

In the New Testament, with restrictions due to symbolism no longer necessary, *both* women and men are called *priests* and *kings* (Rev 1:6), as well as *prophets* and *apostles*. Peter taught (1 Pet 2:5, 9) that all believers are part of a holy priesthood. All believers offer up spiritual sacrifices and are to proclaim the praises of God.

Some may ask, "Why wasn't at least one of the twelve disciples a woman?" It has always been true that discreet men will have only male companions if they want to keep themselves from sexual entanglements and free from the innuendo and accusations of outsiders. Jesus was a male and so he traveled with other males in his immediate group. But outside of his immediate companions, were a number of women who traveled with Jesus. In Luke, women are learn and minister along with the twelve disciples (Luke 8:2-3; 10:38-42; 13:10-11; etc.).

We know the names of the twelve disciples. The names of a number of women are known as well. They are Mary and Martha of Bethany, plus Mary Magdalene, Salome, Johanna, Susanna and Mary the mother of Jesus.

In Acts 1:13-15; 2:1-4, Luke records that a number of women were in the Upper Room on the day of Pentecost. They were part of the 120 who were anointed by the tongues of fire of the Holy Spirit and then went out proclaiming the Gospel in public. Peter explained in Acts 2:17-18 that this had been foretold by Joel.

'And it shall come to pass in the last days,' says God. 'That I will pour out my Spirit on all flesh; Your sons and your daughters shall prophesy, Your young men shall see visions, Your old men shall dream dreams. And on my menservants and on my maidservants I will pour out my Spirit in those days; And they shall prophesy.'

Luke further records in Acts that a number of women were in the forefront of public ministry.

In the Epistles, women were called to minister in every way. The Kroegers (24, 90-92) summed up the situation as follows in this extended quotation:

> The New Testament teaches that individual members, along with their gifts and talents, are God's gift to the church (1 Cor 12:4-11; Eph 4:11-13). There are many gifts ..., (Rom 12:4-8). Among these gifts are those of teaching and administration. No limitation with respect to gender is indicated (Acts 2:17-18; 1 Cor 12:28). Persons endowed with the gift of teaching are expected to develop this potential to the glory of God ... (Rom 12:7-8).
>
> ... Romans 16:1-2 speaks of Phoebe as a deacon (or minister) of the congregation at Cenchrea, and she is also called a *prostates* (overseer, guardian, protector). A verbal form drawn from the same stem ... is used also in the New Testament at 1 Timothy 5:17 for elders who "preside" (or rule) well, and at Romans 12:8 (rule) and 1 Thessalonians 5:12 (hold authority over)." ... Junia is called a noteworthy apostle (Rom 16:7). Paul mentions several women, including Priscilla, as "fellow laborers" and asks that Christians be subject to such as these (Phil 4:2-3; Rom 16:3-4, 6, 12; 1 Cor 16:16,19). A number of Christian women appear to have presided over churches which met in their homes (Acts 12:12; 16:13-15, 40; Rom 16:3-5; 1 Cor 1:11; 16:19; Col 4:15; 2 John).

Why? This question may be asked of interpretations and even translations of the Bible that appear to negate the call of women to all types of ministry. Many times, as I read through a passage of the New Testament using one translation or another I come upon words or phrases that seem to restrict women and/or isolate men.

When that happens, I open up my Greek New Testament to see how these words were said originally. Inevitably, the "apparent difficulties" disappear when the original language version is consulted.

For example, I stumbled when I read a phrase in an English Bible that said "sinful men." I checked the passage in Greek and found the single word "flesh." Apparently the translators thought there was more likelihood of misunderstanding what the word "flesh" stood for, than there was for inserting the word "men."

Any non-student of Greek can gain insight by using a Greek-English Interlinear Version. It will show the approximate English words right below each Greek word. Other resource materials are available for deeper research.

Conclusion

Because of missing quotation marks in our English Bibles, the unwary reader of 1 Corinthians may miss the context of Paul's dialog with persons from the church in Corinth. Not everyone wanted to challenge Paul's teaching (1 Cor 11: 2), but some did. This was also the case in 1 Corinthians 14:34-35. Notably, both quotation sections in 11 and 14 use the ugly Greek word "shame." This is another sign of a common source for these words apart from Paul.

A helpful way to remind oneself of what is happening in these passages is to take out a pen and place quotation marks in your Bible around 14:34-35 (as well as around 11:4-6).

If this Bible study has made it clear that the Bible does not promote the teachings of the Jewish oral law, then those thoughts can be relegated, as Paul did, to the waste file of "human opinion only." No Christian today should propagate or tolerate such teachings either.

Think Again!

1. Various modern translations divide verse 33 and attach the second half to verse 34. How does this change one's impression of what Paul is saying?

2. Some modern translations form one paragraph out of the three verses 34-36. How does this change the meaning? What should be done?

3. Does any spirit of legalism lurk in your heart or in your church, especially in the case of who can and cannot minister and what special requirements may be required of them?

4. If you answered, "yes" to question three, consider Paul's recommended behavior in verses 39-40 and flee from the attitude of the self-righteous legalists.

248

PART IV

How to Spot Heresies for Yourself

250

Chapter 8

"How to" Think Again about the Bible
... and the Seven *Think Again* Bible Study Steps

Chapter Contents:

- The Four Principles and the Seven Steps

- 1. God is the source of all Truth

- 2. Everything in the Bible has its own place

- 3. Everything in the Bible has its own meaning

- 4. The Bible is meant to change me

- The Seven *Think Again* Bible Study Steps

Camp week began with the story about the "lazy looker." It went like this:

There once was a contest for a group of campers. Each one was given a sheet with a numbered list. Hurrying down the path as best they could, they were to spot the numbered items and write down precisely what they saw. A lazy boy determined to win the race. With a burst of speed he soon outdistanced all the rest. When he saw Item #1 he wrote on his list – "tree" – and ran on. When he saw Item #2 he wrote – "rock" – and hurried on. At Item #3 he wrote – "flower" – and dashed ahead. He finished the course in practically no time at all! He handed in his sheet and waited. Fifteen minutes later the next camper arrived!

When everyone was back and the lists had been examined, the leader asked the second one to read his list. The lazy boy was surprised because the winner was supposed to read out what was on his list.

This is what the second one read: "Item #1: sassafras sapling. Item #2: sandstone outcropping with trilobite fossil. Item #3: white trillium, our state flower." And on went the list.

After this story was told, the listening campers understood the lazy boy's mistake. He was a "lazy looker." Then the campers were told not to race through their week at camp but to pay attention. In that way, they would "see" all the richness around them and not be "lazy lookers."

I thought this was a good story for campers. I never suspected it would apply to me. But when I took my first preaching course in seminary, I found out that it did.

Prior to enrolling in seminary, I had been a youth worker. I had learned to stress "the basics" with all my teenage club members. I knew Bible verses for each basic idea: "How to become a Christian," "How to discern God's will," and so on. Whenever I was a guest speaker at various clubs, I picked one of the "basics" and dressed it up with illustrations of my own. In time, I had a half dozen stock messages ready to go and used them often. Sometimes a Bible passage was given for me to speak on. I checked to see which of my six messages best fit the passage and preached away.

In seminary I asked my roommate to check over the sermons I prepared for class. After reading several he was stunned. "All you can see in the whole Bible are your pet topics! There are hundreds or thousands of lessons in there. Let the Bible speak for itself, don't always paste one of your 'basics' over the mouth of the passage!"

I had been a "lazy looker" when I read my Bible! In time, I learned to look more carefully at each passage I read. I began to *think again* about what each passage really was saying.

The following Four Principles sum up "How to" let each passage of the Bible speak for itself: (1) God is the Source of all Truth, (2) Everything in the Bible has its own place, (3) Everything in the Bible has its own meaning, (4) The Bible is meant to change me.

Then, the Seven *Think Again* Bible Study Steps provide an easy roadmap to use in putting the Four Principles into practice.

1. God is the Source of all Truth

To *think again* about any passage in the Bible, it must be decided, "Who is doing the talking?"

-   Is it you, the reader? Consciously, or unconsciously, do you use the pages of the Bible as a springboard for thinking about your *own* ideas?

-   Is it some theologian, or group of theologians, who organize *their* thoughts and tell you what the Bible is saying?

-   Is it some other person – a relative, friend, or person in church – who does a lot of thinking and whose ideas you adopt as your own?

-   Or do you let the Bible speak for itself?

There may be some passages in the Bible where you have not let the Bible speak for itself. In some places you may have followed the ideas of others where their ideas strayed from what the Bible is saying. In such cases it is important to stop and *think again* about the Bible.

When you study a passage, a verse, a phrase, or a word in the Bible, let the Bible itself guide your understanding.

"**Touch and go.**" I grew up in a church where the Bible text for the day was read just before the pastor got up to preach. This pastor had a lot of ideas of his own that he liked to deliver in his sermons. Usually, he would make a glancing reference to the text of the day and then he would leave the Bible's ideas far behind for the rest of his message. Some of us used to joke grimly about his "touch and go sermons."

When a student pilot needs to practice how to land an airplane, and how to take off, the best exercise is the "touch and go." After first taking off, the student pilot circles the airport and comes in for a brief landing – this is the "touch" part of the exercise. As soon as the wheels of the plane touch the ground the student pilot hits the throttle and takes off immediately – this is the "go" part of the exercise. In this way practice is gained on both landing and taking off, but very little time is spent on the runway.

In the church of my childhood, the pastor would "touch and go" with a brief reference made to the Bible verse of the day, followed by a soaring exposition on his own ideas of the moment. We never spent time on what the Bible said. **The Bible teaches us Truth.** It has been said, "All truth is God's truth." This recognition frees the believer to pursue truth in every academic discipline. There is nothing "unspiritual" about learning any truth that comes from God. There is a special branch of knowledge that is all about God. It is called "theology." The word "theology" literally means "a word about God."

Who would know best about God – than God? It can be said that "true Truth" exists in the mind of God. *What God knows* is called Absolute Theology. These are God's ideas, as only God knows them. There are no errors in Absolute Theology.

We humans can see God's creative work revealed in the world around us. In it we see evidence of God's power, precision and joy. We gain an understanding of the depth and complexity of God's ideas. What can be discerned about God from looking at creation is called General Revelation (Rom 1:18-21).

We also learn about God through what is called Special Revelation. It is God's knowledge put into words *by God.* An example of Special Revelation is everything taught by Jesus, who was God in the flesh. Jesus taught God's Truth. He is called "the Word" (John 1:1-3). The Bible is also called God's Word. The Bible says: "All Scripture is inspired by God …" (1 Tim. 2:12). Both the words of Jesus and the Bible, are God's Special Revelation.

Anything we put into words ourselves about God, Jesus and the Bible is called Partial Theology. The closer a person's teachings parallel Revealed Theology, the more True they are. But error can, and does, creep in to Partial Theology.

1. **Absolute Theology** is True and exists in the mind of God.

2. **Revealed Theology** also is True and is inspired by God. General Revelation is revealed in creation. Special Revelation is God's Word, which includes both Jesus and the Bible.

3. **Partial Theology** is made up of human words about God's Truth. The more a partial theology corresponds to God's Revelation, the more True it is.

What God knows and reveals is universally True for all times and places. The difficulty is that Partial Theology is "culture bound." It is skewed by the limited knowledge of a person's time and place.

An example of limited and culture-bound Partial Theology is the theology of Christians who defended the slave trade in England and early America. Their understanding of the Bible was flawed. Their theological statements on slavery were not True for all times nor for all places. Many of their sermons, books, songs, hymns and even prayers, contained flawed Partial Theology.

Issues of Partial Theology should be rooted in Revealed Theology. Partial Theology is developed by humans. All of this should be based on God's part, the inerrant revelation of absolute, and true, Truth. The more Partial Theology is drawn from Absolute and Revealed Theology, the more True it is.

To the extent that theologians grasp God's Truth in such a way that it applies for all times and places, their Partial Theology is True and is "transcultural."

In this way, a number of "great doctrines" have been formulated over the centuries and across cultures. An example of a "great doctrine" is the following balanced statement about the dual nature of Christ:

"Christ is both fully God and fully human."

Partial Theology develops in three stages whenever people in a new culture are introduced to the Bible:

1. Inculturation
2. Indigenization
3. Ethnic theology

Inculturation. Every culture is marked by certain beliefs and certain practices (some of which are sinful) that are prevalent in their time and place. When the Gospel is first presented to people in new culture group, a preliminary Partial Theology is first put into words and action for that culture.

Those who are responsible for putting theology into the new culture are pioneer evangelists and missionaries. They make decisions about what to say and how to say it to the new people group. Often the initial decisions made by missionaries and pioneer evangelists are correct from the start. But sometimes, what they communicate is not fully in keeping with the Truth of Revealed Theology. These errors will need to be recognized and corrected.

Indigenization. This occurs next. The new believers take the inculturated Partial Theology they received and make it their own. At first they simply imitate and repeat what the evangelists and missionaries bring to them. Over time, however, as they pass on their theology, it gets reshaped into their local cultural patterns.

For example, instead of building square buildings topped by steeples, local Christians may begin to hold meetings in buildings that look more like those typically used for religious meetings in their own culture. They also begin to use analogies that exist in their own culture to explain truths about God.

Ethnic theology. This finally develops when local believers find answers in the Bible to questions that the original missionaries and the first local preachers and teachers didn't know to ask. Often this occurs among the second and third generation Christians in a culture.

As these Christians study what the Bible says and apply it to pressing issues in their society, they bring to light aspects of God's Truth that others may have overlooked.

If they succeed in remaining true to Revealed Theology, then the aspect of theology they articulate can be added to the developing transcultural "great doctrines" of the church. An example of this is the development of theology that deals with the missionary movement.

Organizing Partial Theology. Once theological ideas have been developed, they can be organized. Stages in this process include the systematization of theological ideas into doctrines. They also include the development of ways to implement these ideas in everyday life. These are worked out in the fields of Systematic Theology and Practical Theology.

Systematic Theology is passed along in textbooks and in Sunday School lessons. It is also found in the cross-reference notations and footnotes that are added to editions of the Bible. Practical Theology is lived out in various spheres of life. These include getting along with others in the local church, with family members and with others in society.

Ideally, all Systematic and Practical Theology is *drawn from* (the technical word is "exegesis"), God's Revealed Theology. However, in practice, neither corresponds one hundred per cent to Revealed Theology. Sometimes the percentage is much lower. Where doctrines and practices are not drawn from Revealed Theology, as expressed in the context of a particular book or chapter of the Bible, these doctrines need revision.

In Switzerland, I got off the local train that stopped at every station along the north shore of Lake Geneva and walked to a nearby chateau. It belonged to the World Council of Churches and was the summer home of John Samuel Mbiti, an African theologian whose works I had studied for several years.

He was expecting me and invited me to come into the sunroom for a cup of tea. In the course of my research, I had come to the conclusion that one of the doctrines he taught was not from the Bible. In fact, it ran counter to the Bible!

His teaching seemed to be a form of universalism, in that he believed that some day God would draw all souls to Himself, even the ones that had been condemned to hell (for a time).

I attempted to be discreet as I raised the topic with him. I asked him if he had derived this particular doctrine from a passage in the Bible, from one of his own professors, or from a book by some scholar. He paused, tilted his head and thought for a moment. Then he smiled and said, "I guess I made it up." Frankly, his admission startled me.

Many who claim to be "spiritual" in one way or another, may hold beliefs that are not necessarily True. Since experience and intuition can lead a person to hold views that are sincere, but sincerely wrong, it is always important to search the Scriptures to see if a belief is validated by God's Revelation in the Bible.

To sum up:

- **Systematic theology** assembles ideas into systematized themes. This Partial Theology is only dependable to the extent it is drawn from the Bible.

- **Practical theology** is only as dependable as the systematized theology upon which it is built. To the extent that either one is drawn from sources *outside* Scripture, such as cultural norms and myth, or political or ecumenical theology, they may be seriously flawed.

What do we know? When I was a brand new missionary taking language training in Africa, I was urgently asked to preach at a funeral. In America, the Twenty Third Psalm was a favorite passage to use at funerals. I repeated those precious words in my mind, "The Lord is my shepherd, I shall not want. ... Even though I walk through the Valley of the Shadow of Death, I will fear no evil." I accepted the invitation and said I would preach on the Twenty Third Psalm. My choice seemed an obvious one at the time.

Soon I learned that I would be one of a series of speakers who would preach through the entire night at two-hour intervals until the burial the next day. Church choirs would sing in between the sermons. I was to speak at midnight!

I asked if a translator would be available. None was. I would have to use my limited ability in Lingala. I asked for a language helper and got a copy of the Twenty Third Psalm in Lingala to work from. We went over key terms in the passage to make sure I knew how to use and pronounce them.

As we worked through the Psalm, I was surprised to find out this was not a favorite passage of my helper. I then learned that this "Shepherd's Psalm" meant very little to him because, although people owned sheep, they had no shepherds!

Everyone let their sheep forage for themselves. I remembered seeing some very scraggly looking sheep in the area. Now I knew why.

In my message that night, I had to start from scratch and explain how a shepherd in Israel cares for his sheep. Only afterwards could I begin to explain how God wants to care for us in the same way. The response was overwhelming. They were deeply moved. The teachers in the local Bible school even added a lesson to their curriculum on how sheep were cared for in Israel.

Other great passages in the Bible include:

- the Creation (Genesis 1)
- the Ten Commandments (Exodus 10)
- the Suffering Servant (Isaiah 53)
- the Love Chapter (1 Corinthians 13)
- the Hall of Fame of Faith (Hebrews 11)

Great doctrines may be distilled from a great passage, or from more than one passage. For example:

- The doctrine of salvation by faith (Rom. 5-8).

- The doctrine of the Trinity (Luke 3:22, 1 John 5:8)

Church denominations and ministry organizations usually have Statements of Faith. Those that are the most True are drawn from the Bible. Usually they stress one or two doctrines more than other denominations. Here is a balanced one, for example – the Doctrinal Statement of the Willow Creek Association:

The Bible is God's unique revelation to people. It is the inspired, infallible Word of God, and the supreme and final authority on all matters upon which it teaches. No other writings are vested with such divine authority.

There is only one God, creator of heaven and earth, who exists eternally as three persons – Father, Son, and Holy Spirit, each fully God yet each personally distinct from the other.

All people are created in God's image and matter deeply to Him. Central to the message of the Bible is that God loves people, and invites them to live in communion with Himself and in community with each other.

Apart from Jesus Christ, all people are spiritually lost and, because of sin, deserve the judgment of God. However, God gives salvation and eternal life to anyone who trusts in Jesus Christ and in His sacrifice on his or her behalf. Salvation cannot be earned through personal goodness or human effort. It is a gift that must be received by humble repentance and faith in Christ and His finished work on the cross.

Jesus Christ, second Person of the Trinity, was born of the Virgin Mary, lived a sinless human life, willingly took upon Himself all of our sins, died and rose again bodily, and is at the right hand of the Father as our advocate and mediator. Some day, He will return to consummate history and to fulfill the eternal plan of God.

The Holy Spirit, third Person of the Trinity, convicts the world of sin and draws people to Christ. He also indwells all believers. He is available to empower them to lead Christ-like lives, and gives them spiritual gifts with which to serve the church and reach out to a lost and needy world.

Death seals the eternal destiny of each person. At the final judgment, unbelievers will be separated from God into condemnation. Believers will be received into God's loving presence and rewarded for their faithfulness to Him in this life.

All believers are members of the body of Christ, the one true church universal. Spiritual unity is to be expressed among Christians by acceptance and love of one another across ethnic, cultural, socio-economic, national, generational, gender, and denominational lines.

The local church is a congregation of believers who gather for worship, prayer, instruction, encouragement, mutual accountability, and community with each other. Through it, believers invest time, energy, and resources to fulfill the Great Commission — reaching lost people and growing them into fully devoted followers of Christ.

This statement reflects a contemporary summary of the central doctrines in the Bible, which are also presented in the historic creeds of the Christian church (from www.WillowCreek.com).

2. Everything in the Bible has its own place

It is important to keep in mind that each word in the Bible has a context of its own. This context has three dimensions:

1. Literary context
2. Biblical context
3. Context in the world outside the Bible

1. Literary context.

Word. The words in the Bible are linked together by grammatical rules. When they are linked together they form sentences and paragraphs, lists and poems, and more.

The Old Testament was written in Hebrew and some Aramaic, and the New Testament was written in Greek. It is important to understand the meanings of the words in the Bible in their original languages.

Sentence. Each word in the Bible fits into its own home sentence. Sometimes a single word in the Bible can have multiple meanings. When studied in the context of its home sentence, its meaning usually becomes clear.

Passage. A group of sentences that belong together, because they form a statement on a single topic, is called a passage. The technical word for a Bible passage is a "pericope" (peh rih´ cuh pee). In the Book of Proverbs, a pericope may be two lines long. In a New Testament book by Paul, a pericope may run for an entire page.

Context. Each passage has its own place within its book of the Bible. It is helpful to notice in which part of the book it appears because each part may have a specific meaning or emphasis.

For example, in the Book of Romans, the passages in the first 11 chapters are more *theological* in their orientation. The passages in the last five chapters of Romans are more *practical* (see Rom 12:1-2). This is also true of Ephesians. The first three chapters are more *theological* and the last three are more *practical* in content.

2. Biblical context

Book. Each book of the Bible was written by a single author (Revelation: the Apostle John), or by a group of authors (Proverbs: David, Solomon and others). Each author's personality shows through in that book.

It is helpful to take into account *who* is the author of a book of the Bible because each author tended to emphasize certain facts or themes. For example, Luke was a medical doctor. He wrote two books of the Bible: the Gospel of Luke and the Book of Acts. He was a very careful historian (Luke 1:1-4). If a person wants to check for locations where events occurred in the life of Jesus, Luke's gospel is the place to look. Not surprisingly, Luke even included medical details (Luke 8:43, Acts 12:23).

The five books of Moses, Genesis through Deuteronomy, contain many direct quotes made by God. These include a range of quotes running from each word in the Ten Commandments, to detailed rules about cleanliness for those who were authorized to present burnt offerings for sacrifice. Moses was able to write in such detail because he talked with God extensively during forty years in the desert and was a key participant in the events of the Exodus from Egypt.

Isaiah wrote words of prophecy, which he received from God. Some of his prophecies applied to Israel and some applied to other nations. He wrote prophecies that came to pass not long thereafter and some prophecies that have not yet come to pass. He also wrote chapters that recorded historical details.

The Apostle John wrote a gospel, three letters and an eyewitness account in Revelation. These books had very different purposes behind them and represent three very distinct styles of writing: the very theological Gospel of John, the very practical and personal letters of John, and the very detailed symbolism of Revelation. Behind all five letters was the personal touch of the disciple who was part of Jesus' closest inner circle.

Place in the Bible. The Bible is divided into Old and New Testaments. The Old Testament looked forward to the coming of the Messiah. It laid a foundation of laws, symbolism and examples that helped the world to understand the meaning of the sacrificial death of the Messiah. The New Testament tells about the life of Jesus the Messiah and his sacrificial death on the cross for our sins. It also chronicles the beginning and growth of the church, and gives principles for righteous living.

There are distinct groupings of books in both Testaments. In the Old Testament there is historical, prophetic and wisdom literature. In the New Testament there are books on the life of Jesus, the acts of the early Christians, letters to churches and individuals, and the revelation of the end times.

3. Context outside of the Bible

History. Understanding details from past events can help the modern reader better understand the Bible. For example, it is important to have an understanding of the family of Isaac and especially the prophecies made regarding his two sons. What they did afterward, and where they and their descendants settled, can be traced on maps and in the history of the Jews and Arabs. What God said about them helps us to understand the continuing conflict between these two groups.

When reading a prophetic reference to a "bee," it is helpful to know that Egypt was known by that emblem. It also helps to note that Israel was located in the middle of the Fertile Crescent. This placed Israel on the "highway of armies" which was traversed time and time again as nation went to battle nation.

The northern kingdom of Israel was attacked by an empire to its northeast that was later conquered by an empire to the south of it. Later a different empire ruled over the entire area, including Jerusalem, when Nehemiah was sent back to rebuild the city.

Some of these details come to us from indications noted in the Bible itself. Other details come through historical records and from archaeological findings. Modern reference books have maps that show the political divisions of each historical period. These can be used to better understand the interaction of peoples and nations mentioned in the Bible.

Geography. When the Bible says that people went "up" to Jerusalem, it helps to know that Jerusalem was built on top of a mountain. All roads to Jerusalem literally went up!

As surprising as it may seem, in the small area located between the northern and southern borders of Israel at the time of Solomon there is great topographical variety. Simultaneously one can find snows on Mount Hermon in the north, an arid desert south of the brackish Dead Sea, a fresh water Sea in Galilee and salt spray along the coast of Mediterranean Sea.

Culture. The Bible takes us from the peaceful Garden of Eden to the brutal Coliseum of Rome, from the pyramids of Egypt to the Hanging Gardens of Babylon. Each individual culture had a completely different set of rulers, laws, religions and more.

Practice putting a word in its context.

Example 1. In an adult Bible class in our church, after talking about studying a word in its context, we decided to try to practice with a specific word.

Word. Someone in the class suggested the word "healed." We chose to look at the word "healed" in Isaiah 53:5 as our starting point.

Sentence. We noted that the *sentence*, in which the *word* is found, covers more than just one verse. That meant that both verses 4 and 5 would need to be studied together.

Passage. Someone suggested that the *passage* was comprised of the entire fifty-third chapter of Isaiah. Others disagreed. After further discussion the group identified the start of the pericope as 52:13. The passage runs from 52:13 through 53:12.

Context. This passage was known as one of the *Servant Songs*. There are four of them in Isaiah: in chapter 42, 49, 52-53 and 61. All four talk about the promised Messiah as a Suffering Servant.

Book. We studied the Biblical context and the place of Isaiah in the rest of the Bible, and other uses of the Servant Songs. We noted that verses from the last Servant Song were read by Jesus as the assigned passage in the synagogue in Nazareth (Luke 4:18-21). After reading it, he announced that he fulfilled that prophecy!

Historical, geographical, cultural setting. We studied the extra-biblical context of Isaiah and how people had different expectations of the Messiah.

Prior to the successful revolt of the Jews and the independence of Israel as a nation (from 166-37 B.C.), it was understood that the prophecies about the Messiah pointed to his embodiment of *two* different aspects:

1. as the Suffering Servant, and

2. as the conquering King of Kings.

But by the time Jesus came to Israel, the Jews' Messianic hopes were pinned exclusively on an earthly victor who would save their nation from the Romans who had enslaved them some three decades earlier.

When Jesus pointed to the passages that stressed his role as Suffering Servant, the people missed the point. Some even accused him of blasphemy.

Once we had situated the word "healed" in its three contexts – literary, biblical and historical – we recognized that the "healing" referred to in Isaiah 53 was related to the context of the Suffering Servant who would die for our *sins*. We agreed that spiritual healing is certainly intended in the field of meaning of the verse in Isaiah 53:5. We decided we would have to look elsewhere in the Bible if we wanted to find teaching related to physical healing.

Example 2. I asked the class if anyone had another word they wanted to try. The parents of one of the young adults in the class were visiting that day. When no one else suggested a word, our class member's mother said, "I'd like to suggest a word. It has troubled me for years. What does it mean to "be perfect"?

Word. First we had to identify where the words "be perfect" were found. We discovered them in the very last verse of Matthew chapter 5. Jesus told the crowd during his Sermon on the Mount to "be perfect."

Sentence. We noted that these words were in a sentence that began with the word "therefore." We needed to see what the "therefore" was *there for*.

Passage. The "therefore" tied verse 48 with the section of verses that started with verse 43. This passage had to do with loving one's enemies.

Context. The passage started with a phrase that had been repeated over and over again by Jesus in the Sermon on the Mount:

"You have heard it said … but I say to you …."

Jesus was responding to and correcting things that the Jewish Teachers of the Law (Scribes) had been teaching the people. Their teachings were made up of the Jewish oral law and it was flawed.

Book. Matthew wrote the Gospel we were studying. In his Gospel he stressed themes that were especially important to the Jews.

In Matthew 5:48, when Jesus said, "Be perfect," he also referred to "his Father." His hearers would have recognized this as an unmistakable claim that he was the Messiah! This would have astonished and delighted the crowds.

But it angered the Jewish leaders. They believed Jesus was falsely claiming to be God. That was labeled blasphemy, and was punishable by death. The Jewish leaders thought that Jesus had just made himself liable to execution!

In Matthew 5:48, Jesus was instructing his hearers to "be perfect." Only persons made holy by God could ever aspire to being perfect. These words of Jesus placed his hearers under the obligation to recognize Jesus as the Messiah and to trust in Him for forgiveness. They also placed Jesus under the obligation to forgive the sins of those who believed in him. (He soon made that possible by dying on the cross for sins.)

Taking into account the setting.

Here are two examples of how taking into account the historical situation of a passage enriches one's understanding of the Bible.

Example 1. Historically, the Jews executed criminals by stoning. When the Jewish leaders decided to execute Jesus as a blasphemer, they were faced with a roadblock. Their Roman rulers reserved the right to inflict capital punishment.

The Romans did not use stoning. Among other methods, they practiced death by crucifixion. Crucifixion had not yet been invented when the prophets foretold that the Messiah would be pierced (Psalm 22:16, Zech. 12:10 KJV).

These cultural and historical details enrich not only our understanding of what occurred at the time of the crucifixion of Jesus, they also enrich our understanding of how miraculous were the details of the prophecies of old!

Example 2. Much of the teaching in the Old Testament involved "typologies," or concrete examples that stood for spiritual truths. For example, while the Israelites were in the desert, God told Moses to strike a rock. He did as he was told and water poured forth from that rock for everyone to drink. In addition to meeting the immediate need of the thirsty Israelites, Moses' striking the rock represented Jesus (the rock) being struck (crucified) so that all people might drink (of the Holy Spirit) and have (eternal) life.

When God instituted the system of burnt offerings, this served a typological purpose. It taught people about the necessity of a payment for sin. To perform these ritual sacrifices a subgroup of Israelites, the Levites, was set aside. They were trained to do the work of sacrificing the animals and offering them to God on the altar. Everything about this process stood for a spiritual truth related to the future sacrifice of Jesus on the cross. The fire that was used to burn the sacrifices had been lit by God. The blood that was used to cover the altar (and therefore the sins of the people) came from an animal without spot or imperfection. This was symbolic of the sinless Messiah.

No other fire was to be used. No other blood was allowed. There was a penalty for breaking ritual purity.

To ensure that no blood other than that of the sacrificial animal was present in the place of sacrifice, a number of rules were established. No one with a wound or open sore could participate in making a sacrifice.

This led to the unique situation when God was angry with both Miriam and Aaron for *their* sin (Numbers 12). To maintain ritual purity of Aaron, the very first High Priest, *only* Miriam was struck with leprosy when both she and her brother Aaron sinned against God. Her brother would need to be ceremonially clean when it was time to certify her cleansing. But both siblings learned the same lesson.

Jesus demonstrated that the period of symbolic purity was coming to an end when he did a number of things that would have made him ritually "unclean." He touched lepers and made them well. He did not rebuke a woman who had a flow of blood yet touched him, nor did he hesitate to touch a dead body in order to bring a young girl back to life (Luke 8:43-56).

Since the historical events of the death and resurrection of Jesus, no more is a distinction made between Jew and non-Jew, slave or free, male or female (Gal. 3:26-29).

3. Everything in the Bible has its own meaning

Because an English word in the Bible can have one, or several, possible meanings, it is important to determine the specific context in which it appears. Then, after determining a word's context in the Bible, it is time to determine its specific definition.

Here are the basic ingredients that go into building the definition of a given word in the Bible:

- What is its part of speech: verb, noun, adjective, adverb, other? There are only two Hebrew verb tenses, past and non-past. In Greek, there are six. These verbs may be passive or active, continuous or punctiliar, and so on.

- Every word has its own constellation of meanings. No two words in different languages have the same range of meanings. Some of the ideas that "naturally" go with a word in English might not be present in the field of meaning of a Greek word, and vice versa.

- Conjunctions may be emphatic or may serve as mere connectors. Verb prefixes may modify meaning (intensify or attenuate) or may only be exhausted (no longer have the meaning it once had prior to the time it was written in the Bible).

- Frequency of use: common, rare, *hapax* (unique). Study tools may or may not list all occurrences.

- Variations in meaning: unique phrases may modify meaning. Look for the root word behind the English word. Beware of "false friends." Later use of a word does not necessarily define original use.

- Meanings used by a given author: limited or broad. One author may use a nuanced meaning, another may not do so at all (*cf.* Colossians 1:18).

- Other meanings in the Bible: from the same period, or from another time period. For example Moses used words in one way. These words may have been used in a different way later on. Classical, or Attic, Greek was different from the later koiné Greek of the New Testament.

- Meanings in secular literature of the period: relevant, other. For example, Luke wrote the first modern history. This was unique in his day, which was filled with "vanity literature."

Bible dictionaries, commentaries and other references may be helpful in checking one's own work after defining a word.

Grammar and usage affect the meaning of a word. There are at least five elements in grammar and usage to consider.

1. Historical details. It is important to distinguish between a statement of fact (something that is **reported** just the way it happened) and the relating of a detail that serves a purpose (the embodiment of a **principle** to put into practice).

For example, during a Bible study group in an African village, I was asked if polygamy was "biblical." I knew that some individuals in the group came from families where their polygamist father had a number of wives. Historically speaking, polygamy had been reported in the Bible. The Bible reports some men took multiple spouses.

To answer their question using the Four Principles, we looked up the situation of the first person in the Bible who took multiple wives, the bigamist Lamech (Genesis 4:19). I asked the group about the *principle* behind the historical *practice* related in the historical account. It was clear that this example was *not* something to be imitated, especially after we read the sinful boast of Lamech in Genesis 4:23-24,

> Adah and Zillah,
> Listen to my voice,
> You wives of Lamech,
> Give heed to my speech,
> For I have killed a man for wounding me;
> And a boy for striking me.
> If Cain is avenged sevenfold,
> Then Lamech seventy-seven fold." (NASB)

2. Unique complexities may occur in an original language of the Bible that are not used in English. In other words, one cannot assume that the rules of English grammar apply in another language. For example, another language may indicate a detail with more or less precision than is possible in English.

To understand the potentially significant impact of these differences it may be helpful to compare English with the language complexity of a tribe living on the Equator. This people group does not need watches to tell time. A widespread plant growing in their area turns different shades of green depending on the time of day. By noting these shade changes, they can dependably tell what time it is. In their language, they have a series of words to explain throughout the day what "color" (time) it is. If the Bible had been written in the language of this culture, it would be helpful to understand what shade of meaning (literally!) had originally been intended.

3. Patterns common to Hebrew or Greek literature. There are a number special patterns, or constructions, that are hard to translate into English, even though they are important in conveying the meaning of the passage. One example is **parallelism**. Hebrew poetry frequently uses repetition. Usually the second occurrence deepens and enriches the thought that is repeated.

In various passages, the Hebrew and Greek writers used a more complex parallel structure. It was made up of mirrored words or phrases in what is called a "chiasm." A famously complex chiasm occurs in the description of the Flood, in Genesis 7-8. Another occurs in Genesis 2:4-3:19.

In Greek, Paul used a grammatical device called an **anacoluthon**. In this way, a writer interrupted a train of thought and moved to another idea. Sometimes the original thought was picked up later in the passage, but sometimes it was just left hanging.

In some passages the use of an anacoluthon are not reflected in their English translations. These include:

- In Ephesians 5:33, Paul repeats the word "fear" from verse 21 and ties the meaning of verse 33 to the meaning of verse 21.

- In 1 Timothy 1:18, Paul refers to the charge he gave Timothy in the opening verses of the letter.

- In 1 Timothy 2:15*b*, Paul repeats a key word from 2:9 as he leaves behind his discussion on Adam and Eve (2:13-15*a*). When he refers to "they" in the second half of verse 15, Paul refers to women who are righteous, and not to Eve, nor to wives and husbands, nor to mothers and their children, as various theologians (who have missed the anacoluthon) have suggested.

4. Biblical insights. A **parable** is a story that usually has one point, such as answering the question "Who is my neighbor?" (Luke 10:29-37). A **prophecy** on the other hand may have multiple fulfillments.

Multiple prophetic fulfillments have been described as what one might see in the distance when looking across a mountain range. One point on the horizon may look like a single mountaintop, while there may actually be several mountaintops lined up in a row, separated by a series of valleys in between.

Another interesting way of communicating used in the Bible is the **allegory**. In an allegory, the given meaning is not self-evident, and may or may not be explained (Gal. 4:21-31).

5. Theological study needs to be conducted author by author. It should take into account the historical period of the Bible book. Finally, even doctrinal statements need to be considered in the light of the history of the development of doctrine from the early church to the present.

4. The Bible is meant to change me

The Bible is "self-aware" in that it contains statements about how it is to be used and about how its use will change its reader. Perhaps the most complete "user's statement" is to be found in 2 Timothy 3:16-17.

[16]All Scripture is God-breathed and is useful for teaching, rebuking, correcting and training in righteousness, [17]so that all God's people may be thoroughly equipped for every good work. (TNIV)

More "user's statements" are found in John's Gospel:

[20:30]And truly Jesus did many other signs in the presence of His disciples, which are not written in this book; [31]but these are written that you may believe that Jesus is the Christ, the Son of God, and that believing you may have life in His name.

[21:24][I am] the disciple who testifies to these things and who wrote them down. ... [25]Jesus did many other things as well. If every one of them were written down, I suppose that even the whole world would not have room for the books that would be written.

In the Old Testament, Joshua 1:8 gave an example of how God's Word was to be used:

[8]This Book of the Law shall not depart from your mouth, but you shall meditate on it day and night, that you may observe to do according to all that is written in it. For then you will make your way prosperous, and then you will have good success.

Joshua was supposed to meditate on the five books of Moses, out loud. The Hebrew verb "to meditate" in 1:8, literally means "to mumble." Believers were to softly recite the words of God's Law all day long. God attached a strong promise for Joshua if he followed this instruction. This serves as a lesson for Christians today to memorize and review verses of during each day.

David made up poems and sang them to God. These were written down in the Book of Psalms. The original melodies have not been passed down to us, but believers today may add tunes to David's words and sing them to God again!

The Bible speaks from inside history. This means that books in the Old Testament had meaning in the time in which they were written. This was true even though the New Testament was centuries away from being written.

Each Old Testament book contained sufficient revelation that it could be read in its day without referring to the New Testament. In fact, it is best to discern what an Old Testament passage means on its own before doing any cross-referencing to the New Testament.

Cross-referencing from the New Testament will never contradict a truth stated in the Old Testament. It may add to its richness of meaning, but it will never result in what one young Sunday School student called "cross-eyed referencing."

The Bible is meant to change lives. In it is found almost everything a person will ever need to find the answers to the important questions of life.

The Seven *Think Again* Bible Study Steps

How did you do that? What is the method to your studies? Every Bible Study in this book has followed Seven *Think Again* Bible Study Steps. These practical steps incorporate the Four Principles. Following these seven Steps will help you too to take fresh look at one Bible passage at a time and allow each passage to "speak for itself." Here they are with a brief explanation for each one:

Step 1. *Think Again* about what the Bible says. Pick a word, phrase or idea to study. Find a passage where it is located. Set aside preconceived ideas and allow the Bible to speak for itself. Back up and read a page or two in the Bible that leads up to the verse you want to study. Read a page or two after it as well. Make sure you understand the general topic being discussed. Perhaps you will find that the idea or issue that concerns you is not really being addressed in this part of the Bible. If necessary, look for another passage that speaks more specifically to the concern you have.

Even before locating a Bible passage that contains the word to study, a person already has some idea about what the target word or phrase means. The problem is this. Often what is in their mind is *not* what the Bible says in their passage. Only what is in God's Word, the Bible, is "true truth" and can depended on. Their own idea may be very wrong.

Perhaps their idea comes from some other passage in the Bible and is truly an idea from God. But it is possible it does not come from any Bible passage and actually runs counter to God's truth.

Made up ideas often get us into trouble when we try to put them into practice. Major complications arise when they affect other people too.

You can spot such an idea when good people come to different conclusions and harsh divisions arise. You can spot it when some people end up being mistreated, or when God is made out to be very different from what is revealed in other Bible passages.

In cases such as these, it is especially important to make the effort to *Think Again* about the passage in question. The next *Think Again* Study Steps will keep you going in the right direction.

Step 2. *Think Again* about the context. To ensure the Bible makes its own point in a verse, or a series of verses, first find the limits of your passage – the first and last verses. Then, notice how this passage fits into the larger context of the passages that come before and after it. Make sure you know where the flow of ideas is going and pay attention to how your passage fits into that context.

Step 3. *Think Again* about the content. The main points of a passage should receive major attention. Recognize sub-points for what they are. They should receive secondary importance. They will not contradict the main points.

Step 4. *Think Again* about the key image and/or idea. Take literal language literally. If that sense makes no sense, then move to the simplest level of abstraction and see if that fits into the flow of meaning. If not, then and only then, look for a more abstract possible meaning for an image or idea.

Step 5. *Think Again* about the target verse(s). This Step concerns the word, the verse, or the paragraph, that drew your attention from the very beginning. Having taken the three previous Steps, now look at word order, the definition of various words, and come to conclusions about the meaning of the verses of special interest.

Step 6. *Think Again* about the points of application. The Bible was not written only to be studied as an intellectual exercise. It is God's Word to us, communicating to us things God wants us to know, understand, and do.

Step 7. *Think Again* about what the Bible does *not* say. This Step is not often practiced in Bible study. However, if the *Think Again* Study Steps result in a fresh understanding of a Bible passage, previous misunderstandings need to be identified, labeled, rejected and replaced.

The Seven *Think Again* Bible Study Steps in Action

Let's see how these Seven Steps were put in action in the chapter on Ephesians 5:15-6:9: *Think Again about Submission.*

Step 1. *Think Again* about what the Bible says. Suppose a Bible study group wanted to study the relationship between a Christian husband and a Christian wife. They assumed that Ephesians 5:22-25 was a passage that addressed that topic. But they also were willing to set aside their own ideas and see what the Bible had to say for itself in these verses.

They assumed that the passage taught that "the husband is head of the house" and that "a wife is supposed to submit to his will." Happily, they made the effort to follow the *Think Again* Study Steps.

Step 2. *Think Again* **about the context.** This group was aware that a person might approach a verse having already decided what it is all about, and that if a person wasn't careful, the rest of the passage around it could be bent so that it lined up with the incorrect ideas the person brought to the passage.

This has happened in Ephesians. Many people have come to the last section of chapter 5 assuming that "this is the longest passage in the Bible about marriage." They then develop sermons, articles, hymns and recommendations for marriage based on what they wrongly assumed the text was about.

The Bible study group took Step 2 and looked at the context of the verses in chapter 5. They discovered that Paul had divided the second half of Ephesians into six sections and that all the verses in this second half of the book fall into one of these six sections. Since Paul labeled what each section was about, it was easy for the Bible study group to determine the development of his thought.

The Bible study group noted that the verses they wanted to study were located in the fifth section that ran from 5:15-6:9.

They realized they had to take into account the place of verses 22-25 in the whole passage. They also made the surprising discovery that verse 32 says that this passage is not about marriage, but Christ and the church! They wondered if they really should study these verses after all. Finally, they decided to continue.

Step 3. *Think Again* **about the content.** The Bible study group learned that the verses in the second half of Ephesians 5 are part of Paul's explanation on "How to behave as Christians who are walking carefully, filled with the Spirit." Each verse in this passage developed *this* main idea. They wanted to walk this way too, so their enthusiasm level for study of these verses increased.

They found the four "-ing verbs" (in Greek) in verses 19-21 that describe how to behave when one is filled with the Spirit. They noted that the first and fourth actions cannot be done alone, but are done with other Christians. That was fine. They already were meeting in a group. The four actions were:

- (19*a*) Speaking *to one another* with psalms ...
- (19*b*) Singing and making melody ...
- (20) Giving thanks ...
- (21) Being subject *to one another* ...

The list of parallel "-ing" verbs ended with verse 21. At this point they were just one verse away from the first of their target verses. They wanted to dig right in and study verses 22-25 but saved that work until Study Step 5.

Step 4. *Think Again* **about the key image and/or idea.** Often, a reader of a modern language translation assumes that we know all about the meaning of an image or key word used in the Bible. If our translations could exactly replicate the meaning of a word originally used in the Bible, perhaps we could assume that we did understand the meaning of most images right away.

But modern words do not carry the same constellation of meanings as do the biblical Hebrew and Greek words. The word "fire" might have its literal meaning in Greek plus several abstract meanings, while modern English might have a very different set of abstract meanings.

Here is where the Bible study group focused in on the meaning of a key word, "head." The literal meaning of "a real head" was the first sense to try. But, in Ephesians 5:23, a literal "head" is obviously not the intended meaning. An abstract meaning of "head" must be intended. But what abstract meaning?

The group knew that in dealing with abstractions it is best for them to start with the simplest level of abstraction to see if it fit the passage. Only if it did not would they move on looking for a more abstract meaning of the word "head." In this case they found no need to look beyond the simplest level of abstraction – that of the unity of a head and torso that make up one body.

Paul used the metaphor of "the head and torso" to represent the unity of Christians, filled with the Spirit, who are united and therefore can practice the distinctly Christian action of 5:21 of "being subject to one another."

Thus the key image used in the verses in 22-24 is about "unity." A husband and wife are united as one. Christ and the church are also united as one.

In following these preliminary *Think Again* Bible Study Steps, the place and the meaning of their verses of interest were already partly discovered. A closer inspection of these verses was the next step.

Step 5. *Think Again* **about the target verse(s).** Finally, the Bible study group concentrated in depth on verses 22-25. It took them discipline to withhold study of these verses until this Step. But now these verses could be studied in context with at least a preliminary understanding of the imagery used in the text. This was the place to study, in-depth, all aspects of a verse. These include word definition, word order, verb usage, and the place of these words in their context.

Some digging showed them that verse 22 was subordinate to verse 21 since it had no verb. Instead, there was a gap where the verb should be. According to Greek grammar, the previous verb should drop into the gap to complete the sentence. Thus, the verb in verse 21 dropped down into the gap in verse 22. The action in verse 22 then was "being subject to one another" in marriage!

Verse 22 was not about marriage but was one practical example of the redefined reciprocal verb introduced by Paul in verse 21. Verse 22 was not a new main point in the passage but only a sub-point to the key idea in verse 21.

They also discovered that verses 22-24 were but one illustrative subpoint in the passage that illustrated how the new verb in verse 21 can be practiced. Five more subpoints exemplified this verb in the following verses and verse 25 belonged to the second point.

Notice how the inclusion of *Think Again* Study Step 1 kept the interpreters of this passage from going astray, perhaps giving priority to some verses over others, and overlooking some (like 5:32) altogether.

Step 6. *Think Again* **about the points of application.** The Bible is God's Word to us. In it, God communicates to us things to know, understand and to put into practice. In the case of Ephesians 5:22-24, Paul used the reciprocal relationship of a mutually submitting Christian wife and husband to illustrate the practice of reciprocal submission between believers to one another. Thus, an obvious point of application for verses 22-24 was that Spirit-filled wives and husbands in Christ can model Christian reciprocating submission.

Paul used not only the metaphor of those united in Christian marriage, but he also used the metaphor of the unity of Christ and the church. Thus, a second point of application was that Christ and Christians are a model of reciprocal submitting.

In the last part of Ephesians 5:23, Paul reached his main point: Christ's self-submission in the reciprocal relationship, "himself savior of the body." Thus, as Christ practiced self-sacrificing submission so Christians should practice it too.

The Bible study group decided that husbands should humbly step down from any sort of lordly pedestal they may have improperly taken for themselves in their relationship with their wives. This would include the concept of "headship," which is a made up word for a non-biblical and anti-Christian idea.

Husbands should humble themselves to their proper station, that of being co-regents over creation with their own wives, and even further, to the point of intentionally submitting themselves to their wives in an ongoing way. In this reciprocal relationship wives should join their husbands in humbly submitting themselves to their husbands.

The Bible study group felt they had made a major discovery in their study. It meant that they would change the way they related to each other. They felt good about this because they could sense that true love was the underpinning of this kind of living.

Step 7. *Think Again* **about what the Bible does *not* say.** In an international conference held in Lausanne Switzerland, the late Francis Schaeffer warned the more than 4,000 Christian present to beware of the two dragons that attack our faith. One was distrust of the Bible, which is the inerrant, inspired Word of God. The other was misuse of the Word of God, contorting and abusing Scripture in such a way as to promote false doctrine. We must say what we believe and say what we do not believe. This is the thinking that is behind the seventh Study Step. Sadly, it is not often practiced in Bible study.

If any Bible study is to result in a fresh understanding of a Bible passage, false doctrines or erroneous ideas previously attributed to the passage need to be identified, labeled, rejected and corrected.

In the case of verses 22-24, which illustrate how to practice the new Christian verb coined by Paul in verse 21, the Bible study group decided that Paul is *not* dealing with the subject of "obedience" in any way (as in a wife to her husband, or the church to Christ). Questions of "how to obey" were irrelevant and incorrect because the subject was on mutual submission.

Moreover, they saw the passage had nothing to do with issues of hierarchy. Verse 23 is *not* about how Christ is *Lord* of the church, which submits to his Lordship. Retroactively, this idea would make it appear that the words in verses 22 and 24 are about wives submitting to their lordly husbands because they exercise "headship." The idea of these verses was instead how Christ submitted himself – his part of the mutually submissive relationship in one body, which is composed of himself and the church.

The Bible study group decided to reject these erroneous ideas in personal practice and to see if they could be cleansed from all forms of teaching in their church. Any further practice built on these unbiblical (even anti-biblical) concepts needed to be stopped, and corrected, as well.

Final thoughts

Making no distinction among Christians was a key doctrine for Paul, and should be for us today. In 1 Corinthians 12:12-13, Paul wrote:

> [12]The body is a unit, though it is made up of many parts; and though all its parts are many, they form one body. So it is with Christ. [13]For we were all baptized by one Spirit into one body – whether Jews or Greeks, slave or free – and we were all given the one Spirit to drink.

These words echoed his earlier words in Galatians 3:26-29. All believers, whether born Jewish or not, became one in Christ Jesus. Every believer became an heir with Abraham who received the promises. Both men and women believers become "sons" of God:

> [26]You are all sons of God through faith in Christ Jesus, [27]for all of you who were united with Christ in baptism have been clothed with Christ. [28]There is neither Jew nor Greek, slave nor free, male nor female, for you are all one in Christ Jesus. [29]If you belong to Christ, then you are Abraham's seed, and heirs according to the promise. (Gal 3:26-29)